Buttoned Up

NUMBER 157
WILLIAMS-FORD TEXAS A&M UNIVERSITY
MILITARY HISTORY SERIES

Buttoned Up

American Armor and the 781st Tank Battalion in World War II

Westin Ellis Robeson

Texas A&M University Press College Station

First edition

This paper meets the requirements of ANSI/NISO Z39.48–1992
(Permanence of Paper).
Binding materials have been chosen for durability.
Manufactured in the United States of America

Library of Congress Cataloging-in-Publication Data

Names: Robeson, Westin Ellis, 1984– author.
Title: Buttoned up : American armor and the 781st Tank Battalion in World War II / Westin Ellis Robeson.
Other titles: Williams-Ford Texas A&M University military history series ; no. 157.
Description: First edition. | College Station : Texas A&M University Press, [2017] | Series: Williams-Ford Texas A&M University military history series ; number 157 | Includes bibliographical references and index.
Identifiers: LCCN 2017021368| ISBN 9781623495664 (book/cloth : alk. paper) | ISBN 9781623495671 (ebook)
Subjects: LCSH: United States. Army. Tank Battalion, 781st—History. | World War, 1939–1945—Regimental histories—United States. | United States. Army—Armored troops—History—World War, 1939–1945. | World War, 1939–1945—Tank warfare.
Classification: LCC D769.306 781st .R63 2017 | DDC 940.54/1273—dc23 LC record available at https://lccn.loc.gov/2017021368

When fighting is not expected soon, the turret and other openings of the tank can be left open. . . . But when battle is near or going on, the turret is closed and all other openings buttoned up.

—"Armored Forces of the United States Army," *Infantry Journal* (1943)

Contents

Preface

> The story of Xerxes' invasion of Greece, the story of its ultimate failure, cannot be understood without relating it to the arms borne by the opposing sides.
>
> **—Ernle Bradford**

In attempting to comprehend the campaigns and battles of the Second World War and its ultimate outcome, one must be conscious of the various units employed. Just as a mechanic must know the transmission, cylinders, and fuel injectors to grasp which functions are carried out by what parts, appreciating every piece and its purpose, a student of war is required to examine the constituent elements of battle. Only by examining its components under the microscope can he formulate for himself a true understanding of the manner in which a war was fought. Without such understanding, theories, arguments, and opinions are conjectural at best.

Disregarding the men, equipment, logistics, tactics, strategy, politics, and other aspects leaves only the violence, an incomprehensible conflict with a seemingly random outcome. Thus an examination of the components of war is essential to understanding its conduct. The component that this book is concerned with is the tank.

The tank is a combination of battlefield necessities—mobility, armor, and firepower. But a tank operating autonomously is extremely vulnerable to enemy infantry and antitank weapons. As a result, armor is deployed in concert with infantry, where mutual support results in cooperative operations, strengthening the capabilities of both units.

This work is not intended to be a complete study of armor. Rather, my intention, first and foremost, is to enlighten the reader with a *comprehensible* study of the American tank, focusing on its role in the armor battalions of

World War II. This work does not set out to examine the armor divisions in any great detail, for works on these units are numerous. The separate tank battalions, however, exemplify one of the underappreciated fighting units instrumental in the Allied victory. Likewise, this study attempts to shed some light on a campaign that also receives little attention—the Seventh Army and its operations in southern France.

The book is divided into three parts. Part one begins with a general history of the tank and armor doctrine as it developed during the First World War. As the Americans were tardy arrivals to that conflict, their newly founded Tank Corps had to adapt British and French machines and tactics. After the Armistice the future of the tank was in question as armies returned to their peacetime strengths. In the United States the Tank Corps was disbanded, and the vehicles were reassigned to the infantry, where tank development remained in limbo. Yet after the German invasions of Poland and France, it became (mostly) clear that the US Army needed to build an independent tank force. Overall, part one examines the circumstances from which US armor development was cultivated. This context is essential to understand how both merits and demerits in technical and doctrinal thought shaped lasting legacies that assured victory, though at a controversial cost, during the Second World War.

Part two then shifts to America's response to German panzer operations in Europe. After a detailed examination of the development of the US Armored Force, the focus turns to the deserts of North Africa, where the American machines had their baptism by fire with British crews. The experiences and lessons there helped inform the development of new tank models and the standardization in American design. This culminated in the development of the M4 Sherman medium tank, the backbone of American armor during World War II. Part two concludes with an examination of the technical components and specifications that made the Sherman one of the most successful tanks of the war.

Finally, part three focuses on the experience of a US separate tank battalion in the European theater of operations. It should be noted that I have limited the analysis of the Normandy Campaign as its story is readily available in countless other works. Instead this book uses the experience of the Seventh Army as a backdrop for the study of the separate tank battalions, focusing on the notable experience of one such unit—the 781st Tank Battalion. The history of the 781st provides a lens through which we can analyze the average experience of the separate tank battalions during the Second World War.

These final chapters also examine specific confrontations and relevant factors, including the battalion's use of Duplex Drive tanks and T-34 rocket launchers. The experience of the 781st encompassed a variety of engagements, small and large, that provide a feel of the day-to-day operations of the separate tank battalions. Again, this book is not intended to be a complete history of armor but an introduction to armored warfare, providing a basic understanding of the tank as a weapon. The detailed look at the 781st is intended to instill an appreciation for the instrumental role of the separate tank battalions in the Allied victory.

Within the narrative I have included a few fictional anecdotes to help illustrate parts of the narrative. These "scenes" are set apart and presented in italics.

▪ ▪ ▪

First, I must thank my Dad for the many hours he spent poring over my first drafts—his eyes and insight were instrumental and invaluable and saved me from a number of gaffes. Thank you to the Patton Museum Library staff at Fort Knox, Kentucky, for providing me with material and a desk to work at. As far as obtaining sources, I must also mention the Ohio Book Store, located on Main Street in downtown Cincinnati, where I unearthed a number of published primary and out-of-print secondary sources related to armor. To my lovely wife, Annie, I apologize for being late to the table and late to bed, as well as for forgetting to take out the trash on multiple occasions on account of this endeavor. Thank you for your patience. I must also thank a number of faculty members at the University of Cincinnati, including Dr. John McNay and Dr. Susan Longfield Karr, for answering all of my questions, and to Prof. Donald Burns, who encouraged me to write in the first place. Finally, I am truly in debt to the Texas A&M University Press, especially Jay Dew and Pat Clabaugh. To my editor, Kevin Brock, who showed patience and intrepid perseverance in deciphering my words and decoding my notes, thank you for your tremendous help.

While this book attempts to tell the story of unsung military units, I will take this opportunity to honor another group of unsung heroes—our great teachers. The best of our society is in debt to their instruction, guidance, and counsel. We all remember our influential mentors. My own mother is a prime example of an educator whose dedication to her students was always apparent. This book is dedicated to the memory of one such teacher—Dr. Lee Baker of the University of Cincinnati. He not only encouraged me to write this book but also was key in my decision to pursue a new career in education. I have now done both. Thank you, sir.

MAP SYMBOLS

Unit Identification - Unit Size

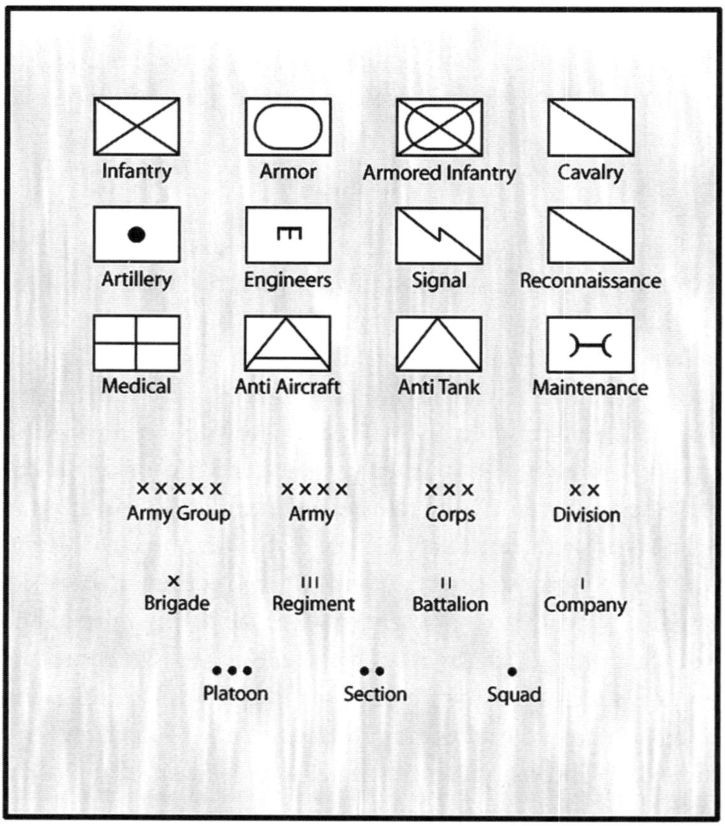

Buttoned Up

Part 1

Origins through 1939

1

An Introduction

> To understand an action that involved artillery, the historian must know the guns themselves. Only then can he judge the competence of the artillerymen or the wisdom of the commanders.
>
> **—Harold Peterson**

The tank is an awe-inspiring piece of equipment. The public has little understanding of its design or capabilities, but an appreciation of its dominance as a weapon is easily perceived by its sheer mass. When one stands underneath the gun barrel of such a hulking machine, there is usually little to say. It is so far removed from any vehicle civilians associate with that imagination alone must fill in the details.

We sometimes see retired tanks in parks or in city centers, quietly immobile in the shade as if sleeping with one eye open, ready to roar back into action. Walking around an olive drab tank, we typically keep our hands in our pockets, except perhaps for a pat on its side to feel how cold and hard the armor is. We gawk at the elevated gun, proudly displaying the authority it once held. Looking at the turret, one envisions it traversing to engage an enemy. The massive wheels and tracks always catch our attention; the vehicle would surely have no trouble crushing a car. Questions abound: How loud was it? How fast could it go? How big is that gun? What is inside? Finally the eyes home in on the worn rubber of the treads, the chipped paint, the rust along the hinges and weld joints, and the inevitable bird droppings on the hatch—we realize this is an old tank.

Moving around toward the front, one usually finds a mounted sign, a typical historical plaque, dark bronze, with embossed shiny text. It might read something like:

> United States M4 Sherman Tank
> HQ Company
> 781st Tank Battalion
> HONORING THE MEN OF ARMORED
> UNITS OF THE SECOND WORLD WAR
> Dedicated May 4, 1995

So where did this tank come from? Who used it and how did they use it? Was it important?

The tank was born in World War I and served as a novelty on that conflict's battlefield. Yet by World War II it had been remolded into a necessity. This book is intended to shed light on the military circumstances that demanded the tank and to give an appreciation for the weapon and the units that controlled them.

In addition, whereas books on particular battleships, infantry divisions, bomb groups, and such are commonplace, armor takes up a rather sparse portion on the shelves of the military history section. The few volumes that are found there tend to revolve around the larger units, such as the historic 3rd Armored Division.

Aside from the sixteen armored divisions that were deployed during World War II, there were sixty-five separate tank battalions that were thrown into the action where and when the US Army saw fit. These self-titled "Bastard Battalions" were attached to infantry divisions throughout the war and have received little recognition, let alone any significant credit, in contemporary works. This is not the "untold story" of these separate tank battalions. Rather, it is a study of armor during the Second World War, revolving around one of those battalions whose story should be told. The objective is to examine the design and development of tanks and armor doctrine, the organization and role of these units during World War II, and the experience of those who served and fought as tank crews in the separate tank battalions.

2

Dawn of the Tank

And the LORD was with Judah; and he drove out the inhabitants of the mountain; but could not drive out the inhabitants of the valley, because they had chariots of iron.

—Judges 1:19

History as a whole is broken up by the rise and fall of nations at the hands of war. Having the advantage of weaponry has long been a deciding factor on the battlefield—the best man did not always win. He sometimes fell to the composite bow, then to the matchlock, and so on.

The tank provides a modern army with a complete suite of battlefield necessities: protection, firepower, and mobility. When welded together, these integral components give birth to an awesome weapon. The tank is at the end of a long line of innovations that have developed around these three keys to military success—thus it is difficult to pinpoint its exact origin. If defined as simply incorporating the previously stated elements, then siege machines and chariots were the great-grandfathers of the tank. If restricted to the era of gunpowder, then the first tanks could presumably be the war wagons fielded during the Hussite Wars of the fifteenth century. One of the most commonly given responses concerning the origins of tank genealogy points to Leonardo da Vinci, whose sketch design for an armored land vehicle appears as a cross between Noah's Ark, a British man-of-war, and a flying saucer. For the purposes of this book, the modern tank is comfortably defined as a fuel-propelled vehicle with tracks that incorporates mobility, firepower, and armor.

The British deployed the first of these weapons in 1916 at the Battle of the Somme. It is not difficult to appreciate the shock value that tanks carried with them during their first engagement. It is easy to draw a comparison between the Germans, their eyes homing in on the steel beasts crawling through the smoke, to the Macedonians laying eyes on Persian war elephants for the first time 2,300 years ago. The tank is quite simply the pinnacle of mobile land-fighting platforms.

Mobility

An army at its heart revolves around the infantry—the sweating foot soldier who wields the most-personal weapons of war. Tactically, the infantry's role has always been the same: to advance on the objective while eliminating the enemy and to take control of territory through occupation. But armies do not solely rely on the foot soldier. They utilize any expedient instrument that will help them defeat their enemy.

The Eurasian civilizations, which relied heavily on the horse for agricultural purposes, were the first to employ these animals on the battlefield. Military historian John Keegan holds that the "long range campaigning, high speed maneuver on the battlefield, effective missile technology, the application of the wheel, and above all, the mutuality between horse and warrior had their origins on the steppe and its borderlands."[1] With the mobility of the horse, a mounted soldier—or cavalryman—could quickly flank a static enemy formation committed to a head-on skirmish. Battlefields soon became two-dimensional as speed and surprise enabled sweeping alternatives to fore and aft charges and retreats.

The Mongolians were among the first to take advantage of the stirrup. Their ingenious short stirrups allowed a mounted archer to stand fully erect and expand his killing radius, thus more easily outmaneuvering his opponent and allowing him to fight during a withdrawal. As for a mounted swordsman, it served as a bridge of energy, transferring the force and power of his speeding animal into the weapon he carried. It is not hard to imagine the blow of a sword from a standing soldier as compared to the same strike with the momentum of a horse behind it.

Before long, as the horse became more domesticated and responsive to man's will and as methods of harnessing were mastered, the chariot emerged as a game-changing weapon. The Chinese, Hittites, and Egyptians relied heavily upon these vehicles. Early designs used one or two horses to pull the two-wheeled carriage, from which the soldier, or charioteer, could fight. The chariot enhanced platform stability over the mounted horseman, improving missile accuracy and rate of fire. It also allowed for a two-man team—one to drive and one to fight—presaging specialization of "crew members" with specific duties in fighting vehicles. Further along, four-horse teams pulled four-wheeled chariots carrying multiple fighters, enabling it to remain effective even if the crew sustained casualties.

Many records of ancient engagements point to the chariot as the deciding factor on the battlefield. In the fifteenth century BC, the army of Thutmose III clashed with a Syrian army in Megiddo (located about twenty miles southwest of the Sea of Galilee). During the battle, the Egyptians deployed their chariots, whose mounted archers outflanked the Assyrian army, securing the victory.[2]

Though chariots would become obsolete by the time of Christ, the horse would remain on battlefields up to and including the twentieth century. Yet following the development of the internal-combustion engine, the flesh, blood, and bones of the horse would prove passé against the hardened steel of modern weapons.

Armor

Protecting oneself in battle is as fundamental a consideration as harming one's opponent. If feasible, men will don armor of some kind prior to an engagement. The use of chainmail, for example, goes back as early as 300 BC. Such armor provided the wearer protection from sword slashes and, to some extent, piercing projectiles. While its use did reduce lacerations, a good blow from a heavy sword would no doubt leave a debilitating bruise, if not a shattered bone, but the wearer probably would retain his limb.[3] With this first line of outer defense, it is easy to understand the reimagining of one prehistoric weapon, the club. As civilizations mastered the arts of metalworking, clubs were reintroduced as a much more lethal tool of war, the mace. But it is difficult to chronicle in any linear fashion the evolution of this weapon and its transformation over time.

The mace proved to be very effective. Simple blunt-force trauma from a weighted ball would easily snap bones or crush skulls. Thus, something stronger was needed for protection. With metalworking came plate body armor, which could distribute a blow over a larger area, thus providing the wearer with protection against blunt-force weapons. But armor plating proved cumbersome to the wearer and was also expensive. In the end it became more practical to continue wearing mail and using only partial plate armor to protect vulnerable limbs or joints. The overlapping use and limited placement of plate and chainmail is an early example of the tailoring of armor to optimize protection while considering costs, comfort, and effectiveness, a technique that continues to the present day.

As projectile technology improved through the ages, with increased velocities and consequently better penetration capabilities, cumbersome body armor slowly made its journey to the dusty shelves of the past. But as militaries deployed new weapons and tactics, armor evolved in material composition and battlefield application.

Firepower

Being able to strike your opponent at a distance is always a preferred advantage, be it through longer limbs, the slinging of a stone, or the use of pikes, javelins, or rifled firearm barrels. If one can wound his opponent at a distance, he will certainly have the advantage by reducing his adversary's effectiveness prior to the commencement of close combat.

Bows were the primary range weapons for thousands of years. As anything else in warfare, the bow advanced technologically and became more deadly over time. Long bows used en masse could rain arrows down on enemy formations with deadly effect, while the composite bow imparted increased energy into a more compact weapon, much to the benefit of cavalrymen or charioteers.

For thousands of years, piercing, slashing, and smashing meted out death on the battlefield. But the definition of weaponry would change during the warring years of the tenth century—the Chinese had created gunpowder. To quote Sir Francis Bacon, "printing, gunpowder, and the [compass] magnet . . . have changed the whole face and state of things throughout the world. . . . [N]o empire, no sect, no star . . . [has] exerted greater power and influence in human affairs than these mechanical discoveries."[4]

Gunpowder made its way across the plains of Asia and into the hands of European armies in the thirteenth and fourteenth centuries. It was not *a* revolution but *the* revolution in weaponry, spawning new killing technology such as handguns, mortars, and cannons.

While the cannon has been used effectively since the fifteenth century, it was the latter part of the seventeenth century when it took on a significant role in warfare. Author Jeremy Black states that during this era in history, the "standardization of artillery pieces led to more regular fire, and encouraged the development of artillery tactics away from the largely desultory and random preliminary bombardment of the seventeenth century, in favor of more efficient exchanges of concentrated and sustained fire."[5] In other words, as cannons became more standard, reliable, and accurate, utilization changed from inaccurate saturation bombardment to more precise direct targeting.

The following century, large-caliber weapons became lighter and often mounted on carriages. In addition, sights were improved using levels and quadrants, range tables were developed, and declination markers appeared, all of these leading to more-accurate fire. This, of course, led to a more refined role for the cannon.

Though the use of artillery dominated the battlefields of World War I, the advancements in gunnery during the American Civil War were tremendous, including the development and standardization of fire control, fuses, and the specialization of projectile types, which allowed a crew to select ammunition most appropriate for a given target.

By 1914, rifled bores, machine guns, artillery, fieldworks, and barbed wire had finally created such an expanse between lines that the span of the disputed ground itself became a major obstacle in warfare. A weapon was needed to cross this open terrain, protected from incoming fire, to punch a hole in the enemy's line. This support weapon would give an assault the edge it needed, expediting infantry movements into the adversary's positions, enabling them to break through into the rear, where it could disrupt lines of communication, rearguard installments, supply depots, and headquarter units.

Bert Chaney, a young signal officer in the 7th London Territorial Battalion, recalled the arrival of the British Army's newest innovation in 1916: "We heard strange throbbing noises, and lumbering slowly towards us came three huge mechanical monsters such as we had never seen before. . . . Big metal things they were, with two sets of caterpillar wheels that went right round the body . . . and machine guns on swivels poked out from either side."[6] The tank had arrived.

J. F. C. Fuller later wrote: "Ever since the introduction of firearms, the two outstanding difficulties in battle tactics had been how to harmonize movement and fire and movement and protection. These were now overcome by the tank. It increased mobility by substituting mechanical power for muscular; it increased security by neutralizing the bullet by armored plate; and it increased offensive power by relieving the soldier from the necessity of carrying his weapons and the horse from hauling them."[7] Machines had produced mass quantities of consumer goods, had moved freight and passengers along the rails dissecting the continents, and powered massive ships across the oceans. It was only a matter of time before machines were drafted by the armies of the world. The tank would crush barbed wire and corpses alike, spray the enemy with machine-gun fire, and then blast away with its cannon. And it would change the face of war forever.

3

The Great War and Its Wake

If the tanks succeed, then victory follows.

—Gen. Heinz Guderian

When someone mentions World War I, our minds call up the scratchy black-and-white footage seen in most documentaries of that conflict. Silhouettes of helmeted figures tread off into the haze with fixed bayonets, moving at a flawed speed due to the awkward frame rate of the film. A soldier peers over the crest of a trench, wounded men stare up from stretchers or the bare ground, eruptions of earth make their way across a plain, and mud latches onto everything like a disease. The pictures continue with a formation of biplanes slowly rolling out and downward. Infantry trot across the landscape, staggering, lifting legs over shredded barbed wire. Another explosion blasts dirt high into the air, followed by a scene of troops scurrying to secure their gas masks. One man hurls a grenade while another helps wounded back to the line. Artillerymen step aside as their big gun recoils, violently jerking its carriage back; instantly the men approach before it settles. Finally, a few officers stand around, one with a pipe, staying clear of the path of a giant steel tank—one man in the background pulls at his mustache gawking at the ugly thing—which lumbers forward, stops, then jolts to the left; all the men are watching.

The tank is most likely the lozenge-shaped British Mark I. Onscreen, this machine looks inept as it awkwardly stirs in the mud. The pictures do not lie, for the Mark I was an antique even at its debut. It would take time for the vehicle designs to match the technology.

The First World War served as the overture for many weapons and doctrines developed in various arsenals across the globe. Artillery was heavily relied upon, softening enemy positions to be assaulted by the infantry. Chemical warfare was unleashed on a large scale. Airplanes of both sides scouted out the lines and circled in the sky, chattering at each other with their machine guns. And the tanks crawled across the muddy fields of no-man's-land like monstrous turtles.

Stagnant Lines and Minds

As the European armies clashed, with waves of infantry flooding futilely through the barbed wire against the machine guns that had infested the battlefield, commanders began to fight a war of attrition. Their strategic objectives shifted from seizing and holding ground to overwhelming their adversary's industrial tolerance, never mind morale and the cost in human lives. The dilemma was that the strategic doctrine had changed, while the tactics remained the same. Technology and machines had advanced at lightning speed since the American Civil War, yet tactical thought had remained mostly dormant.

Capt. B. H. Liddell Hart, in his study of the Great War, referred to this stalemate on the battlefield as a disease and attests that Lt. Col. Ernest Swinton was the "physician" who "diagnosed" the ailment and prescribed the perfect "antidote." At the time, 1914, Swinton (later a major general) was attached to the British general headquarters and serving in France. He saw and understood the quandary faced by the army. The ace in his pocket was knowledge of the American Holt Manufacturing Company's farm tractor, which utilized wide steel tracks to carry it over soft or muddy terrain. On 20 October he met in London with Col. Maurice Hankey, secretary of the Committee of Imperial Defense. Swinton proposed developing this tractor into a fighting vehicle. Hankey was intrigued and moved to write Prime Minister Herbert Asquith about this "antidote" while Swinton returned to France.[1]

The writings to Asquith reached the ears of First Lord of the Admiralty Winston Churchill, who took an immediate interest in the proposal. But Churchill represented a minority view, as most members of the Committee of Imperial Defense showed little enthusiasm for the idea. In the early part of 1915, he nevertheless organized a body, dubbed the Landships Committee, to work on the project.[2]

The committee set forth to develop an armored vehicle capable of crossing the muddy pockets of no-man's-land. Swinton had specified that the machine needed to be capable of crossing over a trench eight feet wide and to overcome a parapet of four and a half feet.[3]

In September 1915 the first prototype was produced. Known as Little Willie, the vehicle weighed twelve tons and had a crew of three. Over rough ground it could only muster about two miles per hour, or thirty yards a minute, though a more accurate estimate, considering battlefield conditions, may be ten to fifteen yards per minute. While it utilized the methods proposed by Swinton, Little Willie showed little potential as a realistic combatant. Yet it laid down the precept that all future designs would build on—the use of tracks to carry the vehicle across the battlefield.

Simultaneously, a new prototype was being forged. Following the classic English habit of droll designations, this vehicle was named Mother and was ready for demonstration by February 1916. It was the first of the traditional rhomboid-type tanks, identifiable by the "sets of caterpillar wheels that [go] right round the body." After some modifications, Mother eventually would be designated officially as the Mark I. The promise of this vehicle's capabilities set in motion the order for 150 to be produced.

Figure 2. The British were the first to bring tanks, such as this Mark IV Male, to the battlefield in 1916. *Courtesy General George Patton Museum, Fort Knox*

The Mark I was thirty-two feet long, fourteen feet wide, and stood eight feet high. It weighed twenty-eight tons and had a maximum speed of roughly four miles an hour. The original design had a turret mounted on top of the body, but to lower the center of gravity, the armaments were moved into two side sponsons.

Two versions of this tank would enter combat—the Male and the Female. The Male tank was armed with machine guns and two naval 6-pounder guns, one on each side of the vehicle located in the sponsons. Its suspension, void of any spring system, provided the crew with a jarring voyage, rendering the 6-pounders inaccurate while the tank was moving. The Female tank was armed only with machine guns and intended to take on infantry or machine-gun nests.

The vehicle was constructed with a combination of bolts and rivets. The eight-man crew was protected by armor that varied from six to ten millimeters thick. This kept them relatively safe from small arms and artillery bursts, though a direct hit from a large-caliber projectile would have no trouble penetrating the tank.

Vision from within the Mark I was very limited. When in action, the crew would button up the tank, limiting the men to seeing only through viewing slits and virtually engulfing them in darkness. With no separate compartment to isolate the crew from the engine or transmission, the interior soon filled with choking fumes. The noise inside could only be described as deafening.

The Mark I underwent a number of modifications, with each bringing a new model designation. These improvements included the installation of a muffler to reduce noise, better armor to counter armor-piercing bullets, the removal of the interior fuel tanks, and placing them outside at the rear of the tank, away from the crew. In response to the threat of German tanks, the Mark IV model saw the upgrade of the Female version to incorporate a Male sponson housing a 6-pounder on one side. This marriage of the two variants was referred to as the Hermaphrodite. Their 6-pounders were also upgraded with shorter barrels.

Baptism at the Somme

The tank made its official debut on 15 September 1916. As the offensive in the Somme valley began to lose its momentum, the British commander in chief, Field Marshal Sir Douglas Haig, ordered up the new weapons.

Swinton, in proper manner, warned that this action might be premature as the tanks and their crews were still in a state of trial and error and fine tuning. These were not serious concerns to the high command, and sixty of the new machines crossed the English Channel for combat in Europe—ready or not.

Of the sixty tanks transported, forty-nine would be thrown forward. Only thirty-two of these, though, actually made it to the front lines; the rest fell victim to mechanical problems. When deployed in action, nine tanks broke down and five became mired in the mud. Of the remaining eighteen, only half moved forward with the infantry while the rest struggled behind, unable to match the speed of the advance.[4]

Among the many problems with this debut was the complete waste of shock value. Haig had been too ambitious and sent the tanks in piecemeal. This gave the Germans time to begin work on antitank defenses. This strategic and tactical blunder squandered the edge typically gained by introducing a new weapon. Historian John Wheldon observed that the tanks, "which had promised a way through the deadlock were now . . . merely incorporated within it, as an added complexity and expense."[5]

The vehicles had been sent into combat in groups of three and were spread out to help support the infantry. Col. John F. C. Fuller had petitioned, like Swinton, that the vehicles, when properly ready, be deployed en masse. He believed that the best way to beat the enemy was to attack his rear. Victory would be achieved not by killing the men in the front lines, but by penetrating those positions and striking at the enemy's command system.

In his work *The Conduct of War*, Fuller emphasized attacking the enemy interior. He also proposed that the real power of an army is the durability of its organization. This can be annihilated by one of two ways: attrition (what he calls "body warfare"), which is more or less the killing of combatants, or disruption, "rendering inoperative [the] power of command—brain warfare." Fuller compared the elimination of an army with that of a man: "the first method may be compared with a succession of wounds which will eventually result in his bleeding to death; the second—a shot through the brain. The brains of an army are its staff—Army, Corps, and Divisional Headquarters."[6] By 1916 the opposing armies were bleeding—severely—but neither side was bleeding out. The tank, as Fuller saw it, was the tool needed to destroy the enemy's brains.

Success at Cambrai

Colonel Fuller proposed that tanks could penetrate the German defenses in the region near the French town of Cambrai by grouping them together and mounting a surprise attack. He envisioned armor and infantry advancing together and calling in artillery fire as targets of opportunity presented themselves. The objective of these assaults, Fuller added, was not to gain ground: after penetrating and disrupting the German positions, the tanks and infantry would withdraw. He believed that these hit-and-run actions, if continued sporadically along the line, would have a tremendous psychological and strategic effect on the enemy.

The lobbies of Fuller and Swinton were finally put to trial on 20 November 1917, when the British mounted an offensive at Cambrai. Though the final plan had little resemblance to the small raids proposed by Fuller, the attack was orchestrated around the mass deployment of tanks, which would take out the antipersonnel barbed wire and machine guns, while the infantry would move against artillery threatening the tanks.

At 6:20 A.M. a short but massive bombardment pounded the German lines. As the defenders peered through their field glasses, they were terror stricken at the sight of hundreds of steel monsters crawling toward them, engaging their strongpoints. Even more disheartening to the Germans was the sight of thousands of infantrymen herding across no-man's-land behind the tanks, virtually unhindered. The barbed wire that had for so long paralyzed the infantry assault was now being smashed into the mud or dragged away by the tanks.

Four hundred and seventy-six tanks, along with infantry, shimmed a 6,000-yard gap in the German line, through which mounted cavalry began to pour. Some units managed to advance five miles into the interior. Yet since the British high command had very low expectations for the attack, they had committed very few resources to exploit any breakthrough. In the end the Germans had time to regroup and counterattack, reclaiming most of what they had lost. Regardless of the strategic failure, the armor had demonstrated both its capabilities and its limitations.

The tanks suffered a fair amount of losses due to breakdowns and concentrated artillery fire, which in some areas, specifically on the left flank of the attack, resulted from sending armor forward without proper close infantry support. Cambrai demonstrated that mass deployment of tanks supported by infantry could form a potentially lethal attack force capable of maintaining its momentum into the enemy's interior if properly coordinated.

Creating the US Tank Corps

American observers had been unimpressed with the first British tanks they had seen, deeming the machines clumsy and unreliable. But once the United States entered the war in April 1917, Gen. John J. Pershing, commander of the American Expeditionary Force (AEF), could not help but wonder at the potential of this new weapon. Pershing had led US forces charged with pursuing Poncho Villa into Mexico in 1916, taking nearly 7,000 soldiers 400 miles into Mexico. The army needed to create a sufficient supply system to maintain this force. While Pershing had 162 trucks at his disposal, these were not enough to transport the necessary supplies; Secretary of War Newton Baker spent $450,000 to purchase 100 additional trucks. Ultimately, thousands of tons of equipment and supplies were transported by these motor vehicles.[7]

No doubt Pershing's dependency on trucks during this campaign would lead him to inquire of future applications for motorized vehicles. Hence, two months after the US entered the Great War, Pershing ordered a team to investigate the utility of British and French tanks. Contrasting with previous attitudes, the subsequent report claimed that the tank must be considered an important element on the battlefield, that US forces should focus on obtaining both heavy and light tanks, and that there must be a centralized command structure for armor. The next month Pershing ordered the creation of the American Tank Board to further investigate the validity of the tank. In a report dated 1 September 1917, the board laid down its findings: the tank was "destined" to become a valuable asset on the battlefield, a separate tank department should be organized immediately, only the French Renault and the British Mark VI were suitable models for American operations, and the American force should consist of 2,000 light and 200 heavy tanks. Pershing ordered Lt. Col. Leroy Eltinge, a member of the Operations Section and who had also served under the general in Mexico, to create a quantitative analysis in order to request tanks from the War Department. Etlinge's plan called for 350 heavy tanks and 1,030 light tanks for combat and 320 tanks for supply, troop transport, and signaling. The requisition totaled 600 heavy and 1,200 light tanks, with a force of nearly 15,000 men.[8]

Figure 3. A young George S. Patton with one of his Renault light tanks. *Courtesy General George Patton Museum, Fort Knox*

While British Mark Vs mostly formed the heavy tank units, the Americans opted to use the French Renault light tanks. These two-man vehicles were sixteen feet, five inches long; five feet, eight inches wide; and seven and a half feet tall. Weighing seven tons, its eighteen-horsepower engine could manage about seven miles per hour. The driver sat in a tub-like compartment in the front of the vehicle, while the gunner operated the weapon, either a Hotchkiss machine gun or a 37-mm cannon, in a turret that could traverse 360 degrees.

Later in September 1917, Lieutenant Colonel Eltinge sought to find someone to command the tanks and serve as director of a new tank school. Though many officers applied for the assignment, Etlinge's attention was drawn to the commander of the AEF Headquarters Company, Capt. George S. Patton Jr. His experience with a machine-gun unit, familiarity and interest with motors, fluency in French, and standing as the only American to have organized combat with motor vehicles against an armed enemy made him an obvious candidate.[9] Patton got the job and a promotion to major.[10]

On 10 November AEF Headquarters ordered Patton to Langres, France, to establish a tank school. The job was immense. Not only did he need to organize and build units and develop doctrinal theory, but he also had to become familiar with the tank itself. He and his new assistant, 1st Lt. Elgin Braine (an artilleryman), were sent to the French Light Tank Training Center at Chamlieu. There, the two Americans were introduced to the Renaults. Patton studied the tanks, learning how to drive the vehicle and how to operate its 37-mm cannon. Together, they observed maneuvers, discussed tactics, toured repair shops, and translated French lesson plans. Meanwhile, tanks were proving their combat capabilities at Cambrai.[11]

In late December Col. Samuel D. Rockenbach, a cavalryman, was assigned chief of the Tank Corps. Having no units organized or even actual tanks, the corps existed only on paper. But the paper was a good start, the result of Braine and Patton having studied the tanks and written reports and proposals concerning organization, training, tactics, and doctrinal theory.

The Tank Corps was officially established on 26 January 1918. Light tank units would be organized in France, while the heavy tank units would be formed across the Channel under the watchful eyes of the British. On 14 February Rockenbach assigned Major Patton to command the 1st Light Tank Center in Langres and Lt. Col. Conrad S. Babcock to command the 2nd Tank Center in Bovington, England.[12]

Throughout January and February, officers and enlisted men, primarily from artillery units, began arriving in Langres. Patton and his command would have to wait until the end of March to receive any tanks. Until then the major busied himself with designing classes, training future instructors, constructing facilities, planning unit organization, and establishing tactical doctrine. In February Patton moved his men, now organized into two companies, five miles south to the small town of Bourg. Still without tanks, he continued to occupy his time with the many details of planning. The burden was enormous but welcomed by the commander, who designed the school free from any prevailing format. Finally on 23 March, after months of languishing, Patton received his first tanks—ten light Renaults. As a testament to his involvement and the work always needed to be done, the major and his men constructed a platform to unload the vehicles from the train. Patton also had to personally drive the tanks off the flatcars since he was the only one there with any experience.[13]

That same day the 1st Heavy Tank Battalion, at Camp Meade, Maryland, received orders to ship out. The men were off to England, where they would train with their tanks. Among them was twenty-seven-year-old Dwight David Eisenhower, a member of the 65th Engineers, the parent unit for the battalion. To the young officer's dismay, when word came for the battalion to ship out, Eisenhower was transferred to a new command, remaining stateside at Camp Colt, Pennsylvania, near Gettysburg, where he would train tankers. Here, he and six hundred officers under him trained ten thousand soldiers, though without a single tank. Instead, the men drilled, learned telegraphy, and became proficient with what cannons and machine guns they could get their hands on. At best they could simulate tank combat by mounting these weapons on trucks.[14]

On 9 April the 1st Heavy Tank Battalion arrived in Wareham, England, where they spent the month learning tank gunnery, driving, maintenance, signaling, compass reading, and other skills. A week after its arrival, the unit was designated the 41st Heavy Tank Battalion. Colonel Rockenbach had ordered that all light battalions to be designated by numbers 1–40, while heavy battalions would be designated 41–50. The system was soon changed again, resulting in the 41st ultimately becoming the 301st Tank Battalion in June. Similarly, the 1st and brand new 2nd Light Tank Battalions became the 326th and 327th, respectively.[15] The 301st was finally equipped with Mark V tanks in July. These newer models were easier to drive than their predecessors, which had required two additional men to operate the gear system.

Once operational, single tank platoons (five tanks) would be attached to attacking infantry battalions. This meant that a company of tanks would accompany an infantry regiment, with a battalion thus assigned to an infantry division. This practice would last through World War II.

The British and the French had very different tanks and thus differing thoughts on their role in combat. The British used their heavy tanks to lead the infantry so they could clear wire and engage strongpoints. French forces, however, employed their light tanks behind the infantry, bringing them up only when necessary to take on strongpoints or machine guns. Developing American doctrine, largely designed by Patton, employed a variation of the two in a combined effort. The ideal formation called for a platoon of heavy tanks and a company of light tanks to support an infantry battalion. The heavy armor would lead the assault, engaging specific, predetermined targets. Two platoons of light tanks would follow one hundred meters behind them, closely followed by the first wave of attacking infantry. The light armor would "clean up" smaller pockets of resistance bypassed by the heavy tanks.

Back in France, Patton, now a lieutenant colonel, commanded three light tank companies, which officially became the 1st Light Tank Battalion (ultimately the 326th Tank Battalion) on 28 April. By this time the unit had started to work with the infantry on maneuvers in order to become familiar with each other's capabilities. Tankers needed to understand the infantry's role in combat, their pace, and their abilities. (As we will see later, the United States would fail to establish such relationships during the Second World War.) "The infantry win the fights," Patton told his students. "The tanks only and always help the infantry to win them."[16] If armor was going to support the infantry, the battalion needed more tanks. By the middle of August, Patton's force had grown to nine hundred men and fifty officers, but only twenty-five tanks. The French guaranteed armor for the command. But these tanks would not be sent to the training center—instead, they would join their crews at the front line.

Baptism of American Light and Heavy Tanks

Rockenbach, now a brigadier general, received orders to plan a role for his tanks in the upcoming offensive near Saint-Mihiel. The armor committed to the assault included his own 326th and 327th Light Tank Battalions and one French light tank regiment. Patton would lead the two American battalions and a smaller group of French Schneider tanks (with French crews), which were organized as the 1st Tank Brigade.[17] On 20 August Patton received orders to "report at once to the Chief of the Tank Corps accompanied by your Reconnaissance officer and equipped for field service."[18]

Pershing planned to deploy three corps—V, IV, and I, from west to east—against the Saint-Mihiel salient. Patton's force, consisting of 144 Renaults and 24 Schneiders, deployed with the IV Corps in the center of the attack. The 326th Battalion would support the 1st Division, while the 327th and French Schneiders would support the 42nd Division.[19]

In the predawn hours of 12 September, Allied artillery opened up along the front. After a four-hour bombardment of German positions, IV Corps began its northern attack into the south side of the salient. The fields in this area were a soggy mess following five days of rain. The Renaults churned through the mud, dragging their bellies, their tracks groping for traction. Scattered artillery came down on the armor, and enemy machine guns opened up on the advancing infantry. When the troops began to take fire, the tanks moved in with their 37-mm cannons and machine guns. Once the enemy guns were silenced, the attack continued. While some tanks became mired in the mud, others struggled to get their bearings through clouds of smoke and ash from burning villages. Many officers lead their vehicles through the mud on foot, guiding them around shell craters and directing fire. The Renaults slowly gained ground, flattening wire and taking out machine-gun nests. Wherever the terrain was suitable, the tanks succeeded in pushing back the Germans. Though some defenders provided resistance, many of the enemy trenches and machine guns were abandoned.

For two days the infantry and tanks advanced through the muddy fields, taking villages where they would reorganize, refit, and press on. On 14 September the tanks were withdrawn in order to prepare for the Meuse-Argonne offensive.

The first experience of the American Tank Corps had been more bitter than sweet. Troop casualties had been light, consisting of five dead and nineteen wounded for the 326th and 327th Battalions. Material losses were much worse. As the assaulting force crossed the battlefield, its wake was littered with dozens of tanks, strewn across the battlefield like dead cattle, abandoned by their crews.[20] Some of the 7.5-ton Renaults slid into shell holes and trenches as the soil sagged under their weight. Others bottomed out as their treads vainly churned the mud beneath them. By the sixteenth there were forty vehicles still stuck. Maj. Sereno Brett, commander of the 326th Battalion, had lost two tanks himself in the mire and a third in the rubble of one village.[21]

Overall, the AEF attack against the Saint-Mihiel salient had been a major success. Though the Germans had been preparing to pull back to take up positions in the Hindenburg Line, they were no doubt taken by surprise by the onslaught, abandoning machine guns and artillery pieces they would have removed otherwise. The Americans captured 466 guns and took more than 13,000 prisoners.[22] Patton concluded that, since the Germans were retreating, "the full value of the tanks was not susceptible of demonstration. In spite of very serious terrain obstacles, the tanks were in a position to aid the Infantry and would have done so had such assistance been necessary. As it was, the tanks entered the towns of Nonsard, Pannes, and Benney ahead of the Infantry and captured the town of Jonville unaided by any Infantry whatever."[23]

As light tanks prepared for what ultimately would be their last battle near the Argonne Forest, the 301st Heavy Tank Battalion anticipated its first action of the war as part of the British 4th Tank Brigade in support of the Fourth Army's attack on the Hindenburg Line. As this German position was known to have much wider trenches—more than ten feet across—the 301st received a number of the new Mark V Star tanks. These were virtually identical to the Mark V except lengthened an extra six feet in order to help cross these trenches.

The 301st, commanded by Maj. Ralph I. Sasse, was to support the 54th Brigade, which would lead the 27th Infantry Division's assault. Sasse and the divisional commander planned for the three tank companies to support the brigade's three infantry regiments, with each battalion supported by a platoon of five tanks. In the case of the heavy tanks, the plan was to have the armor advance one hundred yards in front of the infantry. Sasse, having been a cavalry officer in the 1st Infantry Division, stressed coordination and instructed his company and platoon commanders to meet with their respective infantry commanders to work out last-minute details before the action. He wanted a good relationship between the two arms, for they had to work as a team in order to succeed.[24]

On 29 September the heavy tanks of the 301st began their assault toward the Hindenburg Line. Company A moved up with the 107th Infantry, with Company B and the 105th Infantry following behind; the 108th Infantry, however, was delayed, so the tanks of Company C moved out without infantry support. The first two losses were Company A tanks, which wandered into a British minefield. Once that ordeal had been resolved, mechanical problems began to take a toll. Here and there tanks began to turn back or simply stopped operating. Worse yet, German artillery fire was heavy and increasingly accurate, knocking out a total of sixteen tanks; there was a complete lack of counterbattery fire. Furthermore, the lead infantry units failed to mop up pockets of resistance left by the tanks. Consequently, following troops took unnecessary fire and casualties from these unresolved German positions.[25]

While the light and heavy tanks provided testament to their potential during the Great War, actions such as those at Saint-Mihiel and against the Hindenburg Line lingered in the minds of many commanders who would decide the postwar fate of armored forces. Though the tanks had received their baptism by fire on the battlefield, they would have to prove themselves again in a political battle following the Armistice.

Unlike other weapons used in the "War to End All Wars," the tank resides in the shadows. The war had been the testing ground for these machines, which had proven effective in places like the Somme and Cambrai but whose overall value remained difficult to gauge. They had appeared on the stage but had not caught the eye of the spotlight due to their problematic performance. The interwar years proved to be just as rocky since there was no conflict in which to test the weapons, much less to demand the continuance of production. Tank development was further retarded by diminishing interest, scarce funds, and infighting within and between the different branches of the US Army.

4

American Armor during the Interwar Years

Not one more horse will I give up for a tank.

—Chief of Cavalry Gen. John Herr

Though the battlefields of World War I had given birth to the tank, it remained a bastard to the armies of the world. Generals wondered what to do with this newest military innovation. Was it an infantry-support weapon? Was it simply mobile artillery? Was it a new tool for the cavalry? Unfortunately, the heads of these three branches could only contemplate the tank's lack of potential in relation to their respective arms. This limited their imagination, prompting most to pay disparaging, if any, attention to the new weapon.

The Tank Question

During the interwar years, those who thought that the tank was a revolutionary weapon composed the minority. British colonel Fuller was one of the first to propose that it should be brought up independently within a new branch of the army. This concept failed to materialize in the United States at that time due to personal biases and bureaucratic partisanship, particularly by members of the cavalry.

Logically, it should have been recognized that the retention of the horse as a battle platform into the twentieth century was absurd. While the harnessing of steam in the eighteenth century had paved the way for the industrial revolution, military commanders should have foreseen that the internal-combustion engine would likewise change the world of mobility. Civilizations expanded, cities grew, and all aspects of life began to accelerate. Military leaders worldwide—and especially cavalrymen—should have recognized that conflicts too would become larger in scope and speed, altering the dynamic nature of war.

Straddling the nineteenth and twentieth centuries, the Second Boer War had demonstrated that vast campaigns proved too much for the living blood and muscle of an animal. Of the 500,000 horses the British used during that conflict, more than 300,000 died. Of these, "no more than two percent were lost [due to wounds]. The rest died of overwork, disease or malnutrition, at a rate of 336 for each day of the campaign."[1] One would think that any vehicular innovation, especially the tank would have been a welcome addition to the ranks of the cavalry. This was not so.

The US Tank Corps had come out of the Great War lacking sufficient combat experience on which to base any sound operational doctrine. Its trial-and-error opportunity to develop had been cut short by the Armistice. In 1918 the United States and Great Britain had formed the Anglo-American Tank Commission to study and evaluate armor.[2] In 1919 commission member Maj. R. E. Carlson (American) finished an investigation concerning future development, recommending that the United States pursue fast medium tanks. With support from the Tank Corps and the infantry, the Ordnance Department, the army branch tasked with obtaining, designing, and maintaining nearly every type of fighting equipment, began plans for a new tank.[3]

Any new piece of ordnance required a colossal network of planners to get the job done—and it took time. Every vehicle and weapon design demanded considerable thought to weight and size to accommodate transportation on trucks or railroad cars across bridges and roads and on ships overseas to depots potentially thousands of miles away. And before the Ordnance Department could begin developing a new tank, it needed to know what role the vehicle would play on the battlefield. At that time there was no clear tactical principle from which to guide design: should the emphasis be on speed, armor, or firepower? The US Army General Staff had to determine the tactical role to provide the answer to this question.

While the infantry typically criticized the existing options, some saw a future for the tank as a support weapon. Dwight Eisenhower scrutinized the tank in his article "A Tank Discussion," published in 1920. He believed that the tank had four major limitations. First, it could "not cross deep, un-bridged bodies of water, rocky cliffs, nor deep bogs." Second, any forest with large trees was impassible. Third, the vehicle's range was limited by fuel. Fourth, contrary to the infantry, the tank "has no power of holding a position it has taken." He also summarized the arguments of skeptics, who believed that "(a) tanks are of value only in trench warfare; (b) we will probably never again be engaged in truly 'trench warfare'; and (c) the tank is mechanically untrustworthy and therefore unfit to be depended on in a crisis." These beliefs, Eisenhower pointed out, were based on designs that were the "emergency results of emergency methods." New models, he proposed, would be somewhere between the light Renault and the heavy British tanks, weighing no more than fifteen tons and carrying both machine guns and a 6-pounder cannon, and could potentially replace the divisional machine-gun battalion. In other words, the tank could be the basis of an organic company within the infantry division.[4]

General Pershing also believed the tank to be a tool for infantry. As independent tank units could not hold ground, their only possible role, he believed, was to directly support the foot soldiers. Appearing before a joint session of Congress, Pershing proposed that the infantry absorb the tanks as an auxiliary force. Within the year, Congress made its decision. The National Defense Act of 1920 ordered the Tank Corps disbanded and gave the infantry exclusive rights to operate and develop tanks. The 1,000-odd tanks remaining in the Corps, mostly M1917s (American Renaults), thus were dispersed among the infantry units. The tank school itself was transferred to Fort Meade, Maryland, where infantry commanders governed its operations.[5]

Meanwhile, the Ordnance Department still needed direction regarding the tank's battlefield role. In April 1922 they finally received the guiding principles for development from the War Department:

1. The Primary mission of the tank is to facilitate the uninterrupted advance of the riflemen in the attack. Its size, armament, speed, and all the accessories for making it an offensive force must be approached with the above mission as the final objective to be obtained in development.

2. As a matter of economy and simplicity in organization, the number of types of tanks should be kept at a minimum. Reliance cannot safely be placed on a single type of tank, but two types, a light and a medium, should be capable of fulfilling all assigned missions.

3. These types should be as follows:

    a) the light tank not exceeding 5 tons in weight and capable of being transported on heavy motor trucks.

    b) The medium tank not exceeding 15 tons in weight, thereby bringing it within the limits of average highway bridges, the capacity of railroads and the limit of 15 tons placed by the War Department on the medium pontoon bridge.

4. Inasmuch as certain progress has already been obtained toward developing of the medium type, first consideration should be given to that type. . . . Its speed should be the greatest possible consistent with the limitation in weight, economy and fuel, and radius of action. The control of speed should permit a reduction to that of the advancing rifleman.

5. The armament of medium tanks should consist of machine guns and guns of heavier caliber. The guns should be capable of firing upon enemy troops in trenches and engage hostile tanks on a basis of equality; they should, therefore, be of as large [a] caliber as is consistent with prescribed weight limits and ammunition supply. . . . Auxiliary vehicles, except signal tanks, should not be of a type special to the tank service alone.

6. The tank is not likely to decrease in importance as a war weapon, but tank construction is expensive and it must be expected that funds will be limited. It is, therefore, directed that developments be conducted along the following lines:

    a) The Chief of Ordnance will be allowed great latitude in development of pilot tanks for test purposes, in close cooperation with the Chief of Infantry.

> b) The first program will be the development of suitable medium pilot tanks with their equipment, of a weight not exceeding 15 tons, and of a maximum speed of not less than twelve mph [miles per hour].
>
> c) That for the present funds and effort will be applied principally to development purposes rather than to the construction of complete tank units.
>
> d) The manufacturer of complete tank units will not be undertaken until suitable medium pilot tanks have been developed and have been approved by the War Department as the best available type.
>
> e) Tanks will not be designed with a special adaptation to chemical warfare. . . .
>
> f) The development of special auxiliary vehicles for tank service alone will not be undertaken. . . .
>
> g) Expenditure of funds on existing tanks will be limited to the amount necessary to keep those in actual service in repair, and those in storage from deterioration.[6]

It is significant to note that weight and speed took precedence. Consequently, armament was to be "as large [a] caliber as is consistent with the prescribed weight limits." This decision would have adverse consequences (addressed later in the book). Though a number of designs were on the table, all were over the new weight limits and had to be scrapped. While the weight limits were specific, the chief of ordnance and the chief of infantry would have to determine the other specifications for the tanks themselves. One detail, however, was most clear: the "primary mission of the tank is to facilitate the uninterrupted advance of the riflemen." Any commanding doctrinal concepts were left in the air, as actual tanks were necessary to determine their capabilities, which in turn would help shape their tactical role—and this would determine doctrine. Here, the paradox ensued, for the ordnance developers needed doctrine to begin designing the new tanks.[7]

Into the Mechanized Force

In 1927 the British created the Experimental Tank Force. Secretary of War Dwight Davis observed this force and was convinced that the United States should keep up with its allies across the Atlantic. He instructed Chief of Staff Gen. Charles P. Summerall to organize the Experimental Mechanized Force and conduct a study to assess the validity of armor in future wars. Conducted under the direction of Assistant Chief of Staff Brig. Gen. Frank Parker and cavalryman Maj. Adna Chaffee Jr., the study produced a report entitled *A Mechanized Force*, which laid out some of the foundations for an eventual armored force and argued for an armored corps.[8] Meanwhile, officers and enlisted men from the Infantry Tank Force, infantry, cavalry, artillery, engineers, and the Ordnance Department converged at Camp Meade, Maryland, to establish the Experimental Mechanized Force by July 1928. Though this unit disbanded after only two months, in October 1930 Summerall directed the formation of another unit, the Mechanized Force, at Fort Eustis, Virginia, under the command of cavalryman Col. Daniel Van Voorhis, soon joined by Chaffee. It consisted of a headquarters company, a troop of armored cars, one tank company, a machine-gun company, a self-propelled artillery battery, an engineer company, an ordnance company, and signal, chemical, and quartermaster detachments. While the Mechanized Force was intended to work out tactics and organization, simultaneously testing new machines, its operations inevitably reflected cavalry pursuit and reconnaissance.[9]

Into the Cavalry

The cavalry, specifically its chief, Maj. Gen. Guy V. Henry, felt that the Mechanized Force was intruding in its tactical jurisdiction, for the cavalry was supposed to be the mobile arm, dashing out on reconnaissance missions and penetrating deep into enemy territory. Cavalrymen felt that it was, in essence, taking their job. Thus, after hearing that Pres. Herbert Hoover had employed the newly appointed chief of staff, Gen. Douglas MacArthur, to assess the horsed cavalry and its validity as an arm in modern warfare, Major General Henry feared the worst. Admitting, if only to himself, that a strictly horsed cavalry just might be obsolete, he soon requested that the cavalry absorb the Mechanized Force.

This request was well timed, coinciding with economic strains that tested the practicality of a separate mechanized branch. To Henry's satisfaction, MacArthur concluded: "[The] Cavalry acquired its name when soldiers mounted on horses were able to move more rapidly than any other arm.. . . . Thus there has grown up a very natural conception that cavalry must include the horse. Modern firearms have eliminated the horse as a weapon, and as a means of transportation he has become, next to the dismounted man, the slowest means of transportation. . . . To enable the cavalry to develop its organization and equipment so as to maintain its ability under modern conditions to perform its missions, . . . the Mechanized Force will be reorganized [into a] reinforced cavalry regiment."[10] With that, the Mechanized Force was dissolved, its tanks now forming the new 1st Cavalry Regiment (Mechanized) at Fort Knox, Kentucky. Soon this force grew into the 7th Cavalry Brigade (Mechanized), consisting of the 1st Cavalry Regiment (Mechanized), the 13th Cavalry Regiment (Mechanized), and the 68th Field Artillery Battalion. In order to circumvent congressional policy stating that only the infantry could operate tanks, those transferred into the cavalry were designated "combat cars."[11]

Though the tanks once again had a home, they proved to be the unwanted stepchildren to the cavalry, who still preferred the living breath of the horse. Many of the older heads had a hard time putting any faith in the new weapons. Though they had received reports of the effectiveness of German tanks during the Spanish Civil War (1936–39), they had also heard how those machines had fallen prey to antitank guns. Many cavalrymen, along with artillerymen such as Lesley McNair, felt that the antitank gun nullified armor and would eradicate tanks from future battlefields. Author Robert J. Icks pointed out the heresy of this thought, stating how the "opponents of armor made a great to-do about armor penetration by antitank guns but never made the similar obvious comparison between the thin skin of a man and a rifle."[12] It does not require field experience (or for that matter anything above common sense) to know that men, made of only flesh, were still relied upon to conduct combat operations amid flying bullets. Author John Wheldon has stated that this "absurd" synopsis was so widely accepted among the British that it had worked its way up to the parliamentary secretary of war in 1935.[13] Two years prior, the new chief of infantry in the US Army noted that he doubted "very much if in the next war tanks will be able to go charging about the battlefield in the face of anti-tank weapons."[14] He offered that their success in combat rested solely within the control of the infantry.

To such men the tank had become a burden. It required time, energy, manpower, and most importantly money—funds that various arms sought to obtain for their own projects. Yet while the tank would require these resources at the expense of the other arms, it also represented a psychological threat to infantry and cavalry leaders who felt that armor advocates were quite far reaching in their theories.

Extreme tank lobbyists such as J. F. C Fuller had provoked much of this hostile sentiment, arguing that the tank was the future of warfare. In 1927 Fuller's article "Tactics and Mechanization" suggested that the infantry, artillery, and cavalry were more or less doomed to be replaced by the power of armor. Subsequent to barbed wire and machine guns, the infantry, he argued, had already lost its ability to attack and could only advance after the way had been prepared by artillery.[15]

Regardless of logic, traditions die hard in the military, especially those that have been woven into the tapestry of tactical doctrine since the origins of warring civilization—including the horse. For centuries cavalrymen had developed an umbilical dependency on their animals. The same stubborn nobility that had fought to keep the saber rather than the firearm as their weapon of choice would also carry over to their devout relationship with the steed.

Cavalrymen were, by practice, gentlemen and carried with them an aura of prestige developed over the centuries leading up to World War II. For example, prior to the American Revolution, British colonel John Burgoyne had founded a regiment of light cavalry, the 16th Light Dragoons, insisting that the men be from the high class of society and learn French. The dragoons were to "become highly skilled in tactics, weapons, and horsemanship down to 'each strap and buckle.'" In addition, he wanted them to "practice their writing, to read daily, and [to] refrain from foul language."[16] This type of character profile carried on through the centuries, as evident by Patton's ideal cavalryman. During one of his lectures in 1921, the future general made clear that cavalry officers were to not only be "cold blooded heroes" but also "a horse master; a scholar; [and] a high minded gentleman." He further emphasized the "passion" such a soldier must have for his horse. A cavalryman must be a veterinarian, familiar with horse diseases and conditioning, and above all possess an ardent affection for his mount.[17]

Such passion and affection for the horse left the cavalry wanting nothing to do with the tank. These men believed: "The faster [the tank] moves, the greater her consumption of that fuel which is her life blood; the slower she moves, the less her mobility. The theory of the tank [careening] 'promiscuous-like' about the enemy's country has little relation to fact."[18] This dogma among cavalrymen blinded them from recognizing the potential of the weapon. The eradication of the saddle (as they saw it) in essence would rid them of their entire doctrine of warfare. They felt that the horse was the foundation of the cavalry's very existence as an armed branch of the military; no "tank-man" was going to take away their reins.

The Early Tanks

American tank development had not been completely dormant during the interwar years. The first successful developmental tank was the Cunningham T1. With the vehicle more or less starting out as a tractor, the driver was situated between the tracks at the rear with the engine in front of him. Thinly armored walls were designed to protect him and the engine from small-arms fire. A 37-mm gun and a .30-caliber coaxial machine gun were mounted in a turret at the rear behind the driver. The Cunningham was quite fast compared to the earlier Renaults of the Great War. The eight-cylinder, water-cooled engine was rated at 132 horsepower (hp) at 2,600 revolutions per minute (rpm) and could propel the nine-ton vehicle at eighteen mph.

In 1932 the Rock Island Arsenal introduced the latest version of the T1, the T1E4. This model relocated the turret in the center of the tank while the 37-mm gun was shortened. With a new V-8 engine rated at 140 hp, the T1E4 was capable of twenty mph. While the previous models had four two-wheeled bogies, this one utilized a Vickers-Armstrong leaf-spring suspension consisting of two four-wheel articulated bogies. The drive wheel was at the front, and four return wheels carried the tracks back to the idler wheel. It was seven feet tall and fifteen feet long with a crew of four.

In 1934, improvements on the T1E4 resulted in the T2 light tank. The T2 employed a Continental seven-cylinder, air-cooled radial aircraft engine, instigating the use of lightweight yet powerful aviation motors in tank design. Rated at 250 hp, the T2 could reach a speed of twenty-seven mph. The suspension was the same as that of its predecessor, although it only had two return wheels on either side. Also noteworthy was the tank's use of the rubber bushed track pins that extended the life of the tracks considerably.

The suspension on the T2 was soon redesigned to consist of twin two-wheel bogies employing a vertical volute-spring system (VVSS). In addition,

Figure 4. The T1E3 with turret located at the rear. Note the long 37-mm gun. *Courtesy US Army Ordnance Museum, Aberdeen Proving Ground*

Figure 5. The T1E4 with the new Vickers suspension. Note the shorter 37-mm gun and the repositioning of the turret to the center. *Courtesy US Army Ordnance Museum, Aberdeen Proving Ground*

Figure 6. The T1E4 evolved into what would become the T2, pictured here. *Courtesy US Army Ordnance Museum, Aberdeen Proving Ground*

Figure 7. The T2 (modified). This model marked the first appearance of the two-wheel vertical volute-suspension system (VVSS), a characteristic that would remain on American tanks through World War II. *Courtesy US Army Ordnance Museum, Aberdeen Proving Ground*

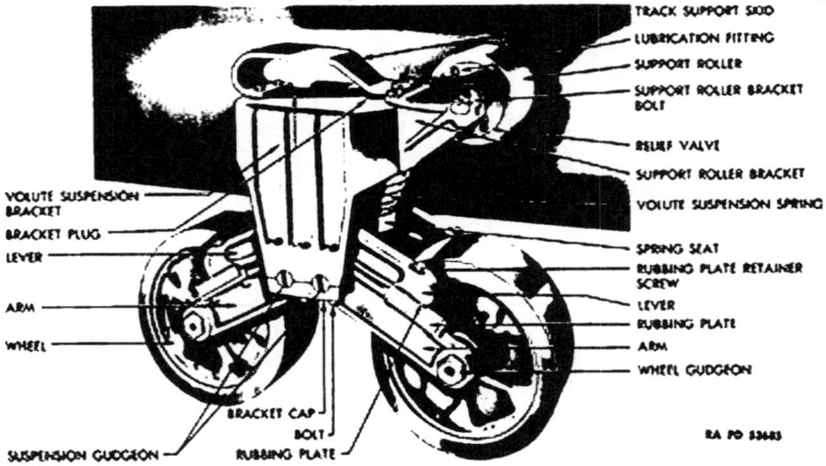

Figure 8. Detailed view of the housing unit (bogie) for the VVSS. *From* Technical Manual 9–1750k

a new track was designed. The T1 and the first T2 models had used forged-steel plates for their tracks, whereas the modified T2 used steel plates with thick rubber pads to reduce wear on the treads.

The M2 Light Tank

After numerous changes and experiments, the T2 gradually evolved into the M2 light tank. The M2A1 had a single turret while the M2A2 had two turrets. Both models had five-eighths-inch armor and weighed approximately nine and a half tons. The M2A3 retained the double turret, with one .50-caliber machine gun in the left turret, one .30-caliber in the right turret, and another .30-caliber in the hull. Armor was slightly increased to nearly nine-tenths of an inch. Eventually this tank would be equipped with an M5 37-mm gun and designated the M2A4. It also carried three .30-caliber machine guns: one located behind the turret on a mount and used for antiaircraft defense, one coaxial, and one located in a ball mount in the right bow of the tank. Its four-man crew consisted of a driver and assistant driver/bow gunner in the hull, and a loader and gunner/commander in the turret. The M2A4 weighed approximately twelve tons and was fourteen feet long. Its maximum armor was just over one-half inch. At the rear of the tank was a Continental WG70 radial aircraft engine that

Figure 9. Crew and equipment for light tank. *Courtesy Davis Memorial Library, Patton Museum, Fort Knox*

Figure 10. A cavalry "combat car." *Courtesy US Army Ordnance Museum, Aberdeen Proving Ground*

Figure 11. Another "combat car" belonging to the cavalry. On the back of this photo is a poem that reads: "My Combat Car. It leaps over the ground, and incidentally through and over these trees, with the greatest of ease. However, it's rough as can be." *Courtesy Davis Memorial Library, Patton Museum, Fort Knox*

Figure 12. The T2 developed into the M2 Light Tank. Note the machine guns in the side sponsons. *Courtesy US Army Ordnance Museum, Aberdeen Proving Ground*

drove the vehicle up to thirty-five mph. Consuming 1.5 gallons per mile, the tanks effective radius was seventy-eight road miles.[19]

The VVSS was retained as it stored significant energy and offered a longer service life compared to other contemporary spring systems. In addition to the suspension, the light tank also kept the rubber-bushed track system of the T2, which allowed the track links to flex. The VVSS and rubber bushings and blocks gave the tracks a useful life of nearly 2,500 miles on paved roads. At this time, most tanks (British and German alike) could only travel roughly 500 miles before their tracks needed service. In contrast, the tracks of World War I tanks were sometimes depleted after only 50 miles.[20]

The M3 Light Tank

The new war in Europe, particularly in Poland and France in 1939–40, had demonstrated that the light armor on the M2A4 was inadequate. Its armor therefore was increased to one and a half inches, while its suspension was also improved. The earlier M2 had four road wheels in addition to the large idler wheel elevated at the rear of the tank, providing a ground-contact length of seven feet. On the M3 the idler wheel was

Figure 13. M3 Light Tank. Note the idler wheel repositioning to provide greater ground contact and the retention of machine guns in the sponsons. *Courtesy Davis Memorial Library, Patton Museum, Fort Knox*

lowered flush to the ground, making it a large road wheel and increasing its track ground-contact length to nine feet. Doing so increased the tank's trench crossing abilities from four feet to six feet as well as its floatation capabilities, allowing it to maneuver over soft terrain.

The M3 was nearly fifteen feet long, seven and a half feet wide, and seven and a half feet tall. Weighing fourteen tons, it could travel one hundred miles on fifty-four gallons of fuel.

The M2 Medium Tank

By 1938 work had started on a medium tank. Basically working from the light M2, designers extended the hull to a length of eighteen feet. To compensate, they added a third bogie with two more road wheels and elevated the idler wheel. The volute springs, located in the bogie housing, were reset parallel to the hull. This configuration would carry on for most of the Second World War, being utilized by multiple vehicles.

It was obvious that a powerful engine was necessary to carry the larger medium tank across the battlefield. According to a powerplant-guidelines memorandum developed by the Armored Force School, six guiding principles had to be followed in order to designate the engine best suited for the tank:

1. POWER—the tank's essence is held in its mobility. Mobility is defined as "the ability to traverse difficult ground and to operate on roads at a high rate of speed."

2. ACCELERATION—closely related to power, the ability of a tank to have the capability to accelerate rapidly. In combat situations, the safety of the crew and tank relied on its ability to speed away or to speed off to the flank of the enemy.

3. MECHANICAL RELIABILITY—Obviously the tank will be subject to rugged conditions; be it weather, terrain, or abuse. A high penalty may be paid for mechanical failure of the engine.

4. WEIGHT AND SPACE—Every pound of weight in the power plant means just that many less which may be used to increase fire power and protection. Space is even more important, for it is not so much the weight of the engine, which increases the overall tank weight; it is the armor plate which must enclose the engine in its compartment.

5. FUEL ECONOMY—A limiting factor in the use of the tank is the amount of fuel the tank can carry. The tank was required to have a cruising range of at least 150 miles. If the engine had a high rate of fuel consumption, the fuel tanks would need to be larger than desired with subsequent increase in the weight of armor plates to protect the tanks.

6. PROCURABILITY—It was necessary to obtain a power plant which is available in quantity without the necessity of tooling a production line.[21]

The Ordnance Department decided to use an air-cooled rather than a water-cooled engine. An air-cooled system was much lighter than a water-cooled system due to the latter's water chambers, pumps, radiator, and associated plumbing. Furthermore, the length of a radial engine was comparatively quite short and would save on space—and consequently weight.

The first tanks were equipped with Continental R-670 radial aircraft engines. While suitable for fifteen-ton tanks, the R-670's 250 horsepower was insufficient for medium tanks nearing thirty tons. Consequently, the Ordnance Department looked to the nine-cylinder Wright R-975 air-cooled radial engine, known as the Whirlwind. (Continental would ultimately produce this engine under license for armored vehicles.) Displacing 973 cubic inches, the R-975 was rated at 400 hp at 2,400 rpm. It was soon married with the new M2 medium tank, where its power-to-weight ratio was sufficient. Nevertheless, American tanks needed to be stronger and more powerful if they were to take on the Germans, who had so quickly defeated the Poles and the French. Eventually the new M3s became much heavier than their predecessors. The Whirlwind engine was "definitely underpowered. Improvements to this installation have increased the horsepower available but the HP/Wt. ratio is still too low to give completely satisfactory performance."[22]

Combined with further unsatisfactory reports from maneuvers, it became clear that more-powerful engines needed to be considered. But by late 1941 the US and its allies were in desperate need of medium tanks; there was no time to re-engineer and test new engines. Budgets still were tight, and unlike other military vehicles, such as trucks, jeeps, planes, and boats, the tank has no civilian equivalent. For this reason, armor units had to make do with what was available. As early as August 1940,

Figure 14. The Wright R-975 engine used in the M3, M4, and M4A2 medium tanks. *Courtesy Davis Memorial Library, Patton Museum, Fort Knox*

Undersecretary of War Robert Patterson had stressed to Supply Arms and Services the necessity to avoid all modifications in tank production unless they were "absolutely necessary." By January 1941 US strategy was settled on producing "thousands of imperfect tanks," capable of gnawing away at the enemy, rather than "scores of perfect tanks" maneuvering on American testing grounds.[23] This philosophy of production and strategy would carry on throughout the war, creating ongoing controversy.

One significant drawback to any large radial engine was its centrally located driveshaft. Most vehicular engines used an inline "V" design, with the driveshaft located on the bottom. While this did not arouse any concern with the smaller M2, it became a problem once engineers wanted to shift to a larger turret design due to the necessity of having the turret basket (where the turret crew operates) above the driveshaft in order to rotate 360 degrees. Using a radial engine would require the turret and overall silhouette of the tank to rise quite high compared to its contemporaries.

The M2A1 was armed with a turret-mounted M3 37-mm cannon and seven .30-caliber machine guns: two in the front glacis plate, one coaxial, and a pair located on either side of the tank in the sponsons. The M3 antitank gun fired a two-pound projectile at 2,900 feet per second (fps), providing an effective range of 750 yards. The M2A1's crew consisted of a driver, a commander, and four gunners. The tanks could tear apart any thinly armored positions or vehicle and decimate enemy troops. From 1939 to 1940 the Rock Island Arsenal built more than two hundred M2s.

War Games and Disunion

While American isolationists dreamt of peace in their time, the US military began to squirm—war was coming. Though Congress acknowledged the need for manpower, the overhaul of equipment and training programs also were critically required. Army Chief of Staff Gen. George C. Marshall wanted to assess his land forces through a series of war games.

These army maneuvers would allow the various arms to test their equipment, gauge the training of their men, find the weak links in their chains of command, and identify any problems the army might face in logistics, communication, and tactics, to name a few. One important question was the tank's capabilities. Could the vehicles maneuver effectively with their limited fuel supply? Could armor units continue with their assaults while simultaneously maintaining their equipment? Could the tank traverse the same ground as the horse?

The maneuvers took place in northern Louisiana during the months of April and May 1940. With nearly 3,500 square miles at their disposal, 70,000 soldiers went to war against each other in mock scenarios. In May the tanks of the 7th Cavalry Brigade and the Provisional Tank Brigade proved their worth. During the last exercise, the two brigades formed a division that was pitted against the 1st Cavalry Division. The tanks carried out rapid thrusts and wide sweeping flank maneuvers, enabling them to defeat the horsed cavalry.

The Third Army's commander, Lt. Gen. Stanley D. Embick, was convinced that the United States must create independent armored divisions. For tank advocates, the Louisiana maneuvers were a validation of their theories.

While the armored division seemed to be an idea for the future, the concept had earnestly been around for at least a decade. An article published in the *Infantry Journal* by Maj. C. C. Benson in 1931 seems to be one of the first to propose the armored division.[24] He began his article modestly: "A few outspoken enthusiasts maintain that most of the fighting in the future wars will be done by machines. Those who rely more upon practical experience than upon imagination can hardly accept this view without important reservations. . . . The ability of mechanized units to operate independently for brief periods should not obscure the fact that they will be organized primarily for co-operation with other arms. Both the old and the new combat elements have their parts to play." Benson reasoned that the role of the tanks would be to lead assault on well-defended ground and to maneuver quickly directly to the enemy's front while also striking the flank and then rear. This concept was nothing novel. Yet, he asserted, "we cannot reasonably expect a single [tank] unit to execute efficiently missions so markedly different; consequently it will be necessary to consider carefully the matter of organization." The "land battleships," as he called tanks, a term left over from World War I, would have various purposes, and the vehicles themselves "may be identical except for thickness of armor and details of armament." This prediction obviously came into fruition with light tanks, medium tanks, and tank destroyers. Benson argued that because tank production would assuredly "affect materially the revision of present plans for mobilization," the organization of these units into an armored division was a subject of "immediate consideration." It was not until after the 1940 maneuvers that these ideas would receive serious consideration.[25]

Armored Force Genesis

Following the maneuvers, Chaffee, Patton, and Embick had a private conference, undisclosed to cavalry and infantry commanders, to discuss the future of armor. Meeting in a school basement in Alexandria, Louisiana, they were also joined by Brig. Gen. Frank Andrews, the War Department assistant chief of staff, G-3. All agreed that there must be an independent armored force—to continue fighting under cavalry control, restricted to its doctrine, would deprive armor of reaching its full military potential. Andrews approved the idea and proposed it to the War Department.[26]

Chaffee went to Washington with a monumental agenda. First, he met with Gen. John K. Herr, the chief of cavalry, to propose that the horse-mounted regiments be overhauled with tanks and then assigned together to form an armored division. After listening to this proposal, Herr "sat there rather straight in his chair, head down—then he looked up." He spoke frankly, stating, "Adna, not one horse will I give up for a tank." Chaffee, perturbed by the general's response, simply replied, "Johnny, if that's the way you feel about it." Turning to Lt. Col. Robert Lee of the Army Air Corps, Chaffee concluded, "Come on Bob, I'm through with him."[27]

With that Chaffee went to speak to Marshall, who had already shown support for the development of an independent armored branch. The argument already had been made that the cavalry replace its horses with tanks, but now Chaffee demanded a bit more—complete independence from the cavalry altogether. Marshall read the proposal and without delay approved the formation of the Armored Force. Its commander would be Adna Chaffee, promoted to brigadier general.

Somewhere in Louisiana in May 1940, an infantry company is informed by the army umpire that it has sustained 20-percent casualties in the recent mock engagement. The company commander walks off with other officers, while the enlisted men stroll into the shade, taking off their helmets, lighting cigarettes, and settling on the ground. Two light tanks come up the road and shut off their engines. The hatches open, and the sweating crewmembers clamber out of their stifling machines. Captivated by the tanks, the infantrymen rise to their feet, leave their gear behind, and approach the vehicles. Some walk around them, while others ask the tankers questions. Two men climb aboard, while another peeks into an open hatch. There are smiles and questions. "We're dead," one of the crewmen jokes.

Five thousand miles away, French soldiers take shelter in a house. Panting, they hug the floor as splinters of plaster and brick spray from the walls as machine-gun bullets whiz in. A 37-mm shell tears into the room, killing one and wounding another. Two men run out but are cut down by machine-gun fire. The shooting stops, the dust settles, but the survivors remain on the floor. Through holes in the wall they can see down the road. Vehicles are approaching fast. The floor shakes as two, three, four German tanks race by, not stopping. After they pass, the Frenchmen rise and run out the back of the house, carrying their wounded. By now the German tanks have moved on to the next town.

While the Americans put theories to the test in a series of exercises, the Germans seemed to have already perfected the art of mechanized warfare. Their tanks had conquered Poland and were busy tearing through France while the Americans fought mosquitoes in Louisiana. The US tank force was in its infancy, and its leaders monitored German operations, taking special note of their machines and organization. How were the tanks deployed? What types of guns did they have? How were they destroyed? The answers to those questions would shape the fate of the Armored Force—for better or for worse.

5

Guderian and the German Attack on Poland

> We conclude that the suggestion that our tanks be divided among infantry divisions is nothing but a return to the original English tactics of 1916–17, which were even then a failure, for the English tanks were not successful until they were used *en masse* at Cambrai.
>
> **—*Journal of the National Union of German Officers* (1937)**

While the British first brought the tank to the battlefield, the Germans first appreciated the full potentials of mobile warfare, a result of the limitations imposed on them by the Versailles Treaty. Since the Germans were limited to a 100,000-man army, they were obliged to become proficient in mechanization, exploiting improved means of deployment to quickly concentrate their few soldiers when necessary. Thus the Germans busied themselves with designs for a mobile army.

Heinz Guderian

In World War I there had been no serious threat to the transportation of troops behind the lines. But the mechanization of armies would present a whole new set of problems in rear-area security afterward. In Germany, future general Heinz Guderian, a student of the theories proposed by Hart and Fuller, recognized this problem early. He had first served in the 5th Cavalry Division during the war, commanding a wireless station. He moved up the ranks through signal units within the Fourth and

Fifth Armies, working for various headquarters units. In 1917 he was transferred to a general-staff position with the 4th Infantry Division, eventually taking over the 2nd Battalion, 14th Infantry Regiment. This assignment was followed by various staff positions, which made him an appropriate candidate for inspectorate of transport troops, Motorized Transport Department. During this assignment, Guderian recalled, "I became for the first time aware of the possibility of employing motorized troops." Following the war, he wrote: "Germany [is now] undefended. . . . We must rely on mobile defense. . . . This [can] only be satisfactorily provided by armored vehicles."[1]

In light of the performance of the tanks during the Great War, Guderian believed that they should not be in auxiliary roles to the infantry but rather in their own divisions, which he felt should include all supporting arms to facilitate armored actions. He, as well as a handful of others, saw that it was the tank that was Germany's best weapon for land warfare. Guderian, while no radical visionary, recognized the potential for theories of this sort of application through the writings of Fuller and Hart. "These farsighted soldiers," he wrote, were "trying to make the tank something more than just an infantry support weapon. They envisaged it in relationship to the growing motorization of our age and thus they became the pioneers of a new type of warfare on the largest scale."[2]

By 1925 Guderian was examining the feasibility of using tanks in a combat role. After using old troop carriers as tanks in field tests, he hoped, "we were on the way to transforming our motorized units from supply troops into combat troops."[3] In 1928 he and his staff began work on tank-unit structures, from platoon to battalion strength.

On 1 February 1931 Guderian was put in command of a motorized battalion. His 1st Company had armored reconnaissance cars, the 2nd had dummy tanks, the 3rd was an antitank unit with wooden guns, and the 4th was equipped with motorcycles. But even with only a battalion-strength command, the inspector of transport troops hindered his efforts to develop it for a combat role.

Guderian remembered that the inspector "had so little faith in this new unit that he forbade us to carry out combined exercises with other battalions stationed in the area." Emphasizing his frustration, he recalled, "when the 3rd Division, of which we formed a part, went on maneuvers, we were not allowed to be employed in units of over platoon strength." Even upon retirement the inspector told Guderian, "neither of us will ever see German tanks in operation in our lifetime."[4] But Guderian continued to pursue his theories.

As the tank advocates worldwide ventured to forge armor into a critical implement of warfare, they also concerned themselves with the commanders who would be wielding this tool. There were many officers who had no faith in such projects, and in many cases the tank would fall into their hands. Since a weapon is only as good as the person who controls it, Guderian stressed the need for independent armor formations under the command of men who understood their capabilities and promise.

In an article for the *Journal of the National Union of German Officers*, dated 1937, Guderian and other advocates for this new arm related their reasons for independent armor units through an "imaginary story":

> Red and blue are at war. Each side has 100 Infantry Divisions and 100 tank Battalions. Red has split up its tanks among its Infantry Divisions: Blue has massed them in Panzer Divisions under direct control of supreme headquarters. On a front of, shall we say, 300 miles, 100 are tank-proof, 100 are difficult for tanks, and 100 are good tank country. So in the battle the following picture emerges: Red has deployed a sizeable proportion of its divisions, along with their tank components, opposite the Blue positions in country where tanks cannot operate and are therefore useless, while a further portion are in difficult tank country where, though not entirely wasted, their chances of successful action are small. Whatever happens, only a fraction of Red's tank forces can be employed in the country for which they are suited. Blue, on the other hand, has collected all its armor in the one place where a decision can be reached and where the ground can be made use of; he therefore has the opportunity of going into battle with at least double his adversary's tank strength while assuming the defensive along the rest of the front against Red's very small-scale tank attacks.[5]

They proposed that the "armored branch will include all other arms. Infantry, artillery, and engineers are necessary to the development of its action, but [armor] will impose upon them its own methods of combat by making them dependent on the motor. Supporting infantry, artillery, and engineers will be motorized and partially armored within the framework of the armored division and the motorized infantry division." Stressing the need for support, the article continued, "the desire to protect the armored weapon against the counter-attack of its most dangerous enemies, the tanks and the plane, will require the incorporation of numerous and powerful anti-tank and anti-aircraft weapons into the panzer division."[6]

Still, the men who had seen the British tanks in the mud twenty years prior could not ignore their own experience. These officers had "built up an entirely fanciful idea of a tank attack in which vast numbers of tanks massed together roll steadily forward to crush the enemy . . . (thus providing a magnificent target for artillery and anti-tank fire)."[7] During the Polish campaign of 1939, the tank's effectiveness—and overall success—would be obstructed by the upper echelon's reckoning that armor be held close to and in support of the infantry.

September 1st 1939. The air is chilly and thick with fog. A German soldier lying on the wet grass wipes the dew from the face of his watch—it is 3:30 in the morning. Carefully walking in the darkness, company commanders return to their troops from their final battalion meetings. A rifleman inspects his bolt, while another tugs on his various buckles and straps—all is secure. A faint command is heard, and a few squads grunt to their feet, gear clicking and rattling, and tread off into the darkness. One soldier lying on his back, propped up by his gear, pretends to be asleep. He hears someone mutter "almost 4:00." Thirty minutes of peace remain. A voice in the darkness curses as its owner's foot finds a hole in the tall grass, followed by a clanking thud—some laughter follows. A tankman's hands and feet have no trouble finding their way up onto his vehicle's hull, like a child who's climbed a backyard tree a hundred times, swiftly climbing into his machine. Tank engines idle.

At 4:29 the men are silent, anticipating the sounds of war. Some hearts start to beat again, and shoulders relax as 4:30 comes—and goes—without a sound. Then it begins. The distant "buh-booms" of the artillery fire pulse through the countryside, one after the other. Moments later the sound is drowned out by the roar of the shells flying overhead on their way to unseen targets. Orders are shouted, men rise up, and tanks bark black smoke out of their exhausts. With a slight jolt the panzers move forward, churning up the wet soil.

The war is on.

The Panzers

As Guderian set about the development of the panzer divisions, it was his opinion that each "would need two types of tanks: a light tank with an armor piercing gun and two machine-guns, one in the turret and the other in the body; and a medium tank with a large caliber gun, and two machine-guns as before." Within a battalion, three companies would be equipped with light tanks and the fourth with medium tanks. The latter would be used to support the light tanks in addition to engaging targets beyond their range.

The Mark I

This first "tank" model began as a small British tractor chassis built by Vickers and shipped to Germany as agricultural equipment or industrial tractors. Using these frames, Guderian and his staff began turning them into light training tanks, eventually becoming the Mark I.[8]

The tank weighed more than six tons and had a crew of two. Its small one-man turret was offset to the starboard side, with two MG-13 machine guns situated at the front. It was fourteen and a half feet long and had a low profile, standing at only six feet tall, and was identifiable by its five open-spoked road wheels.[9] The respectable road speed of twenty-five mph was a tradeoff for the Mark I's thin armor, which peaked at about three-quarters of an inch, offering it protection from small arms and shrapnel only. This was insignificant at the time as it was to be used primarily as a training vehicle. Nevertheless, by September 1939 the Germans had close to 1,500 Mark Is.

The Mark II

The Mark II was designed primarily to serve as a transition between the Mark I and the medium panzers. Its armor ranged from about three-quarters of an inch to one and a quarter inches and consequently weighed in at nine tons. Still keeping a low profile of only six and a half feet, the tank had a crew of three. Its turret was centered and located slightly forward, housing one coaxial machine gun and a 20-mm cannon. While the suspension was slightly different from the Mark I, the arrangement of the drive and road wheels remained unchanged. Its road speed was an impressive thirty-five mph.

The Mark III and Mark IV

Guderian's stress for a medium tank led to the production of two models. Weighing more than twenty tons, the Mark III was three times heavier than the Mark I. It was armed with a 37-mm antitank gun that fired a 1.5-pound shell at 2,500 fps, allowing for an effective range of about 900 yards.

Guderian urged that the tank should be equipped with a 50-mm gun. Due to ongoing production of the 37-mm gun, however, it was expedient to utilize the smaller weapon rather than make factory modifications for manufacturing the larger one.[10] (The effects of such bureaucracy, common in the development process, will be seen again with the design of the American M4.) Standardization is a high priority in weapons development, and only the most brutal lessons from the battlefield can blunt the momentum of uninterrupted production.

The turret of the Mark III had three entrances. On either side was a hatch for the gunner and loader, while a hatch for the tank commander was on top. It was much larger than that of the light panzers, being designed to accommodate larger-caliber cannons once they became available. The Mark III could travel on the road at twenty-five mph on its six small road wheels. It carried a five-man crew: the commander, loader, gunner, radio operator (who also served as the bow gunner), and the driver.

Looking like a big brother to the Mark III, the Mark IV Ausf A distinguished itself with its short-barreled 75-mm howitzer. It had eight road wheels on four bogies that could carry the tank up to twenty-four mph on the road. Intended to make up the fourth company of each tank battalion, its role was to augment attacks made by the Mark IIIs.

The Mark IV also had a five-man crew. The driver and machine gunner/radio operator sat in the hull. In the turret were the loader, gunner, and commander. Maximum armor was about three-quarters of an inch on the turret and five-eighths of an inch on the hull. Only a handful of these initial models were produced by 1937. At that time production switched to the Ausf B, which had increased armor protection and a more powerful engine. The gun and the armor for the Mark IV would be improved throughout the war. It would finally mount the KwK40 cannon, with a muzzle velocity of over 3,000 fps.

The LT 35 and LT 38

In addition to the panzers, German armor formations also employed Czechoslovakian tanks acquired during the occupation. In 1935 the Skoda Company introduced the LT 35. Fifteen feet long, it weighed ten and a half tons. Its hull and turret were riveted with a maximum of about one inch of armor and carried two machine guns and a turret-mounted 37.2-mm gun. With a four-man crew, the LT 35 had a maximum speed of twenty-five mph. But once in the hands of the Czech Army, problems began to arise. The steering and gear-change mechanisms were operated by a pneumatic system that often failed in cold weather. The Czechs fielded three hundred of these tanks in 1938.[11]

By 1939 the LT 35 had benefited from numerous improvements. Engineers removed the pneumatic system and replaced the suspension with four large road wheels. They also exchanged the 120-hp engine for a 125-hp replacement. Further modifications resulted in the LT 35 becoming the LT 38. On 1 July 1938 it was adopted as Czechoslovakia's standard light tank, but fewer than a hundred LT 38s saw service before the Germans took over in March.

In 1939 Germany adopted about 200 of the existing LT 35s into their light divisions, redesignating them, Panzerkampfwagen 35(t)s. They also integrated the LT 38 as the Panzerkampfwagen 38(t) and produced 325 additional tanks of that model.[12] German panzer divisions utilized roughly 300 Czech tanks.

Altogether, more than 2,500 tanks of various models in seven panzer divisions participated in the invasion of Poland. Chiefly the armored forces comprised the light, thinly armored, but fast-moving Mark I and IIs. The heavier Mark IIIs and IVs, limited in numbers, did see action in this campaign.

Poland

The Versailles Treaty had taken roughly 10 percent of Germany's territory and divided it among Poland, Lithuania, and Czechoslovakia. Poland had been resurrected and became an independent republic with the help of the League of Nations following the Armistice. In addition, that country received a corridor of land providing access to the Baltic Sea, splitting East Prussia from the rest of Germany.

To make matters worse, Poland had sought to reclaim further territory in the east during the short Polish-Russian War (1920). From the start then, Poland's independence was stained with German resentment and Russian blood.

Adolf Hitler's signature on a nonaggression pact with Poland in 1934 lulled European leaders into a false sense of security. Even following the annexations of Austria and the Czech Sudetenland in March and September 1938, they felt that perhaps German ambitions were satisfied. But toward the end of the year, the Supreme High Command of the German Army (Oberkommando des Heeres) had spread out maps and positioned divisional markers—their pieces were lined along the Polish border.

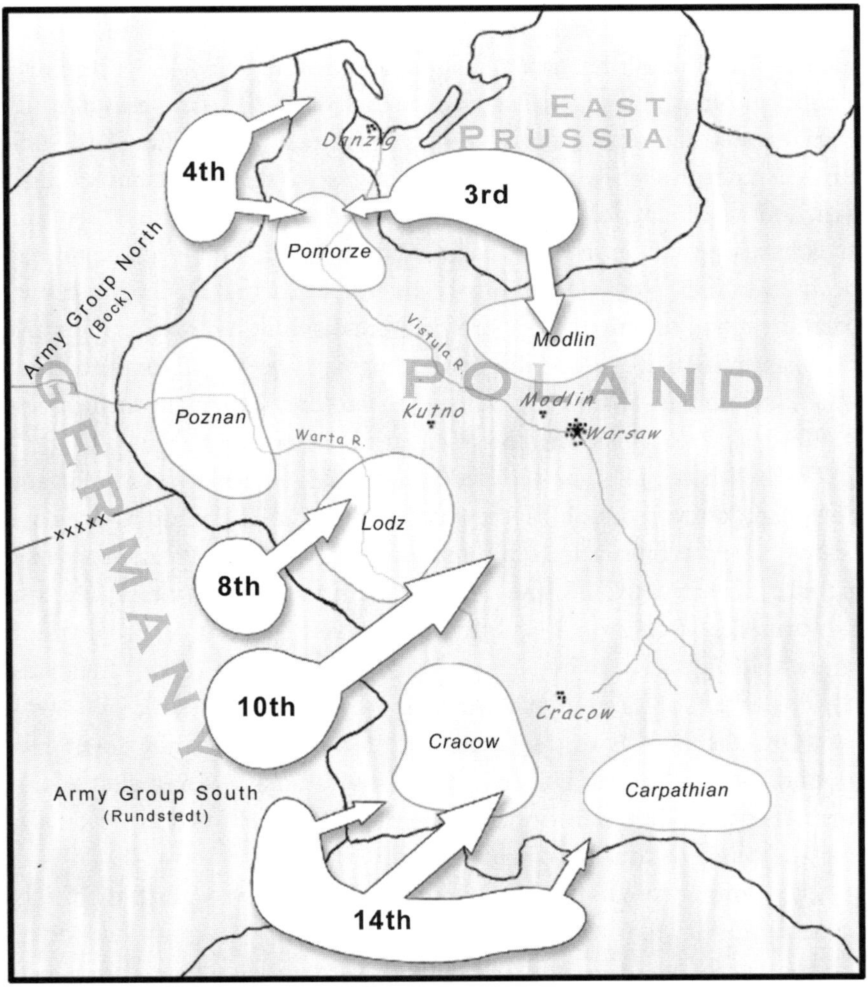

Figure 15. Poland, September 1939.

Without delay, German air-reconnaissance sorties were in the sky over Poland. Plans for the invasion envisioned a two-pronged attack from the north and south along its western border. Two smaller forces coming out of East Prussia would augment these assaults, forming a wide pincer around the western half of Poland.

Army Group North, led by Gen. Fedor von Bock, consisted of the Fourth and Third Armies, with a combined strength of 630,000 men. The Fourth Army's armored units would slice east into the Polish Corridor, racing to meet elements of the Third Army attacking west out of East Prussia. The Third Army would also send a force to attack Warsaw simultaneously with forces from Army Group South.

Gen. Gerd von Rundstedt commanded Army Group South, with 886,000 men at his disposal. His army group was made up of the Eighth, Fourteenth, and the Tenth Armies, with the latter being the main assault force. The Tenth would use its armor to dash northeast to Warsaw. The Eighth Army would protect its northern left flank, while the Fourteenth covered their southern right, taking Cracow.

Polish commander in chief Marshal Edward Rydz-Smigly on paper had nearly two million men to defend his country, but actual combatants numbered less than half that. These troops were dispersed into six armies, five of which were located along the western plains. From north to south, these were the Pomorze, Poznan, Lodz, Cracow, and the Carpathian Armies. The Modlin Army was positioned between East Prussia and Warsaw.

The Polish capital sat 140 miles from the Tenth Army in the west and only 30 miles from the Third Army in East Prussia. The Poznan Army was best prepared to thwart an attack and thus was located in Poland's western extremity, which bulged into Germany. With four infantry divisions and two brigades of cavalry, it expected to receive the brunt of any invasion and would fight a delaying action. With the exception of two divisions, no substantial forces stood between this army and Warsaw, directly to the east. Once engaged with the enemy, the Poznan units would slowly give ground. With all of the Polish armies also gradually withdrawing, commanders hoped that their fronts would mesh together to form a defensive line and thus hold out until help arrived.

Most unfortunate for the Poles, the Poznan Army was positioned right between the German army groups. Together, their attack routes straddled the western bulge of Poland, avoiding direct engagement with Poland's most effective army altogether.

Hitler felt that the only threat from a man in British uniform would come from the sea. As a precaution, he held most of the German navy near the Danish peninsula. In terms of military force, the French posed a great threat, but Hitler was certain they did not have the heart to try and breach his "impregnable" West Wall.

Germany Makes its Move

The Fourth Army deployed the I, II, and III Corps and the XIX Panzer Corps along the corridor. The XIX Corps, under Guderian, comprised the 2nd and 20th Mechanized Divisions along with the 3rd Panzer Division, which was equipped with roughly 300 light tanks, forty-three Mark IIIs, and thirty-two Mark IVs. The Third Army in East Prussia deployed the smaller Kempf Division of I Corps, which consisted of roughly 140 light panzers, three Mark IIIs, and nine Mark IVs.

Clouds of dust and exhaust streak behind the German tanks. The defenders watch helplessly as they approach. One can imagine a Polish infantryman hunkered down in his position. He scans the approaching force for troops—something to aim at with his rifle. The tanks are another 100 yards closer, their engines and tracks now audible. Soon they are so close that he cannot stand up and run. One of the tanks slows to a crawl, its small turret turns to the side—a bright flash erupts from its gun. A second later the report is heard. Another flash from a tank, and a shell shrieks through the air. As the panzers close in, they open up with their machine guns, spitting streaks of tracer bullets and chewing up Polish positions. They creep forward. They are not stopping. The panzers have arrived.

In the north the Fourth Army's I Corps began the thrust toward the port cities of Gdynia and Danzig. The II, III, and XIX Corps pushed into the corridor and began their drive toward the Vistula River. Guderian recalled that "the whole corps moved simultaneously over the frontier. There was a thick ground mist at first, which prevented the air force from giving us any support. I accompanied the 3rd Panzer Brigade, in the first wave." The 3rd Panzer Division moved forward to the vicinity north of Zempelburg, located roughly thirty miles west of the Vistula. Here, elements of the Pomorze Army put up stiff resistance. Guderian continued: "The mist suddenly lifted and the leading tanks found themselves face to face with Polish defense positions. The Polish anti-tank gunners scored many direct hits."[13] The 3rd Division continued its attack until halted at the Brahe River, fifteen miles from the Vistula. The division paused there until a bridge was found still intact in the town of Hammermugle. Troops went across the river in rubber boats to secure the opposite bank, then the panzers crossed on the bridge. By the end of the first day, elements of the division had reached the Vistula.

On 3 September the 3rd Panzer Division, along with the 23rd Infantry Division and the 20th Motorized Division, began to seal in Polish units in the corridor. Guderian recorded that the tanks attacked and destroyed retreating infantry in addition to supply, artillery, and bridging units. This attests to the speed of the panzers and their ability to reach and attack the "interior." Against even the light Mark I and II, Polish units stood no chance. They were, as Guderian put it, "annihilated." Von Bock's North Army Group pushed the Poles out of the corridor in a matter of four days.

While the Third Army's XXI Corps attacked west into the corridor to meet Guderian's forces, its I Corps, with the Kempf Division, attacked south, pushing the Modlin Army out of Mlawa, Przasnysz, and Ciechanow.

In the south Rundstedt's army group also found success. The Eighth Army's X and XIII Corps maneuvered to the Warta River. The VIII and XVII Corps of the Fourteenth Army took Cracow, while the massive Tenth Army pushed toward Radomsko and closed in on Warsaw.

The Tenth Army consisted of three corps that included the following armor units: XVI Corps, with the 1st and 4th Panzer Divisions; IV Corps, with the 3rd Light Division; and XV Corps, which fielded the 1st and 2nd Light Divisions. The panzer divisions had a combined strength of 528 light tanks, twenty-six Mark IIIs, and sixty-eight Mark IVs. The light divisions consisted of 171 light tanks. In addition to their Mark IIs and Mark IIIs, the 3rd Light Division deployed sixty Czechoslovakian 38(t)s.

The Poznan Army, denied the opportunity to fight at the border, raced back toward Warsaw. It came under pressure from the north and in the south near Kutno. There, its units dug in, joined by the remaining elements of the Pomorze Army, which had fallen back seventy miles from the corridor.

On 5 September Guderian's XIX Corps was graced with the presence of the führer. The general joined him for a tour of the recent battlefields. "At the sight of the smashed [Polish] artillery regiment," wrote Guderian, "Hitler had asked me: 'Our dive bombers did that?' When I replied 'No, our panzers!,' he was plainly astonished." Hitler then inquired about the casualties. "I gave him the latest figures I had received, some 150 dead and 700 wounded for all the four divisions under my command during the Battle of the Corridor. He was amazed at the smallness of these figures, contrasting them with the casualties of his own regiment . . . during the First World War." Guderian continued, stressing the importance of the tank: "I was able to show him that the smallness of our casualties in this battle against a tough and courageous enemy was primarily due to the effectiveness of our tanks. Tanks are a life-saving weapon. The men's belief in the superiority of their armored equipment had been greatly strengthened by their successes in the Corridor. The enemy had suffered the total destruction of between two and three infantry divisions and one cavalry brigade." Guderian was speaking of two of the five infantry divisions and the single cavalry brigade of the Pomorze Army. He concluded, "Thousands of prisoners and hundreds of guns had fallen into our hands."[14]

By 7 September the Tenth Army was only thirty-five miles south of Warsaw. The Modlin Army fell back to its fortifications north of Modlin and Warsaw. The defenders were joined by the Narrow Group, composed of two infantry divisions and two cavalry brigades, which had rushed from the border of East Prussia and Lithuania to help defend the capital.

With the motorized and panzer divisions leading the assaults of three of the five invading armies, the Germans moved fast into the Polish interior. The Eighth Army's XVI Panzer Corps plowed through to the capital in seven days—a distance of nearly 150 miles. After driving the Poles south out of the corridor, the Fourth Army's XIX Corps cruised east through East Prussia and resumed the attack, driving south through the center of Poland and forming the northern pincer arm that denied any Polish troops the opportunity of escaping into Lithuania.

By 9 September the Germans were at Warsaw's doorstep, knocking with heavy artillery and dive bombers. Before the Poles could react, the invaders had pushed back, bypassed, and encircled nearly every unit. The Cracow and Carpathian Armies were shoved within nearly one hundred miles of the Russian border. The depleted Modlin, Poznan, and Pomorze Armies took up positions around Kutno and Warsaw, against which Army Groups North and South closed their pincers, their corps clearing out any resistance.

The Pomorze and Poznan Armies were hammered around Kutno by the II, III, X, XIII, XI, and XVI Corps, finally surrendering on 17 September. That same day any existing hope was lost when two Soviet army groups, the White Russian Front and the Ukrainian Front, attacked from the east in the north and south, respectively. A week and a half later, on 27 September, the Modlin Army surrendered at Warsaw after being pounded by I, II, XV, and the Wodrig Corps.

The debut of the panzers was bittersweet. Though the mechanized units carried enough fuel to drive nearly five hundred miles, they were held on a tight leash by the high command and ordered to stay with the infantry units. Throughout the campaign, the debate continued over how armor should be used. Among the upper echelons it was generally accepted that the tanks were only to be used strictly as support for the infantry. General Guderian had requested, to no avail, the opportunity for his XIX Panzer Corps to drive ahead of the infantry divisions. But the high command, fearing an attack from the French in the west, did not want to risk overextending their eastward thrusts.

The initial attack on Warsaw resulted in the loss of fifty-seven tanks. Though this loss has been blamed on tactics, it was also realized that the Mark Is and IIs themselves were obsolete against what antitank weapons the Poles did have. The Germans lost 218 tanks against the deficient Polish Army. The entire operation had demonstrated exactly what Guderian had argued for so long: without infantry support, antitank guns, artillery, engineers, and supply columns, armor could not be employed to its full potential.

While the operations in Poland had demonstrated the tank's capabilities of deep penetration and striking power, the Wehrmacht was far from mechanized and still largely dependent on the horse; the typical infantry division required more than 4,000 of them. In occupied areas the Germans captured tens of thousands of horses, sending them to veterinary units for examination before joining army horse parks. By the time the war ended, they had seized nearly 150,000 horses. Like steel or oil, the horse was a raw material necessary for the Reich's war machine.[15] Consequently, no matter how promising the opportunity for pursuit or exploitation, panzer units could not leave the slower infantry behind.

Though to some in the high command the armored concept was "stillborn," they had unleashed what the rest of the world perceived as a step increase in the intensity and precision of modern warfare. Regardless of fact, the western perception largely perpetuated the notion of blitzkrieg—even the word itself, which was coined by a writer for *Time* magazine. John Keegan has stated that the concentration of "tanks of the panzer division into an offensive phalanx, supported by squadrons of dive bombers as 'flying artillery,' which, when driven against a defended line at a weak spot—any spot was, by definition, weak when struck by such a preponderant force—cracked it, and then swept on to spread confusion in its wake."[16]

Winston Churchill recalled, "We had seen a perfect specimen of the modern Blitzkrieg; the close interaction on the battlefield of Army and Air Force; the violent bombardment of all communications and of any town that seemed an attractive target; the arming of an active Fifth Column; the free use of spies and parachutists; and above all the irresistible forward thrusts of great masses of armor."[17] The Poles were not to be the last to endure this ordeal.

6

Panzers in France

> Over all these activities, military and otherwise, hung the long shadow of the First World War. All around were the awe-inspiring cemeteries—their headstones perfectly dressed, in line and in echelon, for the everlasting parade.
>
> **—Nicholas Harman**

In 1914 French commander Marshal Ferdinand Foch had declared: "My Right is driven in. My center is giving way. The situation is excellent—I attack!" Twenty-five years later the French would not attack. They would sit—and wait.

On 4 September 1939 the voices of Neville Chamberlain and Edouard Daladier crackled on their nations' radios announcing war with Germany. Nearly a year earlier, Hitler had made the following statements: "We have concluded a non-aggression pact with Denmark"; "Germany never had any conflict with the Northern States and has none today"; "The new Reich has endeavored to continue the traditional friendship with Holland"; and "The Reich has put forth no claim which might in any way be regarded as a threat to Belgium." France and England were quick to disregard such oratory and mobilized for the inevitable conflict. Their first order of business was a blockade. The Royal Navy immediately deployed to the North Sea, the English Channel, Malta, Gibraltar, and the Suez Canal.

Norway's coastline offered ideal sites for U-boat stations, and from airfields there the Germans could launch strikes against the British North

Sea blockade and the northern half of Britain itself. On 9 April 1940 Germany attacked and overran Denmark in its march north. Simultaneously, Norway came under attack as nearly 5,500 paratroopers landed in Fornelu and Stavanger while German warships took control of all its ports. Five days later French, British, and Polish troops began landing along the Norwegian coast. Nearly 45,000 Allied troops resisted the German offensive. To combat the dominating Luftwaffe, the British sent the aircraft carrier HMS *Glorious* into the North Sea, where it was promptly intercepted and sunk. By the end of April, the Allies were forced to evacuate Scandinavia.

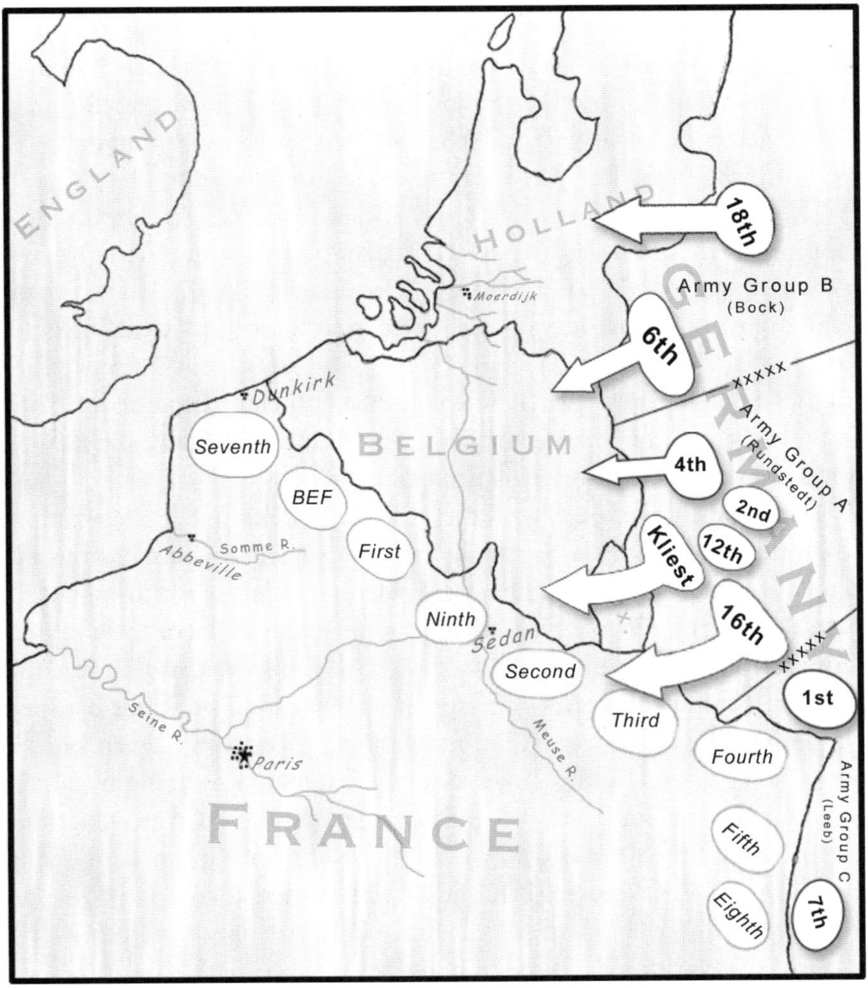

Figure 16. France, May 1940.

Thus, the northern arm of Hitler's pincer to isolate England was set. The left hook would cross through France.

With Germany's attention now shifting west following the fall of Poland—which Gen. Maurice Gamelin, the French commander in chief, saw as the result of that nation's inferior military and lack of adequate material—the French decided to sit behind their formidable fixed positions along the Maginot Line, running the length of their border with Germany; Gen. Alphonse Georges was responsible for defending the line from Switzerland to the Mediterranean Sea. But as the great military theorist Karl von Clausewitz had written the previous century, "If you entrench yourself behind strong fortifications, you compel the enemy to seek a solution elsewhere." Gamelin and his officers believed that this "solution elsewhere" would come through either the Ardennes Forest or Belgium. Since the forest seemed too dense for any army to pass through, the French concluded that the Wehrmacht's only option would be to repeat the Schlieffen Plan of 1914, an invasion through neutral Belgium.

The Maginot Line served as the twentieth century's rendition of the Isthmus Line, which had separated Sparta and Athens during Xerxes' campaign against Greece in 480 BC. The French, like the Spartans and Peloponnesians before them, would have liked to establish a fortified line sealing them off from any enemy. Yet the Belgians, like the ancient Athenians, would consider such action as implying their abandonment. Thus in both cases, no fortified line was constructed; politics had extinguished any comprehensive solution via fixed defenses.

The French, therefore, placed their mobile Seventh Army, consisting of seven divisions, near the North Sea coastline, where it could dash to the rescue of the Belgians once the anticipated German attack commenced. South of the Seventh, the nine divisions of the British Expeditionary Force (BEF), under the command of Field Marshal Lord Gort and numbering nearly half a million men by the spring of 1940, took positions between the Lys and Escaut Rivers. Continuing south along the Belgian border were the First and Ninth Armies, a total of twenty-two divisions, two of which were mechanized, forming the French First Army Group. Continuing south past the Meuse River was the Second Army Group, comprising the Second, Third, Fourth, Fifth, and Eighth Armies; all except the Second were behind the Maginot line. The Sixth Army, with twenty-two divisions, three of them armored, was held in reserve.

In numbers the French had the advantage. Allied forces had a combined strength of nearly 4,000,000 men, while facing them were approximately 2,000,000 Germans. The Luftwaffe would send up 3,200 aircraft against the Allies' 2,400 planes. Numerically, the armor was more evenly matched: the Germans mounted roughly 2,500 tanks, while the Allies had nearly 2,700 total armored vehicles in opposition.[1] Unfortunately for the French, their defensive plan lacked any flexibility. Their armor was also scattered in supporting roles in various units and thus would only be able to fight piecemeal. Finally, the Allies deployed their forces based on the "certainty" that the Germans could only strike through Belgium.

The Attack Plan

With Poland behind them, the Germans crafted the invasion of France with lessons learned—lessons centered on the deployment of armor. Operation Gelb (Yellow), as it was named, had many revisions, many of which involved the grouping and location of the armor. Originally the panzers were dispersed in three groups, again in supporting roles to the infantry, lacking any ingenuity that should have been gained from the experience in Poland. But Gen. Erich von Manstein and armor enthusiasts such as Guderian finally succeeded in giving the tanks their chance.

The final plan organized the panzers into a single striking force named Panzergruppe Kleist, commanded by Lt. Gen. Ewald von Kleist, as part of Army Group A, commanded by General Rundstedt. Army Group A formed the center of the invasion force and would make the main thrust. On its flanks were Army Group B to the north and Army Group C to the south. Army Group B would serve as the diversionary attack, baiting the allies into Belgium and the Netherlands away from the Ardennes, where Kleist's army would spearhead the main assault.

Panzergruppe Kleist consisted of three corps: the XIX Panzer Corps was under Guderian, who commanded the 1st, 2nd, and 10th Panzer Divisions; the XLI Panzer Corps was under Maj. Gen. Georg-Hans Reinhardt, who commanded the 6th and 8th Panzer Divisions; and the XIV Motorized Corps was under Lt. Gen. Gustav Anton von Wietersheim, who commanded the 2nd, 13th, and 29th Motorized Divisions. Rundstedt's army group also included the 5th and 7th Panzer Divisions in Gen. Günther von Kluge's Fourth Army, which would be covering Kleist's right (northern) flank.

In 1940 the panzer division was primarily made up of an artillery regiment, an infantry brigade, and a panzer brigade. The panzer brigade contained two panzer regiments comprising two battalions each. Each battalion had two light and one medium company. Six of the ten panzer divisions (1st–5th and the 10th) of Operation Gelb were organized in this manner. The 9th Panzer Division, however, had only one panzer regiment with two battalions. Finally, the 6th, 7th, and 8th Panzer Divisions each comprised a single panzer regiment of three battalions, all of them fielding Czech tanks. In all, Panzergruppe Kleist consisted of 523 Mark I tanks, 955 Mark IIs, 349 Mark IIIs, 278 Mark IVs, and 328 Czech tanks.[2]

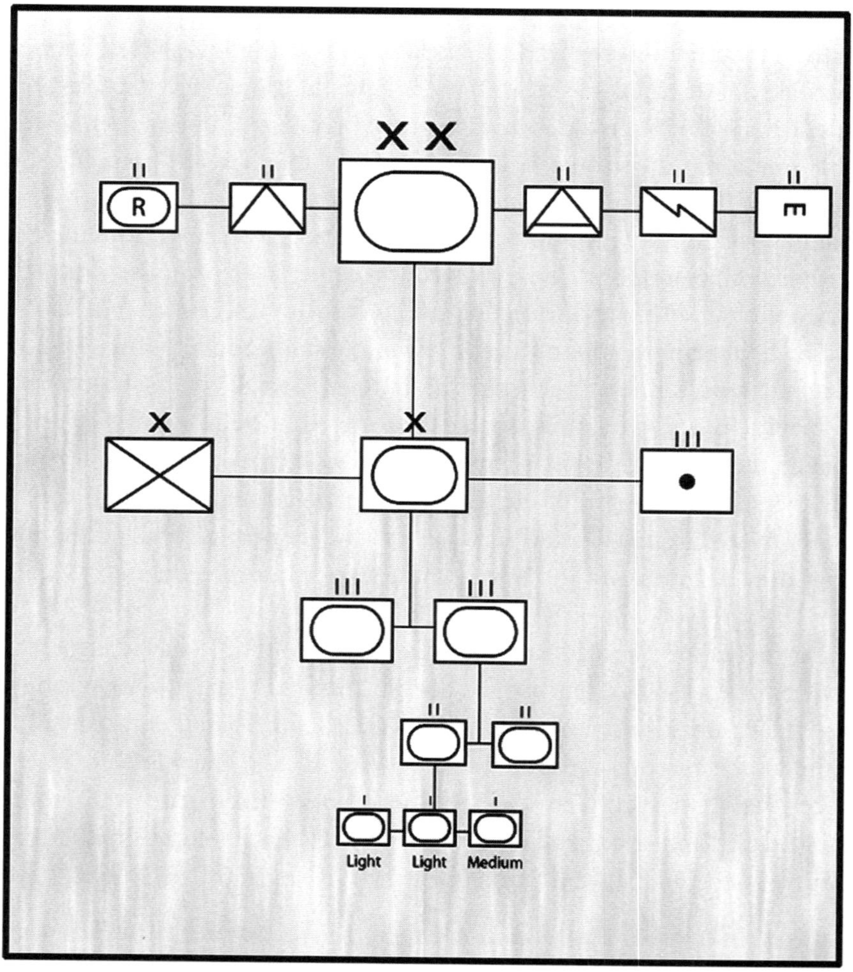

Figure 17. Organization of a panzer division in 1940.

Hitler held a conference in March 1940 for all of the commanders from Army Group A to explain their missions. When it was time for Guderian to speak, he took the opportunity to voice his opinion on the capability of his armor as he outlined his plan for the führer: "I would cross the Luxembourg frontier, drive through southern Belgium towards Sedan, cross the Meuse and establish a bridgehead on the far side so that the infantry corps following behind could get across. I explained briefly that my corps would advance through Luxembourg and south Belgium in three columns; I reckoned on reaching the Belgian frontier posts in the first day and hoped to break through them on that same day; on the second day I would advance as far as Neufchateau; on the third day I would reach Bouillon and cross the Semois; on the fourth day I would arrive at the Meuse; on the fifth day I would cross it. By evening on the fifth day I hoped to have established a bridgehead on the far bank." Guderian was confident in his plans and was likely taken by surprise when Hitler asked, "Then what?"[3]

Guderian looks down at the map, with divisional markers spread along the frontier. Maybe sliding his markers west, he replies: "Unless I receive orders to the contrary, I intend on the next day to continue my advance westward. The supreme leadership must decide whether my objective is to be Amien or Paris." Stepping back, he pauses. "In my opinion," his voice strains as he stretches his arm out, sliding his markers all the way to the blue coast, "the correct course is to drive past Amiens to the English Channel." Guderian straightens up as Hitler now leans over the map with two fists supporting him. His eyes slowly follow the course outlined by Guderian as a growing nod takes over in agreement.

Hitler may have recalled the conversation he had had with Guderian a few months earlier in his car in Poland, reviewing the smashed artillery regiment, leaving the führer with only faith in the capabilities of armor.

The Attack

On 10 May 1940 the Germans attacked. At dawn airborne units dropped into the Netherlands, capturing bridges near Moerdijk that crossed over the Maas River estuary. The Eighteenth Army, Army Group B, moved toward Rotterdam. Two days later the 9th Panzer Division linked up with the 7th Airborne, holding the Moerdijk bridges. The Dutch surrendered on 15 May after sustaining 5,000 casualties.

In Belgium the Sixth Army attacked the Belgian 7th Division, which was stretched along a wide front. Belgium's attempts to deploy counterattacks were met with bombardment from the skies as Stukas whined down from above, releasing their payloads among the Belgian troops. German bombers and airborne troops wiped out communications. Early in the morning on the 11 May, the 4th Panzer Division and the XVI Panzer Corps arrived on the scene. King Leopold ordered the Belgians' withdrawal.

As Army Group B poured into the Low Countries, the Allies quickly counterattacked. The Seventh, Ninth, and First Army, along with the BEF, raced through Belgium to meet the German Sixth Army.

While the Allies concerned themselves with the battle with Bock to the north, Rundstedt thrust his armor dagger into the vulnerable belly of the French Army. The strategic wound was initially created by Kleist's panzers through the Ardennes Forrest in Luxembourg. The wound opened further as Kluge's Fourth, Field Marshal Maximillian von Weichs's Second, Gen. Wilhelm List's Twelfth, and Lt. Gen. Ernst Busch's Sixteenth Armies poured in.

At this point the French Seventh Army turned south to help fight the German breakthrough, but it was too late. Guderian's forces had taken and established a bridgehead at Sedan on the thirteenth, thus locking in the southern pincer. The speed of the German panzers had again proved their worth.

Once across the Meuse, the Germans, with the armor in the lead, had only open country before them most suitable for tank warfare. The remaining French mobile forces not already committed took up positions to block the path to Paris, believing it to be the Germans' objective. They were wrong again. As Guderian had planned, the German drive veered northwest—toward the coast.

The 7th Panzer Division, under the command of Gen. Erwin Rommel, drove northwest from Clairfayts, near the Belgium border, toward Cambrai. Rommel recalled:

> The way to the west was now open. . . . The tanks now rolled in a long column through the line of fortifications and on towards the first houses, which had been set alight by our fire. In the moonlight we could see the men of the 7th Motorcycle Battalion moving forward

> on foot beside us. Occasionally an enemy machine gun or anti-tank gun fired but none of their shots came anywhere near us. Our artillery was dropping heavy harassing fire on villages and the road far ahead of the regiment. Gradually the speed increased. Before long we were 500—1,000—2,000—3,000 yards ahead into the fortified zone. Engines roared, tank tracks clanked and clattered. Whether or not the enemy was firing was impossible to tell in the ear-splitting noise.
>
> The people in the houses were rudely awoken by the din of our tanks, the clatter and roar of tracks and engines. Troops lay bivouacked beside the road, military vehicles stood parked in farmyards and in some places on the road itself. Civilians and French troops, their faces distorted with terror, lay huddled in the ditches, alongside hedges and in every hollow beside the road. We passed a refugee column, the carts abandoned by their owners, who had fled in panic into the fields. On we went, at a steady speed, towards our objective. Every so often a quick glance at the map by a shaded light and a short wireless message to Divisional HQ to report the position and thus the success of the 25th Panzer Regiment. Every so often a look out of the hatch to assure myself that there was still no resistance and that contact was being maintained to the rear. The flat countryside lay spread out around us under the cold light of the moon. We were through the Maginot Line! It was hardly conceivable. Twenty-two years before we had stood for four and a half long years before this self-same enemy and had won victory after victory and yet finally lost the war. And now we had broken through the renowned Maginot Line and were driving deep into enemy territory. It was not just a beautiful dream. It was reality.[4]

This "reality" stood in stark conflict with the words of the inspector of transport troops, who had told Guderian that he would never see German tanks in operation in his lifetime.

From Sedan Guderian's tanks struck west, driving through the country, facing little to no resistance. The leading elements of Panzergruppe Kleist had torn the Allied defenses in two. The deep and narrow penetration had not only shocked the French and the British but also caused the German high command to pause. The panzers had more or less outrun their supporting infantry divisions, which still relied heavily on horse-drawn transportation. The high command, namely General Rundstedt, became increasingly concerned with the vulnerability of the leading units, worried that, should the Allies mount a strong counterattack into their flanks, the panzers would be cut off. According to Army Group A's war diary: "Army group headquarters have no doubt that, if motorized forces were to continue their push in advance of 12th Army, they would probably be able to cross the Oise [River] . . . without difficulty. . . . But looking at operations as a whole, the risk involved does not appear to be justified. The extended flank . . . is too sensitive. The southern flank is simply inviting an enemy attack. . . . If the spearheads of the attack are temporarily halted it will be possible to effect a certain stiffening of threatened flank within twenty four hours."[5] Consequently, on the morning of 17 May, Guderian received orders to halt his advance.

Flabbergasted, Guderian instead resigned his command. The resignation was short lived, however, and his units were soon granted permission to run "reconnaissance" ahead of the main force. On the night of 19 May, Guderian's advanced forces reached Noyelles. The next day the Germans took Abbeville and stretched out their units to the English Channel. From Abbeville, roads and rail lines led straight to Paris. Upon reaching the coast, the Germans did not head south toward the capital but rather headed northeast, back along the coast toward Boulogne and Calais.

On 21 May the anticipated Allied counterattack struck south into the corridor from Arras. The 4th and the 7th Tank Battalions of the British Royal Tank Regiment were ordered to attack, supported by two battalions of infantry and a French tank battalion. The force included fifty-eight Matilda I, sixteen Matilda II, and sixty French Somua tanks.[6] As they attacked south, the Allies encountered an SS motorized-infantry regiment and rifle battalions belonging to the 7th Panzer Division. The Germans turned their antitank guns on the advancing armor. At first the situation looked bleak for the invaders as their 37-mm shells ricocheted off the British and French tanks; the S35 Somuas had up to 2.25 inches of armor. Regardless, the Allied armor were without adequate infantry support, which allowed Rommel to bring up heavier guns. These knocked out eight tanks before the British decided to pull back. The Germans pursued with their Lt 38 tanks, but like the Allied armor, they ran into trouble; British 40-mm antitank guns managed to knock out forty panzers before the Germans withdrew. In both cases antitank guns, rather than enemy tanks, had stopped the attacks. Nevertheless, it was clear that the 37-mm gun lacked sufficient penetrating power against most armor. One British officer counted as many as fourteen hits on his Matilda that had failed to penetrate.[7]

For the Americans, this encounter did not quite demonstrate the ineffectiveness of the 37-mm gun, but rather the effectiveness of a 27-ton tank (the Matilda) against German antitank weapons. One intelligence report stated, "Five hits by German anti-tank guns on a single A-12 caused no damage other than penetration to a depth of about one half inch."[8]

By this time in the operation, the panzers were wearing down. On 24 May Rundstedt issued orders for his armor to stop, advancing no farther than the Aa River toward Dunkirk. Hitler and Guderian wanted the units to regroup and repair in order for a drive farther south into France. In addition, Reichsmarshal Hermann Goering wanted the dive bombers of his Luftwaffe to take care of the roads and beaches congested with Allied troops and material. In addition, whatever Allied forces were left could be eliminated by Army Group B, moving southeast from Holland and Belgium.

This advance came swifter than the British and French anticipated. On the twenty-eighth Belgium, without warning, surrendered. This unexpected capitulation completely exposed the Allies' left flank, further sinking the situation for France.

With the evacuation of more than 300,000 men, mostly from the BEF, from the beaches of Dunkirk completed by 5 June, the Germans pushed into the French interior and were beyond the Somme by the twelfth. Their line ran roughly from Le Havre, down to the outskirts of Paris, and then to Montmedy and the northern flank of the Maginot Line proper. Kleist's panzers, meanwhile, had been transferred to Army Group B under Bock, whose Fourth, Eighteenth, Sixth, and Ninth Armies still retained the German right flank from the coast to roughly sixty miles east of Paris. Just south of the Marne River, Rundstedt's Second and Twelfth Armies, including Guderian, applied pressure to the French Fourth Army Group.

Starting on the thirteenth, the Germans drove south and west, with their armor spearheading the advance. Paris fell on the fourteenth. Army Group B's motorized XV Corps, commanded by Lt. Gen. Herman Hoth, shot north to take the Cotentin Peninsula, where Rommel and his 7th Panzer Division captured Cherbourg on the eighteenth. Hoth then moved on to Brest the next day. The Ninth Army and elements of Kleist's armor drove south to the vicinity of Vichy. On the twenty-first Italy attacked. The following day, 22 June 1940, France surrendered.

Twenty-odd years after the fact, B. H. Liddell Hart concluded: "The dazzling effect of what the new element achieved has obscured not only their relatively small scale but the narrow margin by which success was gained. . . . The Battle of France is one of history's most striking examples of the decisive effect of a new idea, carried out by a dynamic executant."[9] Guderian had filled that role for the Germans. Soon he would have a counterpart in the United States.

Part 2

Summer 1940–Fall 1944

7

Creating the US Armored Force

By command of Brigadier General Chaffee: You will plan, organize, and operate the Armored Force School and Replacement Center.

—Memorandum to Lt. Col. Stephen Henry

On 10 July 1940, eighteen days after France surrendered, the United States established its Armored Force. Five days later this command was activated under the direction of Brigadier General Chaffee. The Armored Force drew its first breath at Fort Knox, a name now synonymous with armor.

Authorized at 530 officers and 9,329 enlisted men, the Armored Force would comprise the already existing mechanized units: the 7th Cavalry Brigade (Mechanized), 6th Armored Infantry Regiment, and the Provisional Tank Brigade—the former two at Fort Knox and the latter at Fort Benning, Georgia. These were reorganized and designated the 1st Armored Division at Fort Knox and the 2nd Armored Division at Fort Benning; the 70th Tank Battalion, a general-headquarters reserve unit attached to the force, was stationed at Fort Meade, Maryland. Together they formed the nucleus of the I Armored Corps.

On paper the divisions fielded an armored brigade and a reconnaissance battalion. The brigade consisted of two regiments of light tanks, one regiment of medium tanks, an artillery regiment, an infantry regiment, and supporting reconnaissance, artillery, and engineer battalions.

Supporting these were signal, ordnance, quartermaster, medical, and service-and-maintenance units.

In reality, at least at first, the divisions were built around one armored and one infantry brigade. George Patton, now a colonel, was assigned to lead the armored brigade of the 2nd Armored Division, under the command of Brig. Gen. Charles L. Scott. His brigade consisted of two light- and one medium-tank regiments, a field-artillery regiment, and a battalion of engineers, a total force of 350 officers, 5,500 men, and 383 tanks. Patton was probably unconcerned at his initial lack of men and tanks, knowing full well that they eventually would come, as had his light Renaults twenty-two years earlier.[1]

As the Allied position in continental Europe collapsed, the War Department began cranking out military "camps" and "forts." From the closing months of 1940 through the summer of 1942, nearly fifty new camps were established. In addition, many older posts, such as Fort Knox, began the necessary expansion of facilities. Nevertheless, Chaffee and his staff were in a desperate race to build up the armored divisions. First, however, they had to create a school that would train the officers and men.[2]

The Armored Force School

Under General Chaffee, the US Armored Force School began to take shape. The first step was establishing the school itself. Upon receiving the memorandum from Chaffee's headquarters, Lt. Col. Stephen G. Henry would reply with his recommendations and proposals concerning the school. This would include a table outlining its organization, the syllabus of courses, the intended utilization of military and civilian institutions and plants, and the buildings and equipment necessary for the training.[3]

Housed on the grounds of Fort Knox, the school set out to find commissioned and enlisted specialists and instructors. Required to provide the instructors and replacement personnel with knowledge in motor mechanics, radio operating, code and cipher operation, motorcycle mechanics and gunnery, the school was divided into three divisions: The Academic Division taught classes through its departments of tank, wheeled vehicle, communication, motorcycle, gunnery, tactics, field engineering, and clerical. The Training Group housed, fed, paid, and provided basic military training to the students. Finally, the Demonstration Regiment was more or less a miniature division that presented tactical demonstrations. Resources from the Tank School at Fort Benning, where the Provisional Tank Brigade had been stationed, and those of the Communications and Motor Schools, already being operated by the 7th Cavalry Brigade, became available to the Armored Force School in September 1940. The school was to open on 1 November 1941.

According to the US recruitment film *The Tanks are Coming*, new recruits arrived at Fort Knox still in their civilian clothes and took their oath of allegiance on base. But by this time, these men were already part of the army. At induction stations across the country, recruits were examined by an army doctor and underwent a physical and psychiatric exam. If passed, each man then received his serial number and took his oath of allegiance. Once recruits were "in the army," they were sent to army reception centers (ARCs), which began to open in 1940; by 1942 there were thirty-six such centers in the United States. When the newly inducted men arrived at an ARC, they were vaccinated, issued their first uniforms, and received their first lessons in army regulations, sanitation, and the Articles of War. Lectures on military courtesy and some instruction on basic drill procedures followed. An army specialist interviewed each enlisted man or inductee to process what he had done as a civilian and to try, as much as possible, to place him in a corresponding position in the army. For example, clerks, cooks, truck drivers, or even mountain climbers could all be placed in some equivalent position in the service—or so it was hoped.[4] Lee Kennett, writing about the experience of American soldiers, noted that overall "the army did a good job of using many of the skills the selectee brought it from a relatively sophisticated and technologically oriented society." But Kennett added the oft-repeated story of a civilian banker becoming an army baker because of a clerical error in his processing.[5]

The soldier also received his soldier's classification card, which would record the "scores received in the Army General Classification Test [AGCT], Trade Tests, and the Aptitude Tests as well as personal, educational, and vocational information, hobbies, etc." The AGCT was an aptitude test that was "nothing more than a sound psychological device to sift recruits and trainees into a few broad groupings with respect to their ability to learn quickly the duties and responsibilities of a soldier."[6] In other words, the test gauged the men's "trainability."

After days or a few weeks of processing, the ARC experience would culminate with the new soldier being assigned to a specific army unit or to one of twenty-eight replacement-training centers (RTCs). These provided basic training for the specific combat arms. For example, Aberdeen

Proving Ground in Maryland was home to the Ordnance RTC, while the cavalry had its RTC at Fort Riley, Kansas. The Armored School and Replacement Training Center was at Fort Knox, Kentucky.

When new trainees arrived at Fort Knox, they again took aptitude tests to determine their abilities in particular courses and consisted of code, clerical, and mechanical categories. This allowed instructors to classify each student and monitor his progress throughout the school. The men would be grouped together based on their individual performances: for example, those who excelled in the mechanical tests were placed together, while those who scored lower on the clerical tests were placed together. The idea was that this would help avoid a "methodical thinker being [placed] with a group of mentally quicker men, and [the] possible [result] of the man obtaining a defeatist attitude and an inferiority complex."[7]

After two weeks of basic training came specialization training. When not doing calisthenics, the men were in class, where they might learn Morse code, study the ins and outs of combustion engines and motor fuels, troubleshoot various engine problems, or qualify for driving school.

At the indoor gunnery range, students learned how to fire weapons accurately, followed by training on how to load, aim, and shoot under "battlefield conditions." These conditions were simulated by "wobbling plates," platforms mounted on hydraulics that would toss and jerk as the men attempted to work with the attached M3 37-mm gun. At the outdoor gunnery range, though, they would fire from the actual tanks at moving targets, large sheets printed with tank silhouettes mounted on a small railway car and gliding down a track parallel to the firing line.[8]

Depending on the area of study, the Academic Division offered programs of varying length. The Tank Department conducted a two-month course to train mechanics and maintenance officers. Similar in length was the Wheeled Vehicle Department's course to educate motor mechanics and officers. The Communication Department, during a fourteen-week course, would produce radio operators and, over a separate ten-week course, radio electricians. The Motorcycle Department conducted a two-month course for its mechanics, while the Gunnery Department trained its men for four weeks. The Tactics Department indoctrinated officers in the combat principals of the Armored Force, offering the basic course for captains and lieutenants. Finally, the Clerical Department, over a course of one month, trained clerks and administrative specialists.

Upon completion of the necessary courses, a soldier still was not considered an expert. "Only the man himself and the opportunities given [to] him by his organization commander can make him that; but he is qualified to do his part in the Armored Force."[9]

The initial target annual output of troops for the Armored Force was 800 officers and 7,200 enlisted men. But with the rapid expansion of that branch, the annual output was soon raised to 4,200 officers and 26,000 enlisted men. Remarkably, such a drastic jump in numbers did not require a physical expansion of the school but merely the reorchestration of class schedules and facility use at a given time. Like production lines that do not wait for the completion of a unit to start work on the next, the Armored Force School applied this method to the training and production of officers and men.

This was accomplished by breaking courses down into phases and making sure that all equipment and facilities were being used all of the time. "The tank department, for example, is divided into eight phases of six days each. Thus, by introducing a new increment of 140 students every six days, a total of 1,120 students could be given training at the same time. As the student successfully completes the first phase, he is moved into the second phase and so on through the course." The school became a factory for producing tankmen. "In industry, raw materials flow through the plant, are worked on by skilled technicians, and emerge as finished articles. In the Armored Force School, the untrained man is the raw material. He moves through the various divisions where instructors impart detailed information and teach operations which he will later perform in his organization. He progresses from phase to phase and emerges with the basic training necessary to work at his specialty."[10]

In addition, the breakdown of courses into weekly phases permitted any student who failed to pass or qualify from a given phase to simply repeat it the following week rather than having to wait weeks or months to continue his training. This was also conducive to training new instructors, allowing them to be fully immersed in a specific phase. They could simply repeat the weekly curriculum two or three times to gain enough experience to teach the phase themselves as experienced instructors were rotated out to field service.

Table 1 shows the courses offered, the length of each, the number of students to be enrolled, and the annual quota of graduates. The average weekly output for enlisted troops was around 540 men, while that for current officers was approximately eighty. The Officer Candidate School

Table 1. Courses of the Armored Force School Replacement Center

COURSE	LENGTH	ENROLLMENT	ANNUAL OUTPUT
Communication Officers	12 weeks	60	240
Tank Maintenance Officers	8 weeks 3 days	120	720
Wheeled Vehicle Maintenance officers	8 weeks	120	720
Gunnery Instructors Officers	4 weeks	75	975
Officers Basic Tactical	8 weeks	200	1,200
Officers Advanced Tactical	6 weeks	50	400
TOTAL OFFICERS		**625**	**4,255**
Radio Operators	14 weeks	1,600	5,440
Radio Electricians	10 weeks	240	1,040
Tank Mechanics	8 weeks 3 days	1,120	6,300
Auto Mechanics	8 weeks	1,000	5,000
Gunnery Instructors	4 weeks	300	2,825
Radiator-Sheet Metal	8 weeks	25	150
Blacksmith and Welders	8 weeks	40	240
Motorcycle Mechanics	8 weeks	156	936
Clerical	4 weeks	356	4,272
TOTAL ENLISTED		**4,837**	**26,203**
Officer Candidate School	12 weeks	2,200	8,250
Teacher Training Department	3 months	300	1,200*
TOTAL ARMORED FORCE SCHOOL		**7,662**	**38,708**

Table recreated from Courses of Instruction Conducted at the Armored Force School Collection, Armored Force School Papers, Patton Museum Archives.

* The teachers are not included in the total number of output for the school. They were reassigned to the school.

output was 160 new lieutenants. Combined, this gave the Armored Force School and Replacement Center a weekly output to the Armored Force of roughly 780 officers and men—nearly the strength of a tank battalion.

A booklet published by the army summarized the role of the school:

> [It] is the great training unit of our Army Ground Forces which organizes and trains large Armored units for use against our enemies. Armored units are fast-moving combat units which attack into enemy territory to overcome his machine guns and other weapons and effect envelopment or otherwise deliver a knockout blow to his forces. They are used primarily in offensive action. Like every other kind of fighting unit, those developed by the Armored Command fight as members of the great war teams which included all combat arms, both air and ground. The men and weapons of armored fighting units are transported in wheeled vehicles—command and reconnaissance trucks, armored scout cars, armored trucks, and ambulances and trailers; and in tracked vehicles—armored halftrack trucks, armored self-propelled artillery guns, and tanks of several kinds. Though they usually fight in co-operation with other branches, Armored units are also trained and equipped to fight by themselves if they need to.[11]

The Armored Force School, and the Armored Force itself, was under the direction of professional soldiers who had come from the cavalry or the infantry. As the force began to take shape, opposing schools of thought surfaced, polarizing the infantrymen and cavalrymen as to the role of armor. The very fundamental principles, such as organization and tactics, inevitably became controversial. Though Chaffee tried to balance and ease the rivalry within his new command, the initial organization and school of thought reflected cavalry doctrine, necessitating fast tanks for deep penetration capable of disrupting the enemy's interior. The Chief of Infantry, Maj. Gen. George A. Lynch, believed that the Armored Force, namely the 1st and 2nd Armored Divisions, directed by mostly old cavalrymen who represented alignment with cavalry thought and therefore allowed no strong voice for the infantry. He feared that the tactics, organization, and the vehicles themselves would be developed with little consideration for the infantry's needs in the field.[12] His concerns were justified, and it turned out, his predictions were accurate.

8

African Desert, British Troops, American Tanks

When the dust and smoke cleared, the Italian forces were seen ranged in a remarkable order.

—Winston Churchill

Libya had been straddled by French Tunisia and British-ruled-Egypt since it was ceded to Italy in 1912. With the French surrender in June 1940, Italian forces there were relieved from any threat from the west, and the door was open to attack to the east. Conquering Egypt and the Suez Canal would inevitably give control of the Mediterranean to Mussolini, thus opening the route to the oilfields of the Middle East to the Axis.

On 13 September 1940 the Italians began their attack into Egypt. After a heavy artillery barrage, Marshal Rodolfo Graziani's invasion force, consisting of six infantry divisions and eight armored battalions, crossed the border near Sollum and Halfaya Pass. The British forces, consisting of three infantry battalions, one armored battalion, three batteries, and two squadrons of armored cars, organized a fighting withdrawal, inflicting heavy casualties on the Italians. After penetrating fifty miles in four days, Graziani stopped at Sidi Barrani in order to regroup and to service his vehicles.

On 8 December the British, under the command of Gen. Archibald Wavell, counterattacked at Sidi Barrani, which they took on the tenth.

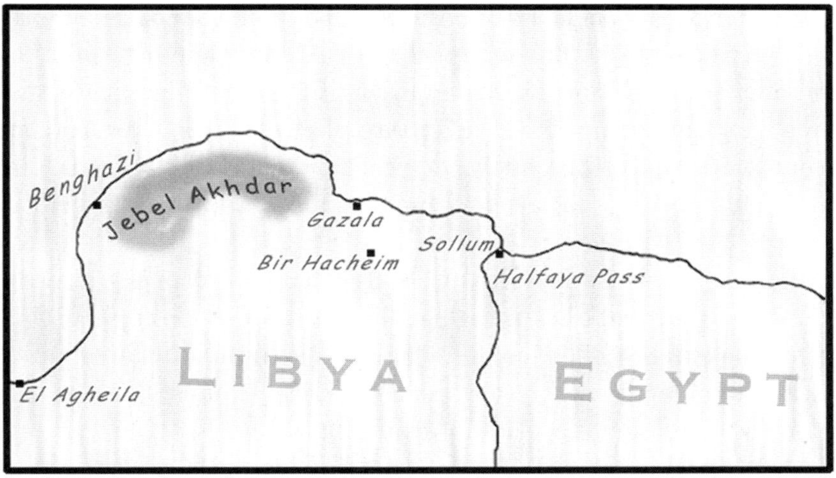

Figure 18. North Africa, 1940–1942.

Pressing the attack, the British removed or neutralized all Italian forces in Egypt by the fifteenth. On 3 January 1941 Wavell's units penetrated into Libya and struck the Italian garrison at Bardia. Supported by British, Indian, and Australian infantry units, British armor entered the city, taking it on the fifth.

The British fielded what they called "cruiser" and "infantry" tanks. The former type was used to penetrate enemy lines and was capable of engaging enemy armor. The latter kept pace with the foot soldiers, supporting them where needed. When the British general staff reorganized the army in 1934, they included designated mechanized divisions, which contained troop transports in addition to a battalion of infantry tanks, such as the Matilda.

At eighteen and a half feet long and eight feet tall, the Matilda infantry tank weighed thirty tons and held a crew of four. On the road its two 87-hp engines could run at fifteen mph but were only capable of eight mph off road. The Matilda's armor, up to just over three inches, was effective against most Italian and German antitank guns. Its turret mounted a 2-pounder (40-mm) gun, with a muzzle velocity of 2,800 fps, and a Besa machine gun.

Wavell's forces further pursued the Italians, taking Tobruk on 22 January. Following the coastal road and cutting across the desert south of Jebel Akhdar, the British moved on to Agedabia and El Agheila. By mid-February, only nine weeks after Wavell attacked, the Italian army was out 400 tanks, 1,300 guns, and 130,000 men.

Armor engagements had demonstrated that the Italian M11/39 tanks were outclassed by the British tanks. Their 37-mm cannons could not penetrate British armor, further testifying to the obsolescence of the weapon. In addition, nearly all the British tanks had radios, allowing them to coordinate movements and react quickly to developing situations. The Italians did not enjoy such a luxury and were thus unable to act in similar fashion.

After this victory in the Western Desert, Churchill stripped his forces in Libya to reinforce the deteriorating Allied situation in Greece. Likewise, Hitler sent panzers to shore up the deteriorated Axis situation in Libya. "A new figure sprang upon the world stage," recalled Churchill, "a German warrior who will hold his place in their military annals."[1] The warrior's name was Erwin Rommel.

Lending aid to Mussolini, Hitler sent Rommel and his Africa Korps to the deserts of North Africa. He arrived in Tripoli in February with 8,000 men of the 5th Light Division, which included the 5th Panzer Regiment with fifty tanks, mostly Mark IIIs and IVs. Wasting no time, Rommel prepared to attack. For the time being, the front had settled around Surt, a coastal town approximately 300 miles east of Tripoli.

The logistical strains in North Africa must be noted. Israeli military historian Martin Van Creveld has noted that "a motorized force of one division, such as the Germans originally sent to Libya, required 350 tons of supplies a day, including water. To transport this quantity over 300 miles of desert [to Surt], the Army High Command calculated that, apart from the troops' organic vehicles and excluding any reserves, thirty-nine columns each consisting of thirty two-ton trucks would be needed."[2] As a result, units in the desert were always short of supply. One understands why it was Rommel who famously said that battles are decided by the quartermasters.

On 31 March the Germans struck at El Agheila. British armor units scrambled but fell prey to the panzers. After the first engagements it was clear that the British tanks, armed with their 2-pounder guns, could still not penetrate the Mark III's or IV's armor at nearly 1,000 yards. In addition, British units suffered heavy losses from Luftwaffe bombers and dive bombers, which had control of the air.

It was now the British who were retreating along the coastal road. They pulled out of the vital port city of Benghazi and were pursued all the way back to Bardia and Sollum. Only Tobruk held out against Rommel's forces.

British forces were in disarray. Their armor had, for the most part, been destroyed. Though they had plenty of men ready to join the fight, they had very few serviceable tanks. On 20 April Wavell sent the prime minister a telegram: "It will be seen that there are only two regiments of cruiser tanks in sight for Egypt by the end of May, and no reserves to replace casualties, whereas there are now in Egypt, trained excellent personnel for six tank regiments. I consider the provision of cruiser tanks vital, in addition to infantry tanks."[3] The result of this plea was Operation Tiger. Churchill planned to ship armor across the Mediterranean to Wavell's depleted forces in order to thwart Rommel's advance. By this time the 15th Panzer Division had reached its full strength and was deployed largely on a line stretching from Fort Capuzzo to Sidi Omar on the Libyan-Egyptian border.

Knowing the material he would receive from Operation Tiger, Wavell attempted to punch a small hole in the German line with his existing forces. His goal was to obtain a small foothold into which he could pour the reinforcements when they arrived. On 15 May Operation Brevity launched, with the small offensive dashing into the Rommel's lines. The Germans counterattacked, and aptly named Brevity was over as fast as it had started. In June the British commenced Operation Battleaxe in hopes of drawing the enemy armor out to engage in a large-scale tank-versus-tank battle. Rommel instead held back his panzers, allowing his infantry and field guns to degrade the British forces first. After two days of the British tanks butting up against his defenses, Rommel sent in his armor, fresh from the rear, into the enemy flank. This again forced the British back to their original lines. Rommel had essentially allowed Wavell's units to blunt "the edge of [their] sword on his own shield, preparatory to the delivery of his thrust."[4]

The British could not break through. Churchill later declared "that after 'Battleaxe' I came to the conclusion that there should be a change." Wavell was out, with no hard feelings, stating: "The Prime Minister is quite right. There ought to be a new eye and a new hand in this theatre."[5] That "new eye" belonged to Gen. Sir Claude Auchinleck, and the "new hand" was the newly formed Eighth Army.

The Eighth Army included the XIII and XXX Corps, each fielding a second generation of tanks. Notable among these are the Mark VI cruiser tank, known as the Crusader, and the American M3 Light Tank, dubbed the Stuart.[6]

The Crusader was an attractive tank, with its low silhouette and angled-armor turret. It had five large road wheels that used a center-guide track system. The drive sprockets were at the rear and propelled the tank at twenty-four mph on the road and fifteen mph off road, utilizing a Nuffield Liberty engine classed at 340 hp.

Previous models were already in action against the Germans, armed with a 2-pounder gun but mounting only about one and a half inches of armor. Immediately upon seeing service, this protection proved obviously inadequate and soon was increased to nearly two inches, thus creating the Crusader II. Finally, when the turret mounted the lethal 6-pounder (57-mm) gun, it became the Crusader III.

The Crusader III had a crew of three and a weight of twenty-two tons. It was twenty feet long and stood just over seven feet. Generally speaking, these tanks were quick and efficiently armed (when fielding the 6-pounder) but were prevented from being totally effective due to a poor engine-cooling system that made them prone to breaking down.

The American M3s were very fast compared to the Matildas. The Stuart's 37-mm gun was adequate for a light tank, and the British fell in love with the reliable track/bogie system that offered them high maneuverability at increased speeds. Auchinleck's forces would field nearly 300 M3s in their next move against the Germans.

With these new and upgraded tanks the British launched Operation Crusader. On 18 November they commenced the attack with a (by now routine) flank attack to the south. Rommel had only 249 panzers there to defend against 738 British tanks. Of these, his units had only a few dozen Mark IIIs and IVs, the remaining force made up of 146 Italian tanks, seventy Mark IIs, and five Mark Is.[7] Near Tobruk on 7 December, after being informed that he would not be receiving any reinforcements in the near future, Rommel decided to withdraw.

By the end of December 1941, the Germans had less than thirty tanks. Their retreat would take them from Benghazi to Agedabia, where they made a stand. By Christmas Rommel's line was flanked, but the situation finally settled with the Africa Korps still holding in El Agheila. By this time the British supply line was so stretched that they also stopped to regroup, rest, and resupply. But the Germans still held Tripoli. As long as the high command saw fit to supply Rommel, Tripoli served as a well from which reinforcements could trickle along the coast to join the ranks near the front.[8]

Shortly after New Year's Day 1942, Rommel's forces began to grow again. On 5 January he received armored cars, field guns, and fifty-five tanks. Like a coiled spring compressed by the British, the German force grew in strength, capitalizing on its proximity to its supply base. On 21 January the spring shot forward. With more than a hundred tanks, Rommel took Agedabia on the twenty-third, and Benghazi six days later. His panzers then raced along the coastal road and hit Gazala on 4 February.

The situation stabilized as both forces took time to reinforce their positions. The Germans up-gunned their numerous Mark IIIs during this lull. The time had come for the 37-mm cannon to be replaced with the 50-mm weapon that Guderian had sought during the Mark III's initial design. In addition to a new gun, extra armor was welded onto the front of the tanks, though leaving four inches between the original armor and the new plates so as to break up an armor-piercing shell prior to its impact with the inner hull.

The British for their part used this pause to bring up their newest Lend-Lease acquisition, the American medium M3.

The Medium M3

The war in Poland, France, and Africa had demonstrated that the American medium M2s were underarmed and inadequately armored.

During the summer of 1940, production began on the new M3 medium tank. After a meeting at Aberdeen Proving Grounds, Chaffee and the Ordnance Department agreed that the new design must have a turret-mounted 75-mm gun. Yet due to the immediate demands of the British Army, production had to move forward without a new turret structure. The design kept the 37-mm gun but was modified to accommodate the 75-mm gun into the starboard-side sponson with limited traverse capabilities.

Due to a lack of R-975 engines, which were also being utilized by the Army Air Corps, the Ordnance Department also developed a powertrain utilizing a commercial diesel engine made by General Motors. The GM model 6–71 was a six-cylinder, liquid-cooled engine rated at 180 hp at 2,100 rpm. Joining two of these engines together allowed the tank to reach speeds of thirty-five mph. In addition, if one engine was knocked out or failed to operate, the vehicle could run on the remaining powerplant. The M3A3 and M3A5 utilized the twin GM diesel engines. The M3A4 mediums, which only saw use as trainers, used a Chrysler Multibank A-57 engine. This was a liquid-cooled, thirty-cylinder engine that was engineered to combine five

Figure 19. The M3 medium tank. Note how much of the vehicle is located above the main gun. *Courtesy US Army Ordnance Museum, Aberdeen Proving Ground*

six-cylinder gasoline engines with a single power output. With 1,253 cubic inches, the Multibank was rated at 425 hp at 2,850 rpm.

The new medium tank, which the British dubbed the Grant, nearly doubled the weight of its predecessor, the medium M2, weighing in at nearly thirty tons. It was eighteen feet long and, in contrast to the stout German panzers, was ten feet tall. On 1 April 1941 the first of the M3s rolled out of the Chrysler Detroit Tank Arsenal.

British spirits rose as they received these thirty-ton mediums with 75-mm guns, which for the first time offered them the option of firing a high-velocity high-explosive or an armor-piercing projectile.

German Tactics in the Desert

While operating in the Western Desert, German gunners typically would open fire at a range of 1,500–2,000 yards. The initial objective was to eliminate British antitank guns and field artillery. German commanders often targeted British 25-pounders first and, once eliminated, would set up their artillery as well as their Mark IVs, which would fire from hull-down defilade positions into the British batteries.[9] Mark IIIs then were sent in to make the main assault. To protect them, the Germans used the 75-mm gun of the Mark IVs, which could engage the British from outside their effective range of antitank fire. At the same time the speed and mobility of the Mark IIIs would provide security from British artillery.[10] The Germans would also use light tanks and other vehicles as bait, luring British armor into antitank traps. The pursuers often found themselves under fire from concealed antitank guns or German tanks.

Rommel Attacks

On 26 May 1942 Rommel again attacked the British positions. At his disposal were 332 German and 228 Italian tanks. Though many Mark IIIs had been up-gunned, only nineteen were available to Rommel by that time. Consequently, the rest of his panzers were Mark IIs along with forty Mark IVs.[11]

As five Italian divisions made the assault on the British lines near the coast, Rommel's tanks swept south. This flank attack consisted of two Italian divisions, one mechanized and one armored, and the 15th and 21st Panzer Divisions along with the 90th Mechanized Division. This southern pincer came wide around Bir Hacheim, then drove north into the British rear.

At Bir Hacheim Rommel first encountered the American-made M3, wielding its 75-mm gun, which he called a "nasty surprise" as its effectiveness against his panzers became apparent.[12] With a muzzle velocity of 1,837 fps, the 75-mm gun's armor-piercing round could penetrate a Mark III at up to 1,650 yards, a new capability for the Allies. In addition, German antitank weapons failed to penetrate the front of the hull or the turret of the M3s.

While the medium M3 initially proved to be an effective war machine in the vast expanse of the desert, where range and maneuverability were key factors, it had one major drawback. The tank towered at ten feet, two feet taller than the Matilda and three feet taller than the light M3. This put the Grant at a significant disadvantage when positioned against the horizon. Even more severe was the flawed placement of the 75-mm gun in the sponson rather than the turret. With the main armament located at nearly half the height of the tank, its ability to fire from a defilade position was compromised.

Though the American medium tank proved effective in the field, there simply were not enough of them to turn the tide of the battle. Rommel's southern pincer rushed into the British rear area and withstood any counterattacks, eventually taking Tobruk. The Germans then pressed on into Egypt, butting up against the British line at El Alamein.

The 88s

At Bir Hacheim the Germans also brought with them the 88-mm dual-purpose gun. One British field report stated: "The greatest single tank destroyer is the German 88mm dual purpose gun. For example, on May 27th at 0800, Axis forces having enveloped Bir Hacheim, a German tank force of 60 tanks attacked the British 22nd Brigade some distance to the northeast. The British moved to attack this force with 50 light and medium American tanks. It soon became apparent that this British force was inadequate and the Brigadier commanding ordered a second regiment of 50 tanks into action. In ten minutes the 88mm German dual-purpose guns destroyed eight American medium tanks of this reinforcing regiment. All day thereafter the British engaged the enemy half-heartedly and finally withdrew. Sixteen American medium tanks were lost in all. These sixteen fell victim, without a single exception, to the 88mm dual-purpose gun."[13]

Designs for the 88-mm antiaircraft gun, designated Flak 18, were underway in the late twenties by Krupp of Essen and Bofors. When Hitler started rearming Germany, the weapon went into full production. Informally named after its caliber, the 88 had its baptism of fire, like the early panzers, during the Spanish Civil War. There it proved to be not only an excellent antiaircraft weapon but also a potential antitank weapon. The high-velocity shell required to engage planes at high altitude validated its potential as a tank killer.

Beginning in 1940, the gun was given a distinct, large armored shield to protect its crew from small-arms fire. In addition, the Germans designed a mount that allowed the 88 to be fired while on its mobile trailer.

Though ammunition varied, the typical armor-piercing round could easily gore nearly four inches of armor at 1,650 yards. This became a vital German weapon, one that would persist until the end of the war. The 88 was ultimately a marriage of a heavy projectile with high muzzle velocity. It fired a 20-pound armor-piercing shell at 2,700 fps. It could easily destroy tanks at over 1,000 yards.

▪ ▪ ▪

The battles in North Africa had demonstrated that German tanks were superior to their American and British counterparts. While the medium M3 could penetrate the Mark IV's armor at over 800 yards, the up-gunned Mark IV could knock out the M3 at a range of 1,000 yards. Though the British were more likely to be destroyed by a Mark IV, the majority of the German tanks were the smaller Mark IIIs, whose 50-mm gun could only penetrate the M3's maximum two inches of armor at 600–700 yards. But at that distance they were halfway within the lethal range of the M3's 75-mm cannon.[14]

Combat in France and Africa had offered a number of lessons for the US Armored Force, not yet in the war, to study. For one, the Americans saw Allied defeats as a result of lack of air support. They also believed that antitank guns had proved their worth as the answer to enemy armor when they were employed against the French at Arras. The United States had purchased a number of antitank guns before the war. The German 37-mm gun was tested and modified, becoming the American M3 antitank gun in late 1939.

In addition, reports from observers noted the lack of reconnaissance, bridging equipment, and mobile artillery units fielded by the Allies. Consequently, the US armored division was equipped with reconnaissance, engineer, and mobile-artillery battalions. Contrarily, the Americans failed to appreciate British reports of the necessity of heavier tanks in combat. Again, the dominantly cavalry-minded Armored Force sought to focus on fast light tanks capable of exploiting breakthroughs and disrupting the enemy's interior. These officers were not interested in heavily armored tanks that would lumber along with the infantry.[15]

9

World War

> The Americans were fantastically well equipped and we had a lot to learn from them organizationally. British experience had been put to good use in the American equipment.
>
> **—Erwin Rommel**

As smoke bellowed from Oahu, Americans sat silently in shock, momentarily befuddled. Since World War I the United States had sat like a cold locomotive in a railyard. But in December 1941 the Japanese had inadvertently ignited the long-dormant but ever-ready coal. Almost immediately, the American war machine cleared its stack, hissed a cloud of smoke and steam, and rumbled into gear.

Only months before the attack on Pearl Harbor, the I Armored Corps had been authorized. This varied command was made up of the Armored Force Board, the Armored Force School and Replacement Training Center, and the new 1st and 2nd Armored Divisions.

The Armored Force Board replaced the technical board, which had been formed to analyze and determine necessary material for mechanized formations. When the Armored Force was authorized, the board became responsible for, among other things, generating training literature. Initially, this material primarily came from cavalry and infantry publications on hand. In 1943 the Armored Force School took over this process and began developing its own publications for the training of armored personnel.[1]

The new armored divisions had been formed from the 7th Cavalry

Brigade and the Provisional Tank Brigade, respectively. Porter Williamson, a member of the I Armored Corps headquarters staff, shed light on the true nature of the unit:

> The term, Corps, meant that we should have two or more tank divisions in our command. A tank division had approximately fifteen thousand men and approximately seventy tanks of light and medium size. We had never seen a medium tank! We had pictures! Everything we did was based on guesswork and on Gen. Patton's memory of his experiences with tanks in World War I. We did not have a guide on how many men or tanks would be needed to make up a corps. We did have trucks and cars. . . . We were the I Armored Corps in name, but we were short fifty thousand men and all of the fighting equipment for war. I Armored Corps was made up of our staff of fifteen officers plus our headquarters Company of approximately two hundred men! All of our "big guns" were six inch stove pipes mounted on trucks![2]

It is tempting to speculate how the American stovepipe guns would have fared against Guderian's wooden guns. Unfortunately for the United States and most of Europe, the Germans' wooden guns had been replaced with real ones well before 1939.

By the time the Japanese brought the war to the United States, the I Armored Corps had five divisions in various stages of development and several battalions in reserve. As the United States simultaneously designed and built its armored force, Brigadier General Chaffee proposed creating armored commands at the corps level, modeled on the panzer corps that had spearheaded the invasions of Poland and France. This separate command would combine armored divisions into a single command "capable of being employed whole or in part as the Germans have organized and used it." These theories had been part of the study concerning the feasibility of tanks as ordered by Chief of Staff Summerall in 1928 that had proposed a force fielding not only tanks but also mechanized infantry, self-propelled artillery, engineers, air elements, and service units. Armor, the study's authors (one of whom was Chaffee) argued, would form the mainstay of future fighting units. They also had called for a fully mechanized corps.[3] In the end, the armored-corps concept floundered in a strong undertow of opposition created by the assistant chiefs of staff, the chiefs of infantry and cavalry, and the lack of support from General Marshall. Historian George Hofmann also has pointed out that "General Macarthur's policy of decentralizing mechanization . . . intensified the autonomy of the combatant arm branches, [reinforcing] their concentric tactical orientation. This action, along with budget restraints, retarded any attempt to establish a unified tank program."[4]

C. C. Benson's call for tank divisions in 1931 had acknowledged the obstacles faced by developing arms and organizations, such as a corps, during a time of peace. Ironically, an Armored Force study entitled "Organization for Command of Large Armored Units in European Armies" determined that the Germans were able to field panzer corps because they *had* trained and organized their forces during times of peace. It is reasonable to conclude that as peace in the United States was marked with economic depression, pacifism, isolationism, and branch infighting, the idea of an armored corps was doomed from the start.

American Armored Division, 1940

While the struggle for an armored corps continued, the army went about planning new and revising old methods of tank operations. Since its formation, the Armored Force had adopted a cavalry role, which was to exploit breakthroughs won by the infantry and penetrate into the enemy's rear to disrupt communications and destroy central-command and logistic centers. To accomplish this, light tanks became the focus of armored units. Raiding and disruption were fitting roles for the relatively speedy light tanks, particularly given the typical lack of antitank guns or enemy tanks in the rear. When planners developed the first American armored divisions in November 1940, they decided to build them around an armored brigade consisting of two light armored regiments and one heavy armored regiment. In addition, the division would field an artillery regiment, an armored reconnaissance battalion, an armored infantry regiment, an engineer battalion, and an artillery battalion. Again, being derived from traditional cavalry precepts, armor's role was to operate as a fast mobile arm to disrupt the enemy's interior.

Antitank Weapons

The Spanish Civil War, Poland, France, and North Africa had demonstrated that the light tank was becoming passé on the modern battlefield. This was the result of the constant remodeling of antitank weapons.

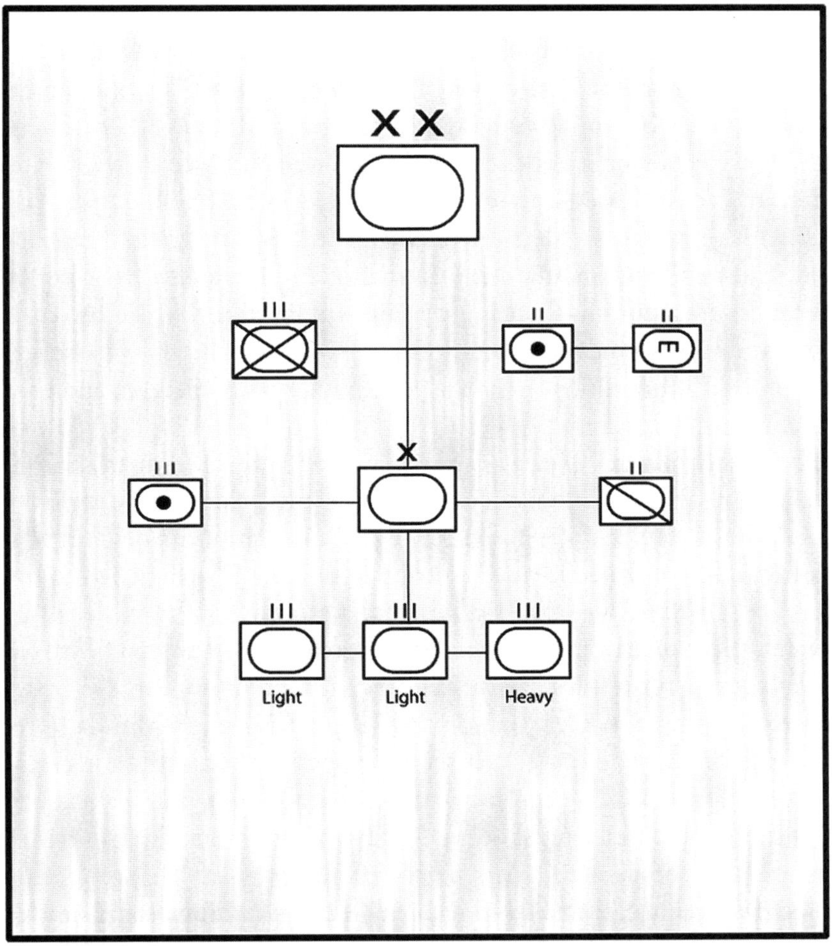

Figure 20. Organization of a US armored division, 1940.

As the tank became more prominent on the battlefield, the demand for tank-killing projectiles followed suit.

As we will later see, a multitude of different projectiles fired from tank and antitank guns existed. The use of various types of shot for different targets dates back hundreds of years. Cartridges were first used in the latter part of the sixteenth century, then typically linen sacks holding the propellant charge. During the first half of the seventeenth century, projectiles were occasionally attached to these sacks, becoming the first forms of fixed ammunition. Doing this allowed a gun crew to increase their rate of fire by loading both the projectile and the propellant as a single unit.

By this time too had emerged a number of shot types to fire: bar, grape, canister, jointed, expanding, chain, explosive, and incendiary.

The French were the first to systemize all aspects of artillery into an organic arm. They began by studying and refining gun tubes and carriages, then developed formulas for determining gun weights based on ball weight and barrel lengths based on the caliber of shot. They were the first to do away with the elaborate decorative casts of tubes for a more simplistic mold, known as the smoothline. Historian Harold Peterson has asserted that the most significant French invention was the sabot, which served as "a wad and also as a means for attaching the powder bag so that an efficient form of fixed ammunition for solid shot could be manufactured and used for field guns."[5]

The American Civil War was on the horizon when Rhode Island militia general Charles T. James developed the rifled cannon. Aside from more-accurate fire and increased range, the innovation made clear that a conical shaped projectile would strike nose first. This logic led to designing a projectile fuse that would detonate on impact rather than by a timing mechanism. The result, Peterson explained, was that "with his multiplicity of projectiles and fuses the civil war cannoneer was better prepared for any possible situation than any artilleryman who had preceded him. In seconds he could select the proper projectile for counterbattery, for anti-personnel work and long range or point blank, for ricochet fire, for battering shot, or for any of the other ways in which artillery might be deployed. And he could quickly insert the proper fuse for just the result desired. The various choices gave him mastery of his profession never before equaled, and in four bloody years he made the most of it."[6] It would not be until World War I when new projectiles would be needed—the armor-piercing shot.

Though armor-piercing projectiles (such as bullets and high-trajectory, low-velocity antitank artillery) had been used during the Great War, they were refined during the interwar years to utilize blunt kinetic energy to achieve penetration. Simple solid-shot rounds fired at high velocity were relied upon to knock out armor. By the time of the invasion of Poland, most armor-piercing projectiles, up to 50-mm in caliber, traveled at 2,800 fps.

The German 50-mm antitank field gun had been issued in the spring of 1941 and was steadily replacing its 37-mm predecessor by the time of the North Africa campaigns. It fired high-explosive and armor-piercing rounds, whose shells weighed 3.25 pounds and 4.5 pounds, respectively.

With a muzzle velocity between 2,953 and 3,280 fps, the gun was fully capable of destroying British infantry and cruiser tanks as well as the American light and medium tanks.

The British 6-pounder antitank weapon was designed to engage enemy armor not vulnerable to their 2-pounders at distances beyond 300 yards. Its projectile traveled at 2,700 fps, yielding an effective range of 875 yards against German tanks. In addition, the British used their 25-pounder howitzer for direct antitank fire when the range was within 1,100 yards. The howitzer's semifixed rounds had four different charges, offering varied shell velocities. Though the supercharge could only give the 20-pound armor-piercing round a muzzle velocity of 1,700 fps, it could easily knock out a German tank with a direct hit, sometimes blowing the turret into the air.

According to a bulletin released by the Military Intelligence Division in 1940, Germany and Britain had conflicting views of the light tank. The British held "that light and medium tanks are of little value," as they were "vulnerable to almost any kind of fire." Contrarily, the report stated that "the Germans found the light tanks extraordinarily effective." Their conflicting views suggest differing outlooks on the machines themselves. Yet the variance actually seems to have been more of a byproduct of how these armies used their antitank guns. For example, German tanks were less likely to run into French or British antitank guns since these were "not distributed sufficiently." Consequently, the German light tank was more likely to maneuver freely on the battlefield. British tanks, however, *were* likely to run into German antitank screens because enemy units "were abundantly equipped with AT weapons."[7] At the time of this report, the United States was still focusing on the production of light tanks. But as antitank weapons became more prominent on the battlefield, Americans began to realize, as the British had in 1940, that light tanks could not represent the vanguard of American armor units.

American Armored Division, 1942

This was not to say that light tanks were obsolete, just that they were no longer suitable for their originally intended role. Because the tactics of an armored division were based on fire and maneuver, it "is not comparable to the cavalry charge," as Chaffee had argued in 1941. He had stated then, "it is the mutual use of armored and air firepower to assist and cover the movement of a maneuvering element."[8] The general believed that tanks used in concentrated mass, accompanied by specially equipped soldiers, could operate as self-sustaining units at the forefront of an attack. The armored division thus began to shift its focus to being a more prominent actor on the battlefield. In August 1941, due to Chaffee's deteriorating health, command of the Armored Force passed to artilleryman Maj. Gen. Jacob Devers. Under Devers, the armored division would take on a new face.

In March 1942 the armored division reversed its light tank/medium tank ratio to be more reliant on the medium tank's firepower rather than the light tank's mobility. The division was also rearranged structurally. The

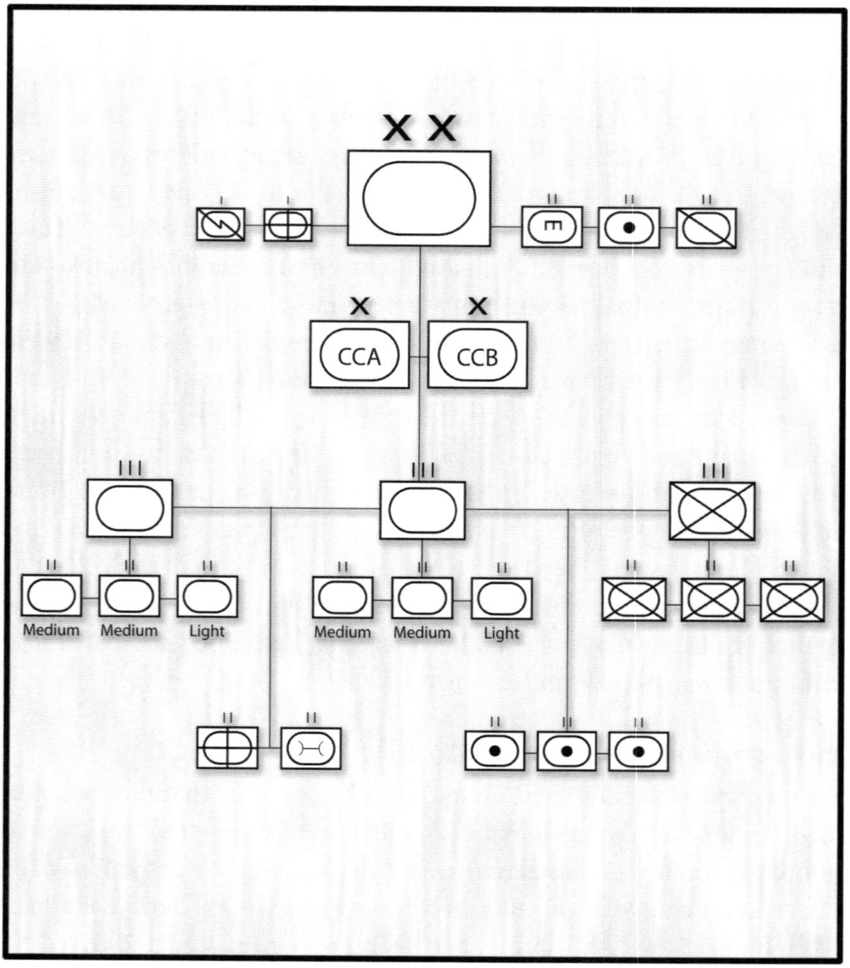

Figure 21. Organization of a US armored division, 1942.

armored brigade was dropped for a more flexible organization consisting of two combat commands. A combat command did not have organic units, rather it was a commanding unit that could control various others from within the division for certain durations of time or for specific missions. This flexible design structure allowed a combat command to draw from the divisional pool of units, primarily two armored regiments—fielding two medium and one light battalion each, consisting of 232 medium tanks and 158 light tanks—and one armored infantry regiment. Each division had two combat commands, CCA and CCB, with a total of 14,620 troops.[9]

After the fall of France, the bulk of the Allied ground fighting had taken place in Libya and, as far as the Americans could see, would likely move into Egypt. The circumstances therefore demanded that the US Army begin training for war in the desert. On 15 January 1942 Major General Patton, the former commander of the 2nd Armored Division, took charge of the I Armored Corps, then stationed at Fort Benning. His new assignment as corps commander was to organize and command the new Desert Training Center. Patton moved the corps to California—into the Mojave Desert. Fifty miles east of Indio, he selected the sites for his camp and the Desert Training Center, which encompassed 18,000 square miles within the borders of California, Arizona, and Nevada. The men began work building kitchens, latrines, and mess shelters while the officers developed the Table of Organization and Equipment for the corps that would assemble and train there.[10]

General Headquarters Battalions—the Bastard Battalions

In addition to the armored division, the Armored Force also built general-headquarters, or "separate," tank battalions. While the division's primary mission was to exploit breakthroughs and penetrate into the enemy's rear, echoing the traditional role of cavalry and mirroring the role of the panzer division, the separate tank battalions were intended as a reserve force to be attached to infantry divisions as needed.

These "bastard battalions," having no mother division, came from various backgrounds. The first separate battalion had been the 70th, formed alongside the 1st and 2nd Armored Divisions, with the purpose of being attached to the infantry. A number of others were created as "reserve battalions" to support infantry and armored divisions when needed. Lastly, many separate tank battalions had their origins in armored divisions. As discussed later, armored divisions went through a number of reorganizations that reduced the number of battalions within them. These "abandoned" units then became separate battalions.

These separate tank battalions were subordinate to what were called armored groups. The command groups were intended to coordinate the armored battalions at corps level, having tactical control over them. In practice, however, the armored groups tended to focus on administration and service issues, such as reequipping units with upgraded vehicles or setting up stage shows for the men. By the latter half of 1944, armored groups were more or less nonessential to operations and thus often absorbed by armored divisions.[11]

The divisions and separate battalions represented the diverging theories on the application of tanks. While the armored division encapsulated total mechanization built around the hard-hitting tanks, the separate battalions served the notion that the infantry was still the principle arm that armor was to support. For both roles, the United States used the M4 Sherman tank.

The Medium M4 Sherman

Due to the immediate need of a medium tank with a 75-mm gun, the Ordnance Department moved ahead with the production of the M3. Simultaneously, work began on designing a medium to mount the 75-mm in a rotating turret. The pilot model was completed in September 1941. After a handful of modifications, the first orders were placed in November for the production of the medium M4 Sherman tank.[12] The Sherman was a little over nineteen feet in length, stood nine feet high, and weighed thirty-three tons. The powertrain, suspension, and tracks were the same as the medium M3. The hull, however, was completely reengineered to accommodate the new turret.

The Sherman turret had a maximum of three inches of armor, located at the front. Its side armor was two inches thick, while that of the roof was only one; an additional three inches protected the gun shield and rotor shield. The glacis (frontal armor plate covering the differential) had two inches of armor, while the sides and rear of the hull had one and a half inches. The turret crew entered and exited through a rotating armored split hatch on the top on the starboard side.

Inside was an electric blower to ventilate the fumes. For improved internal visibility, especially at night, there were three dome lights. Aside from the single split hatch on the roof of the turret, there was a small twelve-inch square hatch on the rear port side called a pistol port. Originally designed as a quasi-solution for close combat against infantry attacks by allowing the loader to fire small arms from within, crews used it instead to help circulate air, allow more light into the turret, and discard spent 75-mm casings or any other material. Most importantly, when loading the tank with its 75-mm ammunition, a man on the ground could hand the rounds directly to the loader through the pistol port rather than handing them to crewmen standing on the hull who then passed the round down through the commander's hatch.

There were two types of hulls for the Shermans. Rolled armor welded together was preferable, but a lack of capable facilities resulted in the Ordnance Department looking to cast hulls as well. The original M4 models used a welded hull, while those with the smooth-cast hull (featuring rounded contours) were designated M4A1. The first of these models to go into production was the M4A1, coming out of the Pressed Steel Car Company in March 1942. Two months later the Pacific Car and Foundry Company began production on the same. In the summer of 1942, the

Figure 22. A column of tanks from the Armored Force School exhibits a variety of medium tanks, including an M4, M3s with welded and cast hulls, and M4A1s. *Courtesy Davis Memorial Library, Patton Museum, Fort Knox*

Pressed Steel Car Company began building the M4s. Throughout the war, the Detroit Tank Arsenal, the Baldwin Locomotive Works, the American Locomotive Company, and the Pullman Standard Manufacturing Company produced the M4.[13]

Early Sherman Engines

Both the M4 and M4A1 utilized the Wright/Continental R-975 engine. But as with the M3, the Ordnance Department made use of other motors then available. Shermans equipped with the twin General Motors diesel, previously used by the M3A3 and M3A5, were designated M4A2s, which began production in April 1942. They were produced by the Grand Blanc Arsenal, the Federal Machine & Welder Company, the American Locomotive

Figure 23. Lt. Gen. George Patton speaks with a mechanic about the Wright engine. *Courtesy Davis Memorial Library, Patton Museum, Fort Knox*

Company, and the Pullman Standard Manufacturing Company while a dozen also rolled out of the Baldwin Locomotive Works by the war's end.[14]

The M4A2 was used to fill Lend-Lease orders and to provide the bulk of the training vehicles in the States. They were not intended to accompany American troops overseas but were eventually used by the Marine Corps later in the war.

Sherman Armament

The army had strict restrictions concerning the specifications of vehicles relating to size and weight, which limited the tank and its turret to be no wider than 124 inches and in turn dictated the size of its main armament. This consequently resulted in the use of the M3 75-mm gun, a single-shot, flat-trajectory weapon. The gun tube was nine feet in length and weighed just over three tons. It used a horizontal sliding breech block with a recoil of twelve inches and could fire three types of ammunition: armor piercing, high explosive, and white phosphorus.

Against tanks or hardened targets, gunners would use the APC (armor-piercing capped) M61 or the AP (armor piercing) M72. Both were solid "shot" rounds, having no explosive filler. The APC M61 shell had a steel-alloy cap and windshield that was designed to lessen the "stress on impact by spreading the energy transfer over a large area and for a longer period of time, allowing the mostly undamaged projectile to penetrate the armor."[15] This cap gave it a longer, sharper, and more aerodynamic appearance. According to a War Department technical manual, the production of the "more complex M61 projectile could not meet requirements; therefore, a simpler round was developed." The result was the AP M72, which lacked the steel-alloy cap and the windshield, giving it a much stubbier appearance. Both rounds came out of the bore with a muzzle velocity of 2,030 fps; their predecessor on the M3 had a muzzle velocity of only 1,850 fps. According to the field manual for tank platoons published in 1944, the armor-piercing ammunition was "effective against most hostile tanks up to a range of 1,600 yards." Tankers would discover that this was far from true.[16]

The M48 was the high-explosive round for the 75-mm gun. Its fuse, which screwed onto the head of the shell, had a small slotted disk that could be turned with a flathead screwdriver to one of two detonation settings stamped on it—"SQ" (super quick) or "Delay."[17] Setting the fuse to "SQ" would cause the round to detonate at the exact point of impact.

So whether it struck a tree, the ground, or a building, the shell would detonate on the exterior, scattering its deadly fragments through the air. This setting was most effective for antipersonnel attack. Setting the fuse for "Delay" would detonate the burst .05 seconds after impact, allowing the projectile to penetrate before exploding to expel its lethal blast on the interior of a given target, such as a building or stone wall. Later this delay would be increased to .15 seconds. The entire round weighed 18.8 pounds and contained 1.5 pounds of TNT.[18]

Not only were their two types of fuses, but the cartridges also had two different propelling charges available—"Normal" and "Super Charge"; the brass casing would be labeled with one or the other. The *normal* charge produced a muzzle velocity of 1,470 fps, whereas the *super charge* had a muzzle velocity of 1,885 fps. They could be used for direct- or indirect-fire missions, capable of reaching targets more than 7,000 yards distant.[19]

As the M4 and M4A1 had different hulls, they differed in ammunition capacity for their main gun. The M4, with its angled armor, had room for ninety-seven rounds of 75-mm ammunition, while the M4A1, with its curved hull, held only ninety rounds. A trained crew could fire twenty rounds per minute under nominal conditions, though training emphasized the conservation of ammunition. Field tests dictated that a usable rate of fire should be around six rounds per minute. At this rate a Sherman would fire all of its ammunition in a total of sixteen minutes of combat.

In addition to the main armament, each tank crew was issued twelve hand grenades, consisting of fragmentation, incendiary, and smoke grenades; a submachine gun; and tripods for the Sherman's .50-caliber and .30-caliber machine guns. The .30-caliber machine gun was the air-cooled M1919A4, classified at being effective up to 2,500 yards, though realistically not used beyond 1,000 yards. Its armor-piercing ammunition could be used against most antitank-gun shields at a range of 200 yards or less.

Sherman Tank Crew

The Sherman had a crew of five. The driver was seated on the port side of the tank and the assistant driver/bow gunner (BOG) to the starboard, both located in the hull with the transmission between them.[20] In the turret were the loader, gunner, and commander. The loader sat on the port side of the turret and the gunner on the starboard side, with the 75-mm gun between them. Seated in the back behind the gunner was the commander.

Figure 24. Crew and equipment for medium tank. *Courtesy Davis Memorial Library, Patton Museum, Fort Knox*

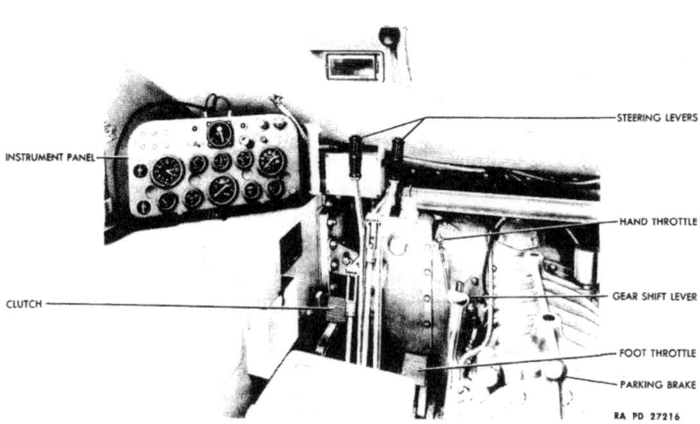

Figure 25. The driver's compartment of a Sherman. Note the transmission directly to the right of the driver's seat. *From* Technical Manual 9–759

The driver and the BOG sat forward of the turret. Both had padded seats and backrests, each with a hatch located directly above him to enter and exit the tank. The driver's instrument panel was located in the sponson to his left. To drive the tank, he had two brake-steering levers. Pulling back on the right lever would turn the tank to the right, while pulling on the left lever would turn the tank left. In order to stop, he would pull back on both levers simultaneously.

Shermans had five forward gears and one reverse. The gearshift was located near the driver's right knee, while he operated the clutch with his left foot. To accelerate, the driver would depress a pedal underneath his right foot.

The driver and the BOG each had a periscope fitted in the hatches directly above them. Weather permitting, tank crews typically traveled with these hatches open, allowing them to ride with their heads out and providing a much better view of the surroundings. Driving this way also allowed more light to come into the tank and promoted better ventilation, especially for the two in the hull. When the tank engaged in combat, the crew would close all hatches, or "button up." If not under small-arms fire, the commander usually kept his hatch open, though, allowing him to constantly, and cautiously, evaluate the battlefield situation as it developed around him.

The BOG operated the .30-caliber M1919A4 machine gun, which was installed in a ball mount on the starboard side of the hull. If the tank was making a long march, the BOG could trade places with the driver and take a turn at the controls to give him a break. He would also fill in if the gunner or loader were wounded or otherwise no longer capable of carrying out his duty.

In the turret the tank commander either sat in the rear or stood with his head protruding out of the main split hatch. Typically he kept this hatch open, even in combat, offering him the greatest view of the terrain and targets. Commanders were responsible for communication with other tanks of their platoon, for directing the driver on which course to take, and for guiding the gunner to a target and estimating the range.

The gunner sat on a backless seat to the starboard side of the 75-mm gun. Taking directions from the commander, who had the best all-around view, he would orient the turret and gun to the desired target. To the gunner's right was a vertical pistol-grip joystick mounted on a horizontal control wheel. Utilizing the electro-hydraulic power-traverse system, he simply had to turn the joystick left or right for the turret to move in that direction. The system was pressure sensitive, and the farther the gunner turned the joystick, the faster the turret spun. If he wanted (or had) to rotate the turret manually, he could do so by grabbing the same joystick and use it as a handle to spin the traverse wheel. With the electro-hydraulics, it took fifteen seconds for the turret to traverse 360 degrees. Manually, it would take the gunner seventy-four rotations to turn the turret just 90 degrees. While allowed for accurate settings, manual operation would be a last resort if engaging a threat, when speed is essential.

To set the elevation of the gun, the gunner operated a vertical hand wheel, located in front of him, with his left hand. During this time he would have his face against a periscope, looking for the target.

At the gunner's feet were, from left to right, a pedal and two buttons protruding from a small control box. The button on the right fired the main gun, while the button on the left fired the coaxial machine gun. The pedal was for manually firing the main gun in case the electric systems failed.

The loader was responsible for loading the 75-mm and the coaxial machine gun situated in front of his position. In the early Sherman tanks loaders had the bad luck of not having easy access to the turret hatch. While the commander was located in or under the hatch and the gunner situated in front of it, the loader was on the opposite side of the gun. In the event of the tank being knocked out, he would have to squeeze by or under the breech and recoil guard to climb out of the vehicle. This would be very difficult if he was wounded, blinded, or knocked senseless from a blast. Loaders were usually the last of the crewmen to get out.

To communicate with the platoon, the tank commander had a handheld T-17 microphone. Other crewmembers wore T-30 throat microphones, which used two small transmitters held against the throat by a small elastic band. All crewmembers had receivers mounted into the side flaps of their crash helmets.

Communication between vehicles or units could be carried out by foot, by motorcycle, or by jeep. When companies were in a static position, such as an assembly area, crews could lay wire for communication between vehicles. In action, the tanks used a few different radios. FM models included the SCR-508, SCR-528, and the SCR-68B. Under ideal conditions these could transmit messages up to twenty miles.[21]

Tankers wore an assortment of uniforms that differed from those typically worn in other army units. The general ground-forces uniform

Figure 26. These crew members wear the one-piece HBT coveralls while holding their M1942 crash helmets.

Figure 27. Tank crewmen wore a variety of uniform pieces. Two of the soldiers (far left and second from right) wear the lightweight cotton HBT coveralls, while the rest are wearing winter-combat trousers. All but the man on the left wear winter-combat jackets. Only one crewman wears his crash helmet, while the others don M1 steel helmets or winter-combat helmets.

consisted of a wool shirt, a wool-lined M41 jacket, wool trousers, canvas leggings, and service shoes. All of these items would be worn by the tankmen too, but they were also issued a number of specialized items.

Whether training in the States, racing through North Africa, or fighting in Normandy, many tankers wore the single-piece cotton HBT overalls during warm weather.[22] Though typically worn by mechanics of all fields in the army, they were perfect for the tankers, as the snug coveralls were not likely to get caught on the miscellaneous parts inside their vehicle.

The tankmen were also issued a short, winter combat jacket, dubbed the "tanker jacket," comprising a cotton exterior with a wool liner. The zipper easily distinguished it from other army jackets, most of which had buttons. Furthermore, unlike other service jackets, the tanker stood out with its knit collar, cuffs, and waistband, which again helped prevent snagging within the tank, and was devoid of epaulets and chest pockets. It was common to see this jacket worn with the winter combat trousers, which were actually overalls. These matched the jacket in materials, being made of cotton with a wool liner. Two suspenders attached to the front bib, which had a zipper running down the center. Designed to be worn over standard-issue wool trousers, they had two openings that unzipped to give the wearer access to his pockets in his regular trousers. Lastly, they also came with a zipper fly.

From a distance, the most distinguishing feature of a tanker was his headgear. The winter combat helmet was in no way a helmet; one might reasonably call it a hood or even a hat. Coordinating with the winter combat trousers and jacket, this headgear was a snug-fitting cotton hood with a wool or blanket-type liner. It had a chinstrap and an attached collar that was to be tucked into the jacket, keeping the wind and elements out of the uniform.

The signature item, though, was the M1942 tanker, or crash, helmet. These were basically olive drab Rawlings football helmets. They had vulcanized fiber shells with an adjustable leather liner, and two side flaps for protection that also housed headphones connected into the tank's radio system. These helmets were not designed to protect the tankers from enemy fire but simply to protect their heads when bumping into the tank's metal interior. If the men were outside of the vehicle or otherwise exposed, as a driver or commander often were through an open hatch, they had the option of wearing the standard-issue M1 steel helmet. When used it often was worn without its liner and over a crash helmet.

The Tank Destroyer

American tanks, both light and medium, were designed to penetrate enemy lines and disrupt rear installations—not engage with armor. The German blitzkrieg had the immediate effect of compelling US officers to look for other measures for stopping tanks. To begin they looked toward antitank guns. The theory of these weapons was often corollary to antitank sentiment. One article written in the *Infantry Journal* in 1938 by one "Captain X" provides a window into the reasoning for the lack of enthusiasm for the tank while simultaneously insisting that antitank weapons would always devastate their prey.

Captain X formed the basis of his argument on a comparative analysis, focusing primarily on vulnerability based on audibility, visibility, and mobility of the respective weapons. It is given, he stated, that tanks are more vulnerable at greater distances, while antitank guns are more vulnerable at short range. He based this on the fact that antitank guns can conceal their positions, while tanks are "about as capable of a stealthy approach as a herd of elephants charging through a [field of sugar cane]." Regardless of whether the gun crews hear or see the approaching vehicles, "they have the drop on the tanks, and a big one it is." This advantage allows the defenders to "get a jump in opening fire." As discussed more fully in chapter 19, the first-to-fire phenomenon is a determinable factor on the battlefield.

Visibility was a major factor for Captain X in comparing antitank guns with tanks. "The tank has been nearsighted from birth," he argued. "Seldom, if ever," he continued, "will tank crews detect a gun in concealed or prepared positions until it has opened fire."[23] This observation was no stretch of the imagination, keeping in mind that the US Army had yet to work out tank-infantry teams. But it was this type of thought that led officials to focus more on the development of mobile antitank weapons—the tank destroyers.

While Captain X had faith in the promise apparently guaranteed by antitank guns, Maj. Gen. Lesley McNair lamented in April 1941: "It is beyond belief that so little could be done on the question in view of all that has happened and is happening abroad. I for one have missed no opportunity to hammer for something real in the way of anti-tank defense, but so far have gotten nowhere. I have no reason now to feel encouraged."[24] For others, the answer was clearly in tank-destroyer formations. Hugh A. Drum, the commanding general of the First Army, spearheaded this concept. A tank-destroyer center was created at Fort Meade just before Pearl Harbor but was quickly moved to Camp Hood, Texas.[25]

The tank destroyer was designed as a highly mobile antitank gun, specifically intended for use against enemy armor. As antitank guns increased in caliber, they were often mounted on trucks, halftracks, and eventually all-tracked vehicles, thus giving the appearance of a tank. But tank destroyers are simply vehicles that carry an antitank gun. For protection, some had only a thin gun shield, behind which the crew operated more or less in the open (such as the gun motor carriage M6), while others had an open-top armored turret (such as the M10 Wolverine). Regardless, their mobility came at the price of limited armor. But this was a fair tradeoff if the tank destroyer was used properly, so it was thought, as a hit-and-run weapon. Where tanks were used to move in and exploit any gains, the tank destroyer was only to be employed against known enemy armor units.

The first American tank destroyer, or gun motor carriage, was the 75-mm gun motor carriage M3. This was simply a World War I 75-mm field gun mounted on the M3 halftrack. The army also developed the 37-mm

Figure 28. Early M3 75-mm gun motor carriage tank destroyer. *Courtesy US Army Ordnance Museum, Aberdeen Proving Ground*

gun motor carriage M6, a Dodge ¾-ton truck with the gun mounted in its bed. But as the 37-mm was more or less useless, and having a ¾-ton truck available to move material was more desirable, most M6s were disarmed.

In September 1942 the army began production of the 3-inch gun motor carriage M10 (Wolverine). It had a large, thinly armored open turret to give the crew a full view of their surroundings. The M10 utilized the same chassis and powertrain of the medium M3 and M4 but was equipped with the M7 3-inch antitank gun. The fifteen-pound shell was capable of penetrating over three and a half inches of armor at 1,000 yards.[26]

The story of the tank destroyers is one of polarizing doctrinal theory. One of the most detrimental effects of these weapons was that they misappropriated progress in tank development. As discussed in chapter 11, US tankers came into World War II outgunned and outarmored. Generally speaking, things would not improve until the war was near its end because tank destroyers were the units, in theory, that would engage enemy armor. In practice, though, this was seldom the case.

Figure 29. M10 3-inch gun motor carriage. *Courtesy US Army Ordnance Museum, Aberdeen Proving Ground*

10

El Alamein

It may almost be said, "Before Alamein we never had a victory. After Alamein we never had a defeat."

—Winston Churchill

When Tobruk fell, roughly 35,000 Allied troops surrendered as well. On 24 June 1942 General Rommel continued his drive east. Also at this time, command of the British forces in North Africa passed to General Auchinleck. The British had since settled into Mersa Matruh, 140 miles into Egypt, to catch their breath. But Auchinleck felt that it would be better for them to continue their retreat as a means to buy time and gather strength for the inevitable struggle against the pursuing Desert Fox.

Only 40 miles stretched between the Mediterranean and the 7,000-square-mile Qatar Depression. These two natural boundaries formed a bottleneck for any army advancing on Cairo. Resting on the coastal road between these obstacles was the small city of El Alamein; Auchinleck decided to regroup the Eighth Army there. A successful defense there would put a stop to the wide flanking maneuvers that had dominated the battlefields of North Africa.

El Alamein was the last steppingstone across the Egyptian frontier before reaching Alexandria. Both Auchinleck and Rommel knew that the town was key to the defense of Alexandria, which in turn was the key to Cairo. Whoever held the Egyptian capital controlled the Suez Canal, the gate to the East.

The fighting in the desert was ultimately a war of logistics. As each army advanced along the coastal road, they would in turn stretch their supply lines. The British now had Alexandria, their key supply depot, at their backs, only 70 miles away. The Germans, on the other hand, had to move their material from depots in Tripoli, Benghazi, and Tobruk; Tobruk being the closest was still nearly 350 miles from the front. This was a battle of attrition that would be decided by who had the most supplies, who received them first, and who had the more reliable machines of war.

The British set up multiple strongpoints and held their limited armor in the rear. On the first of July Rommel attacked. Yet the British were prepared, having laid down a heavy string of minefields and positioned their artillery where it could lay down a devastating rain of fire on the approaching enemy. Due to these defenses, Axis forces were forced to stop.

Rommel then tried a strike from the south, but his units were attacked from their rear and again forced to withdraw. Exhausting men and material daily against the British line, Rommel had to temper his offensive.

Throughout the month of July, the forces battled it out with continuous attacks and counterattacks in the vicinity of El Alamein. The last of the German assaults took place on 31 August, when the British 7th and 10th Armoured Divisions staved off the panzers again attacking from the south.

On 3 August Churchill arrived in Cairo. Subsequently, Lt. Gen. Sir Harold Alexander replaced Auchinleck and Lt. Gen. Bernard Montgomery received command of the Eighth Army. On 23 September Rommel, with ailing health, handed over the command of the Afrika Korps to Gen. Georg Stumme. In the end the contest came down to these two commanders: General Stumme and Lieutenant General Montgomery.

Prior to El Alamein, the opposing armies had used their armor to facilitate envelopment attacks. The previous battles were also aimed at victory through attrition, hoping that one side would exhaust its men and material before the other. At El Alamein both sides were obliged to prepare for a battle of breakthrough and annihilation. For the Germans, their resources were low due to the diversion of men and material for the "big show" against Russia. The Afrika Korps had to break through to Alexandria—and soon. For Montgomery, he had to break out and push Germans away from the Suez and, hopefully, out of Africa. And he felt that he had the material to do just that.

Axis forces consisted of 104,000 men; a little over half were Italian. They had eighty-five standard Mark IIIs and eighty-eight Mark IIIs equipped with the 50-mm gun. In addition, they fielded eight Mark IVs and thirty others upgraded with the long 75-mm gun. With an additional 278 Italian tanks, primarily M13/40s, General Stumme had 489 tanks at his command.

Montgomery had close to 200,000 men and more than 1,000 tanks. Ready for battle were 194 Valentines, 216 Crusaders with 2-pounder guns, and seventy-eight Crusaders with 6-pounders. In addition, the British had at hand their gifts from Lend-Lease: 119 light M3 tanks (Stuarts), 170 medium M3s (Grants), and 252 of the newly arrived medium M4s (Shermans). Montgomery had sufficient forces to go on the offensive.

On 6 October the British issued the plan of attack. The initial assault would be spearheaded by XXX Corps on the right, west of El Alamein, while XIII Corps would strike on the left, to the south, along the Qatar Depression. Commanders hoped that XIII Corps would draw enemy forces away to the south, for they expected the XXX Corps to achieve the main breakthrough in its sector. The 9th Australian Division, 51st Highland Division, and 1st South African Division, composing part of XXX Corps, were to clear two corridors through the German minefields down which the 1st and 10th Armored Divisions from X Corps would surge ahead. The armor would initially protect XXX Corps, then attack the Axis panzers.

In the darkness of 23 October, the Allies attacked. At exactly 9:40 p.m. the horizon lit up as 882 British artillery pieces opened up. Each gun fired roughly two rounds every minute for five and half hours. The troops of XXX Corps went to work in the minefields at this time, while XIII Corps occupied the 21st Panzer Division in the south.

One of Rommel's favorite defensive weapons was the mine, using them abundantly in North Africa. In front of their lines around El Alamein, Axis troops laid no less than three million mines in what was dubbed "the Devil's Garden." To help cut through this extensive patch of death, the British 1st Army Tank Brigade put to use two dozen newly introduced flail tanks.

Using the chassis of the Matilda, the design featured a large spinning drum, off of which hung three veils of chains, positioned out in front of the tank. Running off auxiliary power installed in the sponsons of the vehicle, the drum would spin at eighty rpm as the tank crept ahead at two mph. The chains would pound the earth, detonating any mines that lay in its path and thus creating a safe single lane for following tanks and infantry to pass. While ingenious in conception, the flail tanks proved to be quite a burden. The tremendous amount of dust and dirt churned up clogged the air intakes, causing the vehicles to frequently break down from overheating.[1]

Initial progress in the corridor was slow due to concentrated enemy artillery and mortar fire, but by nightfall the 1st Armoured Division was through.

By the following morning, both the 1st and 10th Armoured Divisions were nearly a mile beyond the minefields. Unbelieving, Stumme needed to see the situation for himself and headed for the front in his command car. His vehicle came under fire, and his driver was shot and killed. Shock and fear overtook the general, who collapsed, dying of a heart attack. Rommel had to go back to North Africa despite his poor health.

The Desert Fox returned on the evening of 25 October. His 15th Panzer Division had been decimated, with only thirty-eight tanks remaining. He promptly withdrew the 21st Panzer Division from the south and ordered it north, where he anticipated the main attack would occur. Simultaneously, Montgomery decided to shift his armor strength toward the south. On the night of the twenty-seventh, the 1st Armoured Division withdrew under the cover of darkness.

Montgomery threw his armor into the southern bulge in the German line. The attack was carried out by infantry and 132 tanks, of which only 19 survived, and punctured the German defenses, allowing the 1st Armoured Division to pour through. The Axis forces began to withdraw—they were finished.

Rommel was forced to withdraw his remaining panzers westward, nearly 1,500 miles, through Libya and into Tunisia.

Meanwhile, the Doolittle Raid over Tokyo in May 1942 had given the United States its first heroes and provided Japan a preview of American strength and ingenuity. The US Pacific Fleet soon afterward thwarted the Japanese attack on Port Moresby, New Guinea, at the Battle of Coral Sea, losing one carrier. Then in June the US Navy had turned the tide in the Pacific at the Battle of Midway. In August American troops landed at Guadalcanal, securing the airfield the Japanese had constructed there to support their New Guinea campaign. Thus by late 1942, the United States had battled it out with the Japanese for almost a year. But this was not the case with Germany. Churchill had to wait until November 1942 for his American allies to join the fight in North Africa and Europe.

11

Disaster in Tunisia

You folks at home must be disappointed at what happened to our American troops in Tunisia.

—Ernie Pyle

As the Eighth Army pursued Rommel along the coastal road through Egypt, three Allied task forces began landing in Morocco and Algeria as part of Operation Torch. The British and American invasion of North Africa was the first strategic action toward the US global strategy of "Germany First." Though talks about and plans for a "Germany First" policy had existed as far back as 1938 by a joint army-navy board, the strategy was not officially adopted until March 1941. The US Navy had at first challenged the plan, but Chief of Naval Operations Adm. Harold R. Stark came to believe that the most fundamental interests of the United States were the security of "territorial, economic and ideological integrity," which were dependent on Europe and the survival of England.[1] Operation Torch was chiefly an American endeavor, with Dwight Eisenhower, now a lieutenant general, as commander in chief. His orders were to move through Morocco and Algeria and strike at Rommel's rear, which would soon be in Tunisia.

Before dawn on 8 November, three Allied task forces began landing operations in North Africa. The Eastern Task Force, made up of British and American units, the latter from the 34th Infantry Division, was commanded by Maj. Gen. Charles Ryder. Their landing took place in and around Algiers. The Center Task Force, built around the American 1st

Infantry Division and 1st Armored Division, commanded by Maj. Gen. Lloyd Fredendall, landed near Oran. The Western Task Force, under Major General Patton, consisted of the 3rd and 9th Infantry Divisions and the 2nd Armored Division. The assault waves were supported by tanks from Company B of the separate 70th Tank Battalion. They went ashore along the Atlantic coast in Morocco near Casablanca.

British units continued landing farther east during the next few days, taking Djidielli and Bone. On 15 November they moved into Tunisia for the first time at Tabarka. That same day the 2nd Battalion of the American 509th Parachute Regiment landed in Algeria, near Tebessa, capturing two airfields near the Tunisian border.

In December Rommel was west of El Agheila when the Fifth Panzer Army, under Lt. Gen. Walther Nehring, arrived in Tunisia. The Germans intended to hold their new bridgehead in Tunisia and build up their forces to contest the Allies once again in North Africa.

The newly arrived Fifth Panzer Army was composed of the German Korpsgruppe Fischer and the Italian XXX Corps. Korpsrgruppe Fischer was made up of the 5th Fallschirmjäger Regiment, Division Von Broich, the 334th Infantry Division, and the 10th Panzer Division. In addition to the standard two regiments of tanks, the 10th Panzer Division also brought an extra battalion—the 501st Tiger Battalion.

The Tiger Tank

Prior to the campaign in Poland, German planners realized that there would be a demand for a tank heavier than the medium Mark IV. Numerous companies went to work developing a new breed of armor, a heavy tank to be armed with the high-velocity 88-mm gun. Two companies led the way in progress, Henschel and Porsche. Both submitted their prototypes to the army on the deadline, 20 April 1942—Hitler's fifty-third birthday. After presentations, analyses, and demonstrations, officials decided to move ahead with the Henschel design. Thus production began on the Mark VI in August 1942.

The new tank was fitted with a dynamic suspension, utilizing a torsion-bar system and interleafed road-wheel placement. Three road wheels were fitted to each torsion bar, of which there were eight on each side of the tank, amounting to twenty-four road wheels per side. But these were not the stout road wheels as those on the early panzers or Sherman tanks—the Mark VI's were 31 inches in diameter. The ninety-six steel tracks that spun around these wheels were enormous, measuring 28.5 inches wide.[2] This suspension provided the crew with a comfortable and efficient off-road capability.

The Tiger was equipped with a water-cooled Maybach HL 230, 1,410-cubic-inch V-12 engine. The HL 230 had an output of 690 hp at 3,000 rpm. One drawback for this engine was its consumption of approximately 2.75 gallons per mile. In comparison, the Sherman's fuel consumption was roughly 1.1 gallons per mile.

A massive turret sat atop the Mark VI to house the 88-mm gun. The hydraulics, powered by the main engine, strained to turn the eleven-ton turret 360 degrees in sixty seconds.

Unprecedented armor protected the tank, with just over 3 inches on the turret sides and the rear hull, nearly 4 inches on the front hull, and up to 4.7 inches on the gun mantle.[3] Most important was the 88-mm gun. Its Pzgr.40 round, weighing sixteen pounds and shot with a muzzle velocity of 3,050 fps, could penetrate armor 4.3 inches thick at a range of nearly 2,200 yards.

The debut of the Tiger occurred on the eastern front at Leningrad in August 1942. But it was not until a few months later that British intelligence discovered the tank for themselves, releasing a report in November that the Germans had a "new type of tank." The Russians would withhold their information concerning this "new type of tank" until April 1943.[4]

This fifty-seven-ton German behemoth was already leaving charred Soviet tanks in the East. Now it was going into the desert to fight the Americans' prized thirty-ton, 75-mm-armed Sherman.

Tunisia

By November 1942 Germans were in retreat in North Africa. Their defeat at El Alamein had precipitated a long withdrawal toward Tunisia, where Axis forces could receive supplies and reinforcements at Tunis and Bizerte. In addition, the mountains of Tunisia could provide Rommel an excellent defensive advantage. Knowing that the Germans were on their way, the Allied forces of Operation Torch headed east to try and beat them to these vital cities. But marred by foul weather that turned the roads into impassible mud fields, the Allies failed to reach Tunis and Bizerte before the Germans.

American forces in Tunisia consisted of the 1st and 34th Infantry Divisions and the 1st Armored Division under Maj. Gen. Orlando Ward.

These units made up the US II Corps, which would fight alongside the French XIX Corps d'Armee.

Due to a serious strain on logistics, the Americans were stretched dangerously thin along a line from approximately the northernmost part of Tunisia down to the dry lakebed of Chott Djerid. The 1942 organization of a typical US armored division consisted of two combat commands working with two armored and one mechanized infantry regiment. As a result of the limited number of infantry within the 1st Armored Division, commanders had to pull battalions from the 34th and 1st Infantry Divisions to provide adequate support for the extenuated tank units. If this was altering the official armored-division structure, then the creation of two more combat commands, necessary to direct this force, simply eradicated it.

On 26 January 1943 Rommel established his headquarters in Tunisia. His command, the German-Italian Panzer Army, was reorganized into three corps: the Deutsches Afrika Korps, XX Corps, and XXI Corps. The combined strength of the Fifth Panzer Army and the German-Italian Panzer Army numbered roughly 100,000 men, three quarters of whom were German troops.

Rommel identified the greatest threat to the Axis foothold in Tunisia as the US forces around Gafsa, especially those in the north at Kasserine, Sbeitla, and the small town of Sidi Bou Zid. He was concerned that the Americans might mount a concentrated attack against the German lines and penetrate all the way to the sea, thus splitting the Axis armies. "Accordingly," wrote Rommel, "the 21st Panzer with elements of the 10th Panzer Division was ordered to attack the Americans at Sidi Bouzid and Sbeitla, with the object of breaking up and as far as possible destroying their concentrations."[5]

The German Attack at Sidi Bou Zid

Located just west of the German lines around Faid is a stout eminence named Jebel Lessouda. There the 2nd Battalion of the 168th Infantry Regiment (abbreviated 2/168), an organic unit of the 34th Division (but at this time operating under Combat Command A of the 1st Armored Division), was dug in. Alongside the infantry in this position were Company G of the 1st Armored Regiment and a platoon of tank destroyers. On 14 February the Americans were enduring a large sandstorm. But the winds brought more than just Tunisian sand.

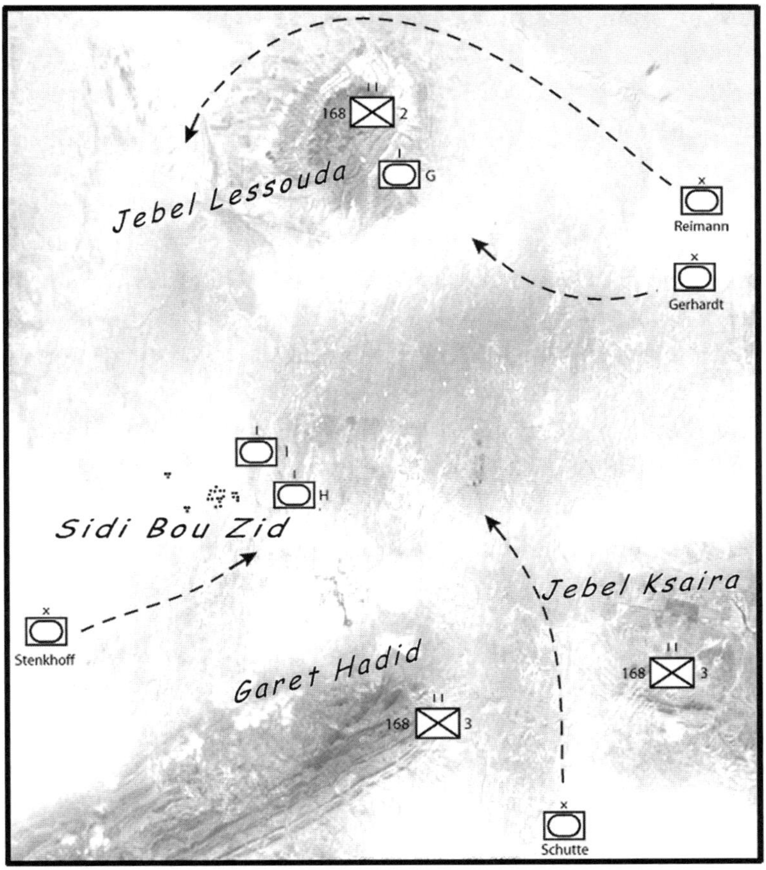

Figure 30. German Attack at Sidi Bou Zid, 14 February 1943.

Maneuvering within the storm was the 10th Panzer Division. Prior to closing in on Jebel Lessouda, the division split, with Kampfgruppe Reimann, consisting of the Panzer Grenadier Regiment 69 and the 501st Tiger Battalion, heading to the right to envelop the mountain along its northern edge, while Kampfgruppe Gerhardt, consisting of Panzer Regiment 7 and Panzergrenadier Regiment 86, moved to the southwest.

Troops on Jebel Lessouda spotted elements of the enemy force, and the tanks of Company G raced into action. Soon after black smoke poured from many American tank hulls.

To the south of Jebel Lessouda, 3/168 (positioned on both sides of a pass) came under attack by the 21st Panzer Division, which was coming in from the south. Panzergrenadier Regiment 104 pierced the American line between Garet Hadid and Jebel Ksaira. Simultaneously, elements of Panzer Regiment 5, also part of the 21st Panzer Division, drove in from the southeast.

The Germans struck hard and fast. At once they disposed of armor threats and encircled the 2/168 while panzers headed toward the town of Sidi Bou Zid. Responding to the attack on the Jebel Lessouda position, two medium-tank companies, I and H, set out to counter the advancing panzers. They immediately took fire from a battery of 88s the Germans had positioned around Jebel Ksaira in anticipation of such a counterattack. The Shermans also came under fire from the Mark VIs of 501st Tiger Battalion. Soon an array of high-velocity antitank guns joined the action. Shells streaked through the air. A number of cruising tanks took shots through their hulls and slowed to a stop in clouds of dust. Wounded tankers scrambled out of the hatches, quickly followed by smoke and flame. Some slowly crawled out, bleeding, falling from their vehicle, and rolling in agony, while others ran for cover. The remaining Shermans continued to fight, but the hopelessness of the situation became apparent as tank after tank came to a halt, their crews forced to abandon the smoking hulks.

The American armor force was decimated. Of the forty-four tanks entering action, all but seven were knocked out. Their protective armor proved insufficient to withstand German armor-piercing shells. Belton Y. Cooper, who served in a maintenance battalion, recalled the effects of a shell that penetrated the front of one Sherman. The round pierced the tip of the differential cover, or glacis plate, "at its thickest point, which was about four and a half inches. The projectile penetrated the armor, passed through about a foot of fifty-weight oil, severed a five-and-a-half-inch steel driveshaft, then passed through another eight to ten inches of oil and a one-inch armored back plate before entering the driver's compartment."[6] Comparing this effect to the American rounds, which merely bounced off the German tanks, explains the heavy losses suffered by the tank force. That night elements of the 10th and 21st Panzer Divisions linked up west of Sidi Bou Zid, enveloping it and sealing off the remaining Americans.

The Germans came to a halt and shifted their focus to the annihilation of the American infantry left in the surrounding hills. US commanders were equally concerned upon learning about this situation. Major General Ward hastily conjured up a plan founded on the erroneous assumption that German tank strength was around forty vehicles.

American Counterattack

At 4:00 a.m. Combat Command C received its orders from division to "move south, and by fire and maneuver, destroy the enemy armored forces which have threatened our hold on the Sbjeitla area." Doing so, Ward and his officers hoped, would allow the trapped infantry to withdraw.

Shermans, not tank destroyers, again went out to fight Axis tanks, a mission that exactly contradicts their designed purpose. A single battalion from Combat Command C—the 2nd Battalion of the 1st Armored Regiment under Lt. Col. James Alger—drew the assignment. This unit was supported by one tank-destroyer company consisting of M3 halftracks with 75-mm guns, a battalion of armored infantry, and one battalion of artillery. This may have been sufficient to combat forty light and medium tanks—but the enemy force proved to be more formidable. To cap off this developing debacle, the few maps available provided limited information of the terrain. Worse yet, no reconnaissance was conducted.

Alger organized his attack. Company D would lead the assault, followed by Company F. The assault guns and self-propelled artillery would follow, trailed by Company E. In the rear would be the armored infantry and two companies of artillery. As if to reiterate this inappropriate deployment of tanks, the 1st Armored Regiment's commander dismissed Alger with the orders, "Seek enemy armor and destroy it."

Foreshadowing things to come, fourteen Junkers Ju-87s strafed and bombed Alger's units. Damage was minimal, but the planes radioed back a warning of the approaching force. At 1:00 p.m. the first two platoons of Company D moved out. German 88s and Italian 47-mm field guns opened up on the tanks. The Shermans returned fire and managed to knock out a number of enemy guns. Soon Company F came under heavy artillery fire, which the supporting artillery battalion returned.

As the American tanks advanced, elements of the 21st Panzer Division crept around to the west, while units of the 10th Panzer Division prepared an ambush from the north. After the first Shermans passed through the open claws of the German pincer, the panzers opened up. Alger's men spotted roughly thirty tanks to the north and twenty-five to the south. Initially the Americans saw some success, knocking out a dozen of the panzers, but heavy tank and artillery fire began taking out the Shermans one by one.

One gunner recalled being hit. In his turret was "a little wheel that you could use to traverse it manually. I remember that little wheel very well, because when the tank got hit, that wheel was right in front of me and it knocked four of my front teeth out." He recalled the impact lifting "the tank about two feet off the ground." They were hit again, and "that one came through the turret. There was this goddamn humongous explosion and racket and heat. . . . It immediately caught fire."[7]

The 21st and 10th Panzer Divisions closed in behind the tanks, severing them from their infantry support. By midday the battle was over, and the entire American tank battalion was written off. The 1st Armored Division had lost 184 vehicles, including ninety-eight tanks, in a matter of forty-eight hours.

Sidi Bou Zid in Review

The US tanks and their crews suffered a humiliating defeat at Sidi Bou Zid. The 1st Armored Division had been stretched beyond its limit when tasked to cover a sixty-mile front. Subsequently, its desperately needed infantry support had to be brought in from other outfits, requiring the improvisation of two extra combat commands.

Once attacked, these ad-hoc commands responded at once with a poorly conceived counterattack. Its character echoed a mounted cavalry charge. The Shermans were sent to their doom in a textbook V formation, speeding toward an unknown enemy of unknown number. The crews were certain in their training, confident in their machines, and carried with them a feeling of superiority that had been fostered on untested grounds—a recipe for disaster. It is difficult to blame the tankers for having such trust in their methods and machines. One account from the 743rd Tank Battalion recorded the skewed reality of armored potential as it was perceived during training: during one of their training maneuvers in the States, the battalion destroyed (theoretically) thirty-six enemy tanks and eleven other enemy vehicles, suffering the loss of one tank and one vehicle. But they really were operating on guesswork. The Germans, however, were veterans. Rommel wrote that the "inexperienced Americans were steadily battered down by my tankmen—veterans of hundreds of desert battles."[8]

12

Lessons from the Desert

Get first-hand information. Get the story at the front.
Go to the enlisted man. See what he knows.

—Lt. Gen. Jacob Devers

Action in the deserts had produced significant feedback from the tankers, much of which revolved around the Sherman's armor protection.

During initial production, the turret's electric traverse system butted up very close to the turret wall on the gunner's right side. Thus the interior wall was cast considerably thinner to accommodate the gunner and his instruments. One report indicated that the "frequency of penetration by enemy shell-fire on the turret of the M4 tank indicates that the recess of indentation formed thereon for the filling of appliances has dangerously weakened the vehicle's armor in a critical area."[1] Consequently, armor plates began to appear on the exterior front of the turret to the immediate starboard side of the gun, where the gunner and the power traverse system were located.

Additional plates were also welded onto the hull in front of the driver and BOG. The armor in front of their hatches protruded out from the slope of the hull, resulting in a steep angle much more susceptible to penetration from a flat-trajectory projectile. In the field, armor plates were more or less slapped on by service units. Production in the factories was no different, and soon all M4s had crude plates welded onto the hulls.

Identification of the pistol port as another ballistic weak spot resulted in its removal from future production.

Ronsons and Tommy Cookers

The most significant feedback concerned the Sherman's tendency to "brew up" after being hit—often instantaneously. Many tankers believed that this was the result of gasoline. But upon analyzing the tanks that had burned, investigators discovered that the stored 75-mm ammunition was the culprit.

The M4 carried ninety-seven rounds for its main gun in thin sheet-metal bins located in various parts of the tank. These were placed in racks

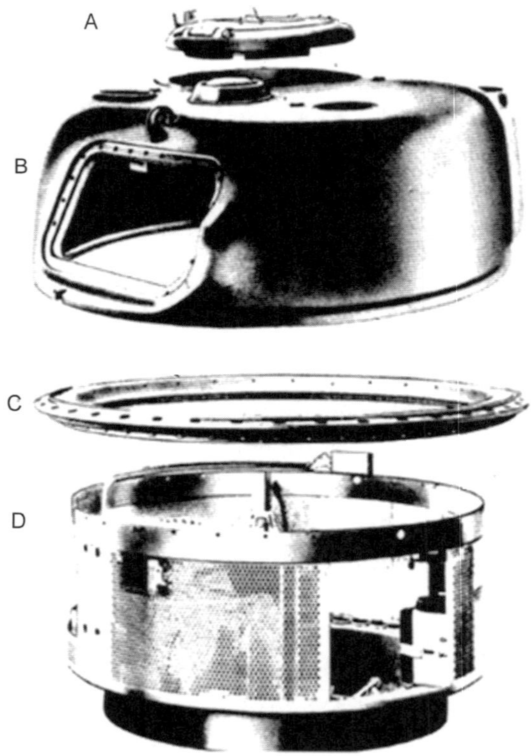

Figure 31. An exploded view of the turret assembly for the first-generation Shermans: (a) single split hatch, (b) cast turret without a pistol port, (c) race assembly ring, and (d) turret platform, or basket. Note the basket's steel-mesh walls; the crews occasionally removed these to expedite passing ammunition from the hull to the turret. *From* Technical Manual 9–1750k

in the turret, in the sponsons, on the turret floor, and also along the interior of the turret-basket wall for quick access. Some tankers had discerned that this was the true source of ignition. One remembered that a round had penetrated his vehicle "through the right sponson where a bunch of the ammunition is stored and ignited the propelling charge in this 75mm ammunition, . . . and I suppose that it [the round] probably went out the other side. Instantaneously, the tank was a ball of fire."[2]

As a result, ammunition racks mounted in the turret basket were removed from the design. This decreased the 75-mm ammunition capacity from ninety-seven to eighty-five rounds. In addition, production improved upon the ammunition bins, which were replaced with heavier quarter-inch steel compartments. Lastly, more armor plates were welded onto the sponsons where ammunition was stored, two on the starboard side and one on the port side.

Voices from the Front

In the summer of 1943, the Armored Replacement and Training Center (ARTC) published a manual documenting the experiences of tankers who had seen action in Tunisia. Lieutenant General Devers, chief of the Armored Force, had initiated the process by sending Brig. Gen. T. J. Camp to North Africa with the order: "Get first-hand information. Get the story at the front. Go to the enlisted man. See what he knows."[3]

Camp conducted his interviews in an informal fashion, asking the tankers, hypothetically, what helpful information they would share with a "younger brother just entering the Replacement Center at Fort Knox." So casual and "first hand" were these discussions that enemy activity sometimes interrupted them, the men used vocabulary such as "half-assed," and interviewees sometimes could simply point to the hills where they had just seen action. The introduction to this study concludes with words from Maj. Gen. C. L. Scott: "The men who talk to you in this book won the hard way; heart and soul they hope you will learn from them how to win easier than they did. You had better learn now to kill or be killed or else you'll learn the hard way in battle."

Although the reports are in no specific order, many share overlapping concerns. Arranging these into groups, one notices recurring themes concerning suggestions for training, an emphasis on reconnaissance, their experience with the tanks, the German use of antitank weapons, and tactics in the field.

On Training

Concerning the training conducted at the ARTC, a Colonel Haines of the 3rd Battalion, 1st Armored Regiment, Combat Command B, 1st Armored Division, offered his opinions. One suggestion was that the soldiers receive more training in first aid. Many times the tankers had to help themselves or their fellow crewmembers without the aid of medics. In most cases, especially in the desert, the tanks were not within close proximity of supporting infantry. Furthermore, when hit by enemy armor, a tank crew had to worry about exiting their vehicle under fire from the enemy tank's machine guns. Thus it was necessary for them to be able to treat themselves until either they could get away or someone could rescue them. The colonel also suggested that recruits increase their level of physical conditioning and their amount of gunnery practice. A Lieutenant Colonel Hightower of the 1st Armored Division added, "it is better to miss 500 rounds in the United States than one round here."

Some of the tankers had opinions about the methods of teaching. One lieutenant from Company D, 1st Armored Regiment, felt that the school taught too many things at one time. He understood that the concept was to "hold interest" but felt it "really accomplishes nothing." A number of the interviewees wanted to impress upon the ARTC that all crewmen should be able to drive their tank. They felt that each member should understand the others' responsibilities and be capable of doing them in the event of casualties. Again, often left in a virtual no-man's-land if their tank was hit, tankers had to be self-reliant.

On Reconnaissance

It seems that the tankers in Tunisia could not overemphasize the importance of field reconnaissance. Lieutenant Colonel Hightower called it the most important thing he could think of. Staff Sgt. W. Hagler of Company E, 1st Armored Regiment, blamed the lack of scouting for his loss of two tanks to fire from 88s and the subsequent deaths of a number of the crewmembers to heavy mortar fire. Hagler concluded that he was "confident that reconnaissance would have saved" the tanks and the men. The lack of reconnaissance sometimes led to confusion of the whereabouts of friendly units. This resulted in Shermans opening up on friendly vehicles while at other times leaving them to watch unidentified tanks advance through the desert, realizing too late that they were enemy armor. One man declared, "it all simmers down to the fact that you can't beat that personal reconnaissance."

Staff Sgt. L. Shelton of Company I, 13th Armored Regiment, reported that he often never knew the location of the front line. "I think if our boys knew where our troops were," he said, "they would be mentally set to go to work, and would at least have a half-assed idea of where to look for the enemy." One soldier put it in the simplest of terms: "We will have a much better chance if we know what we are doing."

On Tanks

Overall, the men were satisfied with their medium tanks. They recommended that traveling in a low gear should be common practice. First, keeping it slow and steady kept the tank from churning up lots of dust, therefore preventing them from disclosing their positions to the enemy. Second, shifting gears could produce jets of flame from the exhaust that could give away their position in darkness.

A few tank commanders and loaders suggested testing the fit of every round of 75-mm ammunition in the chamber before moving out. Occasionally, a casing would get stuck in the breech, and it was unpleasant for a commander to get out of his vehicle and ram the shell or casing out while under fire.

On desert terrain tankers preferred steel tracks over rubber tracks. The steel worked much better over natural surfaces, while rubber was better suited for roads.

Some tank commanders emphasized the great reliance they placed on their drivers, explaining that "you can't do nothing unless you have a good driver." Some drivers in turn lent support to this, stating that their commanders fully trusted them to get the tank where it needed to go.

Many tankers complained about the orientation of the mufflers in desert warfare. While panzers had their mufflers pointing skyward, US tank mufflers pointed downward, directly toward the desert surface. This kicked up tremendous amounts of dust and made concealment rather difficult, particularly during the day.

Several US units used the M4A2, referring to them as "swell" tanks and preferring them over the M3s, which "looked good but should be three feet lower." But one drawback to the Sherman was the placement of its driver and BOG hatches. On the A2 model the elongated doors were set parallel to the length of the tank, making them perpendicular to the crewmen's shoulders below. Exiting required twisting one's body to the left or right before actually leaving the tank; a wounded man would have a very difficult time getting out. Another problem was that if the turret was in the six-o'clock position, it blocked the hatches from opening. One tanker recalled having to return to his burning vehicle to traverse the turret so the driver could get out.

When their tank was hit, the crew had a few options. If it was hit in the tracks and immobilized, the men might remain inside and continue firing at the enemy. Other times, especially if a round came into the crew compartment, the commander would order surviving crewmembers out. Sometimes the tank would be hit and immediately catch fire, at which point the crew would always bail out. In some cases the men reported that after exiting the vehicle, it would crawl on for another four or five hundred yards before stopping. Often after abandoning a disabled vehicle the crew would have to hide in brush or ditches until nightfall, afterward walking or crawling, sometimes many miles, back to their lines. This again stressed the importance of self-reliance on first aid.

Forced to leave their burning tanks in such a hurry, crewmen might forget to grab their steel helmets and submachine guns, not to mention other belongings. First Lt. G. Dempsey of Company I, 13th Armored Regiment, hoped that "supply sections [understood] that when a tank [was] knocked out, even if the crew escapes, they invariably lost all their personal equipment."

One British general (whose name was not mentioned) provided some suggestions for tank crews. He advised moving the ammunition, at every opportunity, from the bins throughout the tank to the racks in the turret. He also strongly encouraged a tank commander to always wear a steel helmet when looking around outside the hatch, exposing his head. As for rescuing casualties, the general explained that the tank should move over the wounded man, straddling him so that he is directly under the escape hatch in the floor, so that the BOG could "reach down . . . and roll the wounded man face down, and then pull him in shoulders first."

On German Antitank Fire

Most of the tankers warned about "jumping on" lone German tanks, which were often bait to draw the Americans into an antitank trap. Lieutenant Colonel Hightower warned that German light tanks would try to entice opponents "by playing around just outside effective range." Once American tanks drove after them, "they turn tail and draw you in within range of their 88mm guns." When crews then tried to flank these positions, they were hit at nearly point blank by undetected antitank guns. The tankers asserted that the Germans were excellent at concealing their guns (usually 88s), which often were towed in behind panzers. The crews would then dig a twelve-by-twelve-foot hole six feet deep. Once the gun was in position, the tanks would leave. Even trained eyes using excellent field glasses had difficulty spotting their muzzles, resting just a foot or so above the ground. Hightower compared this chore to looking for a pencil that was pointing directly at the observer—the only sign is the minuscule black point of lead, in this case a conspicuously floating black dot that is actually the muzzle of an antitank gun.

But firing at such a low trajectory, the 88 mm shell would kick up dust as it nicked the desert floor. To further conceal its position, the Germans (as did the Italians and the Allies) commonly worked to dampen the amount of dust raised from the discharge. According to some of the men in the Tunisia, the Germans used mats to reduce the kick up of dust.

The 88s were to be respected, not feared, noted a Sergeant Lasley of the 1st Armored Regiment. He reminded tankers to stay turret-down defilade since the 88 could "knock you out at 3,000 yards." To deal with these dug-in positions, experienced Americans recommended calling in an artillery barrage. The tanks themselves could not take these positions out due to the low trajectory of their own rounds. High-trajectory howitzer fire was most effective to "root them out."

On Tactics

Finally, nearly all of the men had something to say about tactics. Lieutenant Colonel Hightower instructed ARTC students that in the desert they should not travel in column but instead in a wedge formation. Advancing on an enemy that had time to set up his defenses, Hightower recommended that infantry follow immediately behind the tanks. This way, when an antitank screen took the tanks under fire, the infantry could readily engage the enemy positions.

When engaging Mark IVs, Hightower shared his practical knowledge "that a high explosive shell will crack a [Mark IV]." With this method, the gunner "should shoot low and it will ricochet and kill them in the turret, or damage them so they will be of no use." To accomplish this successfully, it was necessary to throw the delayed-fuse shell into the ground sixty or eighty yards in front of the target. A Lieutenant McCracken of the 1st Armored Regiment explained that, as opposed to a ground burst from a high-explosive round, a ricochet shot would detonate in "a half-moon pattern [burst] and has five or six times more explosive force." Ricochet fire was intended, not to knock out a tank (though it may happen), but to unnerve its crew and cause them to button up, thus limiting their vision.

American tankers realized that lone armor charges were not a feasible method of attack. Though the wide-open terrain could afford navy-like tactics of fire and maneuver, German camouflaging of positions required the eyes of infantrymen to recognize them. The anonymous British general accordingly reported: "We must get away from the idea that tanks can work alone. Tanks can take terrain but can't hold it"—a principle already formulated during World War I.

A few of the men talked of the simplicity of avoiding the 88-mm gun mounted on the Tiger. The Germans would often use their coaxial machine gun to acquire the range of a Sherman. Once the American crew started to be pelted with machine-gun fire, they would take immediate action, turning sharply to the left or right and thus avoiding the 88-mm round that would soon follow. Many tankers discussed the range and angle with which to knock out a Tiger. Author Robert Kershaw shared a number of tankers' theories and ideas on what to do when encountering the formidable German tank. He closes with, "The best outcome was not to meet one."[4]

Many of the American crewmen advised the continuance of fire on a panzer that might appear to be knocked out since the enemy often would "play dead" after receiving a hit. They recommend firing until the tank caught fire. One tanker recalled throwing eighteen shells into a panzer after it was immobilized.

Though canister rounds were rarely used, a lieutenant from the 751st Tank Battalion suggested using machine guns and canister shot as a means of reconnaissance by fire, also known as prophylactic fire. He recommended firing on anything and everything that could have been a German position.

Mobility versus Firepower

In hindsight, one lesson not fully appreciated was the Sherman's lack of firepower. The low-velocity 75-mm gun and the woefully obsolete 37-mm had shown their worth and come up short in the face of the Mark IV's long-barreled, high-velocity 75-mm. Though the Tiger too had made an appearance, the Americans thought that encounters with this behemoth would be few and far between. Nevertheless, Lieutenant General McNair felt that greater mobility was key to defeating the enemy. Since larger tanks would be slow and less maneuverable, he sought to improve existing vehicles and guns. Army Ground Forces sought to keep light ground pressure and speed but increase firepower and armor. The Ordnance Department considered these elements "mutually irreconcilable."[5] While the two bureaus fought over theories and practicalities, Shermans continued to be the workhorse of the Armored Force. While these tanks would eventually receive a number of improvements (examined in later chapters), McNair felt that tank destroyers would be sufficient to take on German armor in the future. The war would be over before this preference for using tank destroyers and faster, lightly armed and armored tanks would be reversed.

Part 3

The 781st Tank Battalion,
Fall 1944–VE Day

13

The Mediterranean and France

All our divisions were short in infantry replacements in total numerical strength. . . . [C]ounting all types of divisions—infantry, armored, and airborne—we could, on average, deploy less than one division to each 10 miles of front.

—Gen. Dwight D. Eisenhower

Following a number of defeats in Tunisia, General Patton was called in to whip American forces there into shape. Coordinated attacks orchestrated by Patton and Montgomery, whose British Eighth Army was advancing from the south, ultimately forced the enemy back against the Mediterranean. The Axis troops in Tunisia surrendered on 13 May 1943.

Sicily and Italy

The Casablanca Conference in January had determined that the Allies would invade Sicily. The capture of that island would give them a perfect jumping-off point for an assault on Italy. While Sicily served as a bottleneck to any naval traffic in the Mediterranean while in Axis hands, for the Allies it would be an ideal base from which to launch naval and air attacks against Italy.

Operation Husky, the codename for the invasion of Sicily, was launched on 10 July 1943. The 1st, 3rd, and 45th Infantry Divisions of the Seventh Army, under Patton, landed in the southwest while the Montgomery's

Eighth Army landed in the southeast. The 2nd Armored Division and the 753rd Tank Battalion were intended to support the US infantry divisions, but on D-Day the tanks unloaded from LSTs and LCTs bogged down in the soft sand of the beaches.[1] The infantry thus had to press ahead without armor support. Consequently, when the tanks finally made their way off the beaches, they had to rush to catch up with the infantry then facing German counterattacks. In order to support the threatened units, the 2nd Armored Division's battalions were assigned to infantry regiments rather than fighting as a division. The separate light 70th Tank Battalion began coming ashore on D+3 and prepared to move up to support the 26th Infantry Regiment, 1st Division. The force set out to take Barrafranca, located near the center of Sicily, in order to thwart an anticipated German attack on the beachheads. Two companies from the 70th Tank Battalion took to the high ground on either side of a road and overlooking the area where they expected the counterattack.

On the sixteenth the Americans spotted a German column with sixteen Mark IVs coming down the road. As the enemy tanks crept into range below, the light M3s opened up with their 37-mm guns. The panzers stopped and faced the American tanks but could not elevate their guns high enough. The M3s fired from the ridges, backed out of sight, moved to a different position, and then moved up again to fire. This concealment and movement allowed them to hit the German tanks in the rear and knock them out. The M3s destroyed five Mark IVs before Allied artillery fire rained in, taking out four more. The remaining seven panzers withdrew.[2] Though the M3s had performed well, they had three uncommon advantages that gave them the upper hand in the engagement: the Americans had good intelligence, were on the defensive with good concealment, and held the high ground. All three of these elements provided them the means of firing first, a significant factor in securing victory (as discussed in chapter 18). US armor would continue to support the infantry in Sicily, but the fact that the 70th Light Tank Battalion soon had a medium company from the 753rd Tank Battalion attached to it testifies to the shortcomings of the light tank. When the battalion reached England later that year in preparation for Operation Overlord, it was reorganized as a medium-tank unit.

In September 1943 British and American forces landed in Italy, commencing Operation Avalanche. The US Fifth Army's main assault around Salerno landed on 9 September, with the British X Corps on its left and the American VI Corps on its right. Though the landing troops faced some heavy opposition at first, they soon gained ground and established a beachhead. The main objective of the operation was to secure Naples and its port as well as the airfields at Foggia, from which Allied air power could strike at central Europe.

On 22 January 1944 the Allies landed at Anzio in order to outflank the Gustav Line, the Axis defensive position that stretched across the Italian peninsula. The 756th Tank Battalion at this time was attached to the 34th Infantry Division, which had the task of crossing the Rapido River. While many battalions were split up and committed piecemeal in the rugged Italian terrain, where vehicle movements were often constrained to narrow roads, there were some opportunities for the infantry to work with large concentrations of armor. For example, elements of the 756th and 760th Tank Battalions supported the 168th Infantry Regiment's actions near the Rapido. When twenty-six Shermans "hoisted themselves onto the flat and began running wild across the mine-fields . . . and German machine gun positions," the infantry "failed to get out of their holes to follow up the advantage the sudden appearance of the tanks had created." The tankers began pouring fire from their machine guns and 75-mm cannons into

Figure 32. An M4A3 tank dozer waits in hedgerow country. These modified Shermans were first used in Italy. *Courtesy National Archives and Records Administration, Washington DC*

the enemy positions. Finally, the infantry were "shocked" into action and began filing in behind the tanks, which continued firing, pinning down the Germans, allowing the men to "swarm up the hill, taking over."[3] The infantry were learning to work with the tanks and vice versa.

Italy was a quagmire for armor maneuverability. The Apennine Mountains, stretching from the southern tip up into the Po River valley, proved treacherous for any army, mechanized or not, trying to navigate the peninsula. The fact that drivers could sometimes not avoid running over dead soldiers, German and American alike, is a gruesome testament to the fact that the tanks were often constrained to narrow roads or paths.[4]

Due to the initial lack of forward momentum in the campaign, many tank battalions, including those of the 1st Armored Division, were committed to indirect-fire missions, augmenting infantry division artillery units. Light tank battalions received the new M8 motor carriages, while medium units received Shermans equipped with 105-mm guns.[5] In addition, Americans began using their new tank dozers, which General Eisenhower called a "godsend." Prior to these, the Americans relied on regular tractors and bulldozers, even on the front lines. On steep mountainsides these tractors were sometimes right up with the fighting units, where their operators were easy and vulnerable targets.[6]

American Armored Division, 1943

In September 1943 the army reorganized the armored divisions to reduce it to a more manageable size. The three regiments of armor were replaced with more evenly balanced tank and infantry battalions. The new formation was built around three battalions of tanks, three battalions of armored infantry, and three battalions of armored artillery. As a result of these changes, the number of tanks within the division dropped from 390 to 245 (168 medium and 77 light). The 1943 organizational model retained the medical, maintenance, reconnaissance, and engineer battalions along with the signal company. The only other major change was adding a third combat command, designated for reserves.

Separate tank battalions were also reorganized. These units had been composed entirely of either light or medium tanks. But based on the combat experience in North Africa, most of the light tank battalions were reorganized as medium battalions. Each separate battalion now consisted of three medium companies and one light company.

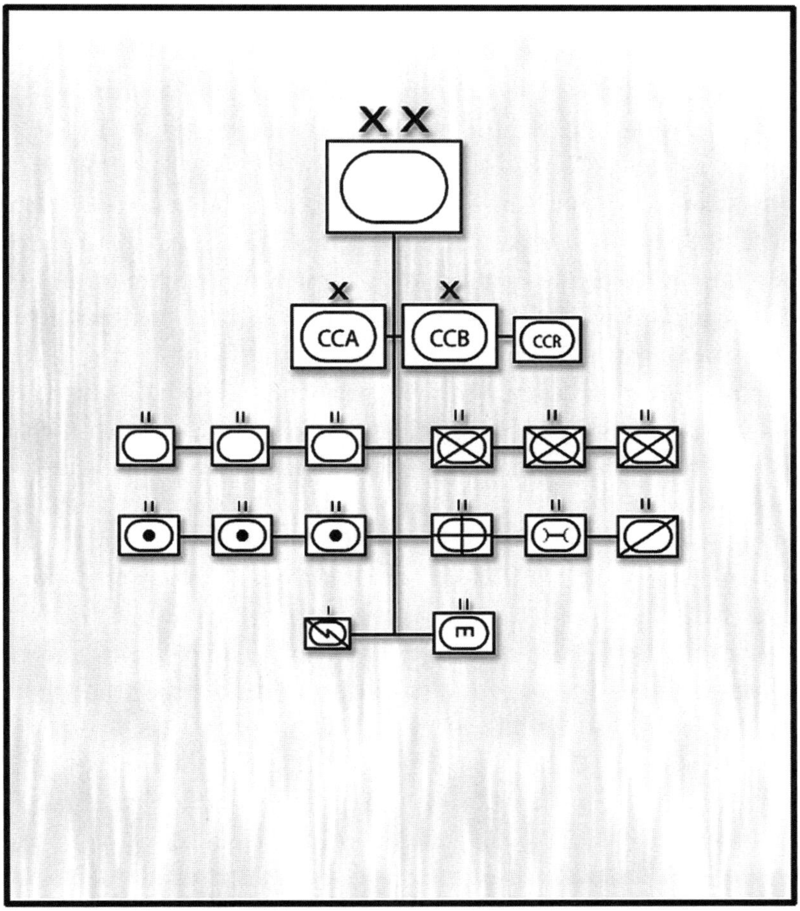

Figure 33. Organization of a US armored division, 1943.

France

On 6 June 1944 the thunder of war again erupted in France. Allied troops and armor poured out of LCVPs, C-47s, and gliders, seizing bridges, eliminating gun batteries, and clinging on to vulnerable beachheads. Under the overall command of General Eisenhower, with General Montgomery in operational command, the massive invasion force prepared to move inland.

Lt. Gen. Omar Bradley and the American First Army began to drive south and west. V Corps had managed to penetrate nearly twenty miles directly south from the beaches, while VII Corps in the west was checked by a number of German divisions rushing north. The latter finally moved into the Cotentin Peninsula, cutting it off by 19 June.

The British Second Army, under the command of Lt. Gen. Sir Miles Dempsey, was beating its head against the defenses of Caen, where the Germans had pulled in seven panzer divisions. It was not until late July that the American and British armies took Saint-Lô and Caen, respectively. Once Saint-Lô was secure, the 1st Infantry Division and four US armored divisions drove farther into the interior. The American forces pivoted southeast, while the British, who were caught up in heavy fighting around Caen, acted as the hinge of the assault east toward Paris.

During Operation Cobra, Maj. Gen. J. Lawton Collins's VII corps broke out of Normandy west of Saint-Lô. The attack route had been prepared by a massive aerial bombardment, which had devastated an area of six square miles.[7] On 25 July three divisions, the 3rd, 9th, and 40th, with their respective supporting tank battalions, the 743rd, 746th, and the 70th, spearheaded the assault. Initial progress was slow due to some surprisingly stiff resistance and the rough terrain resulting from the bombardment. But believing the Germans were desperate for reinforcements and fearing their potential to regroup and establish another defensive line, Collins made the decision to send in his armor. The next day the 2nd and 3rd Armored Divisions, under Maj. Gen. Edward H. Brooks and Maj. Gen. Leroy Watson, drove toward Marigny, Saint-Gilles, and Canisy. Units from the 2nd Armored Division had penetrated fourteen miles by the end of 27 July.

General Patton, who had been in "command" of the fictitious First Army Group leading up to the invasion, now entered the campaign with his growing Third Army. His 4th and 6th Armored Divisions were committed west of Collins's forces, springing into the interior with the mission of sealing off the Brittany Peninsula. Two combat commands from Maj. Gen. John S. Wood's 4th Armored Division pushed the Germans south of Coutances on the twenty-eighth. In only a week the 6th Armored Division raced to the city of Brest, while the 4th Armored Division took Vannes and then Nantes a week later. Meanwhile, Brig. Gen. Maurice Rose, commanding two combat commands of the 2nd Armored Division, cut southwest, sealing off the escape routes of the German LXXXIV Corps, trapping three infantry divisions and two panzer divisions.

After the liberation of Brittany, the Allies began a rapid campaign that lasted a mere twelve days, again covering more than a hundred miles in a week, bringing the American Army to Paris. Yet while the rest of the army received flowers and wine from the Parisians, the 4th Armored Division continued its advance as far as Troyes, nearly a hundred miles farther to the southeast. By 25 August northwestern France, including all its vital ports (with the exception of Le Havre), was in the Allied hands.

Operation Dragoon

By the end of August, the Allies had pushed their advance to the Seine River. Some intelligence officers looked toward the next few months with optimism, foreseeing the end of the war by the beginning of 1945, convinced that the Germans would fold under the weight of Allied forces pressing against them. Others were more conservative, anticipating a hard road ahead and believing that the enemy would fight even harder as the Allies closed in on Germany. Indeed, the Germans were far from capitulation. In the final months of 1944, the Allies would fail to take Arnhem and would suffer tens of thousands of casualties in the Huertgen Forest. In the south of France, the US Seventh Army would soon be engaged with a determined enemy in the woods and villages of the Vosges Mountains.

The invasion of southern France, codenamed Operation Dragoon (originally Anvil), was a subject of contention between the United States and Britain from both political and strategic standpoints.[8] Churchill and his chiefs of staff were concerned about the state of affairs in the postwar Balkan states if the Russians decided to move into that region and therefore felt that pushing through Italy would be the best means to guard against such undesirable ends. The Americans, including President Roosevelt, viewed an enhanced Italian campaign as a long operation with questionable aims. At a minimum they felt that it would consume time and material that instead could be used directly against the Germans in southern France, with the strategic aim of forcing the Germans to pull divisions from the north. This more direct assault in support of Overlord would aim straight at Germany and more quickly end the war, which was first and foremost in US global strategy.[9]

As far as immediate strategic aims, the Americans felt that securing the large Mediterranean port of Marseille would help alleviate the growing logistical strains being faced by the advancing armies in France, constantly stretching their supply lines. While the port at Antwerp had been captured on 4 September, the Allies had yet to secure the Schelde Estuary, thus leaving the Belgian port unusable. Capt. Harry Butcher, Eisenhower's naval aide, recorded that the general insisted to Churchill that "he needed an additional big port into which to pour American divisions now awaiting action at home. By getting another port, such as Marseille, he told the [prime minister], our forces could be augmented by perhaps twelve divisions." In the end, the Americans and Operation Dragoon prevailed, with a French and American task force scheduled to commence landing operations on 15 August. Eisenhower wanted to drive toward the Ruhr and the Saar Valley. Responsible for opening this campaign was the US Seventh Army, under the command of Lt. Gen. Alexander Patch.

Following an aerial and naval bombardment, the invasion force headed toward the beaches. The assault was carried out by Maj. Gen. Lucian Truscott's VI Corps, which consisted of the 3rd, 36th, and 45th Infantry Divisions, supported by the French 1st Armored Division. These divisions and supporting raids landed on a front stretching from Cavalaire-sur-Mer in the west to Saint-Raphaël in the east. The landing was a major success against only light resistance. Within weeks, four more French divisions had joined the fight. The Seventh Army moved with lightning speed, taking Lyon, Toulon, and the all-important port at Marseilles. On 11 September elements of the Seventh Army linked up with those of Patton's Third. Soon after, French Army B and the Seventh Army were organized into the Sixth Army Group, under the command of Lieutenant General Devers.

Even with an additional army group now on the continent, victory was not a foregone conclusion. At the beginning of August, the Allies had thirty-five divisions in the field, with six more in England. By the end of September, with the addition of the Sixth Army Group, they had fifty-four divisions. While Allied strength had seen a spike, the Germans still had more men and material to hold, and even push back, the Allies. "All our divisions were short in infantry replacements," Eisenhower recalled, "in total numerical strength of ground forces the Germans still had a marked advantage. We were disposed along a line which, beginning in the north on the banks of the Rhine, stretched 500 miles southward to the border of Switzerland. . . . [T]his meant that, counting all types of divisions—infantry, armored, and airborne—we could, on average, deploy less than one division to each 10 miles of front." The strategy, therefore, was to continue an "unremitting offensive" across a broad front to constantly strike the enemy where intelligence projected the Allies to have superiority.[10] By the end of October and early November, the situation across the entire front had deteriorated due to increased German resistance, bad weather, and the strain on supplies. Eisenhower met with Montgomery (Twenty-First Army Group), Bradley (Twelfth Army Group), and Devers (Sixth Army Group) to revive the offensive in France. The result was a directive, dated 28 October, which ordered Montgomery to secure the approaches to Antwerp and to clear the area west of the Rhine. Similarly, Bradley would push toward the Rhine and attempt to secure beachheads south of Cologne. Devers would secure Bradley's southern flank, push to the Rhine, and secure crossings near Karlsruhe and Mannheim. Actual assaults across the Rhine would have to wait for better weather, a drastic improvement in supply, and fresh units.

Some of these needed reinforcements had just arrived via Marseilles. The untried 14th Armored Division and 100th and 103rd Infantry Divisions were moving north to join the fight with the Seventh Army. Attached to the 100th Infantry Division, and also having just arrived in Europe, was the 781st Tank Battalion, a new and untested separate tank battalion.

14

The Separate Tank Battalion

> It is particularly important that the [separate tank battalions] be available in quantities to permit all infantry divisions to work with them freely and frequently.
>
> **—Lt. Gen. Leslie McNair**

Following the fall of France and Poland, largely to German panzer commands, the United States went to work building its version of panzer divisions while scuttling the prototype armor corps. Responding to infantry demands for organic armor units attached to its divisions, the army formed what were called general-headquarters battalions, organized into tank groups. The tactical premise was that these groups would deploy their battalions en masse under the control of a single commanding headquarters on an "as-needed" basis by infantry and armor divisions.

Yet actual combat in North Africa had demonstrated that the infantry constantly needed tanks, which themselves constantly needed infantry. Furthermore, the army recognized that the armor division, under its current organization with two regiments of tanks, was quite unwieldy. Thus, as Lieutenant General McNair wrote in the aftermath: "It is believed that our 1943 troop basis has entirely too many armored divisions, considering their proper tactical employment, and too few general-headquarters tank battalions. It is particularly important that the latter be available in quantities to permit all infantry divisions to work with them freely and frequently."[1] Consequently, armored divisions reduced their strength from two armored regiments to one. This resulted in a surplus of unassigned tank battalions.

The reorganization of armored divisions combined with the infantry's growing demand for tanks resulted in the formation of the new separate tank battalion, of which there would be sixty-five by war's end. These units had to be self-sufficient and thus were equipped with their own headquarters, maintenance, and supply organizations. These units would be assigned to infantry commands, where their medium and light tanks could provide the extra firepower needed to break through stubborn resistance when encountered.

Organization and Equipment

Six companies composed each separate tank battalion: battalion headquarters and headquarters company, three medium tank companies, the light tank company, and the service company. The battalion headquarters section had four ½-ton trucks, three M3 halftracks, and two Shermans. The headquarters company had four organic units: a reconnaissance platoon, a mortar platoon, an assault-gun platoon, and company headquarters, which included a headquarters section; an administrative, mess, and supply (AM&S) section; and a maintenance section. In all, the headquarters company had a total of three halftracks, a jeep, one ½-ton truck, one 2½-ton truck and trailer, and two Shermans for the battalion commander and the battalion's executive officer.

The reconnaissance platoon had five ¼-ton trucks (jeeps) and one M3 halftrack, while the mortar platoon had four halftracks, three of which were M21 mortar carriers. Lastly, the assault-gun platoon consisted of two M3 halftracks and three M4s equipped with 105-mm guns. In theory the tanks were to tow ammunition trailers that could carry an additional fifty-four rounds. But the trailers were more often a burden on maneuver and a potential risk if struck by enemy fire. Consequently, they were seldom used.

Three medium tank companies formed the nucleus of the battalion. Each had a company headquarters equipped with two Sherman tanks, one M4 (105-mm), and one jeep. Headquarters also had a maintenance section consisting of one jeep, one M3 halftrack, and one M32 Armored Recovery Vehicle (ARV). Each company had an AM&S section with one

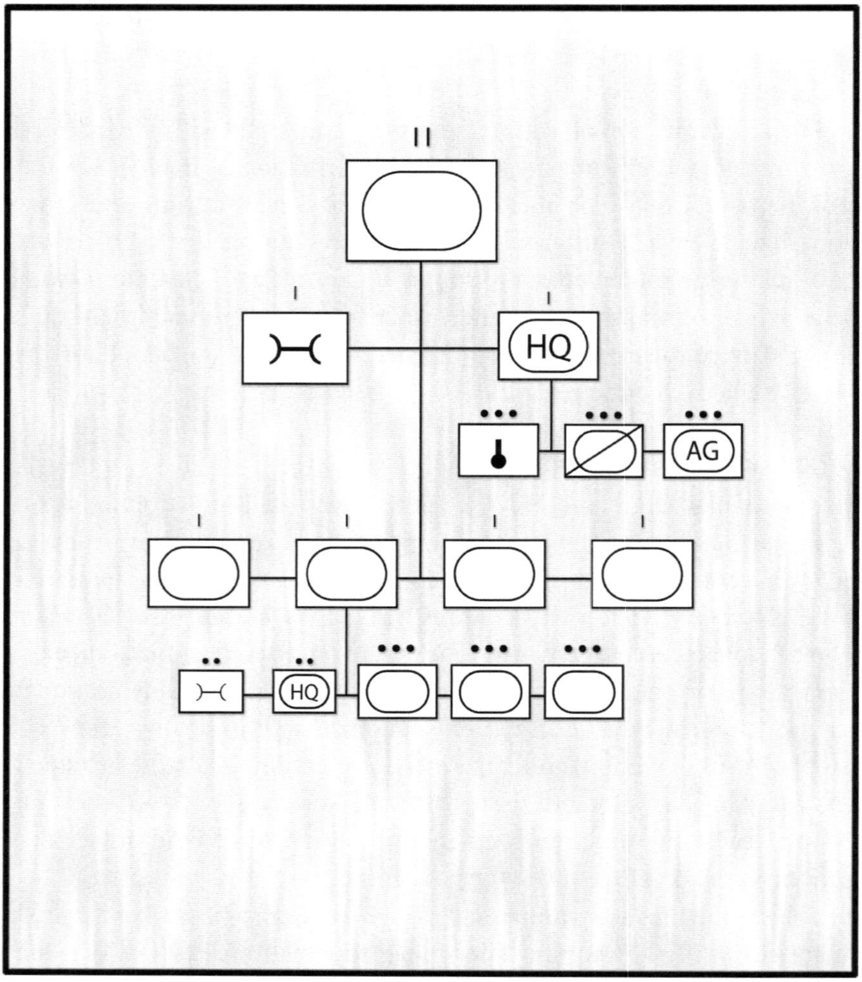

Figure 34. Organization of a US separate tank battalion, 1943.

2½-ton truck and trailer. Lastly, there were three medium tank platoons. Each was made up of five Shermans, one for the platoon leader as his headquarters and two each in two sections.

Shermans equipped with the 105-mm howitzer were virtually the same as other M4s other than their armament. The battalion had a total of six tanks with 105s; three in the assault-gun platoon and one for each of the three medium companies. The gun could be elevated to 35 degrees and could fire indirectly on targets at 12,000 yards, though crews found their fire to be less then accurate beyond 1,000 yards. Each tank had storage for

Figure 35. A crew chief (sergeant) instructs two students on how to remove the tracks from a medium tank in less than thirty minutes. *Courtesy Davis Memorial Library, Patton Museum, Fort Knox*

Figure 36. A staff sergeant trains this crew on how to "pull" the Wright Radial engine in fifty minutes, utilizing an improvised A-frame. *Courtesy Davis Memorial Library, Patton Museum, Fort Knox*

Table 2. Separate tank battalion table of organization and equipment, 18 November 1944

	HQ & HQ Co.	Med. Co. (x3)	Light Co.	Service Co.	Medical Det.	Total
Officers	13	5	5	4	2	39
Enlisted Men	127	112	89	108	18	678
.45-cal. Pistol	3	0	0	0	0	3
.45-cal. SMG	47	92	70	44	0	437
.30-cal. Carbine	70	25	24	71	0	240
.30-cal. M1 Rifle	20	0	0	0	0	20
.50-cal. M2 HMG	5	1	2	10	0	20
2.36-inch Bazooka	12	3	2	12	0	35
M5A1 Light Tank	0	0	17	0	0	17
M4 Medium Tank	2	17	0	0	0	53
M4 (105-mm) Tank	3	1	0	0	0	6
M21 81-mm	3	0	0	0	0	3
Halftrack	8	1	1	1	0	13
M32 TRV	0	1	0	2	0	5
Light TRV	0	0	1	0	0	1
¼-ton Jeep	11	2	2	3	4	26
¾-ton Ambulance	0	0	0	0	1	1
¾-ton WC Truck	0	0	0	2	1	3
2½-ton Truck	1	1	1	34	0	39
Heavy Wrecking Truck	0	0	0	2	0	2
M10 Ammo Trailer	4	0	0	13	0	17
¼-ton Trailer	11	2	2	3	4	26
1-ton Trailer	2	1	1	20	0	26

sixty-six rounds. These six 105s could, and often were, used as an armored artillery battalion to support the infantry's artillery units.[2]

The light tank company was identical to its medium counterparts except that it consisted of light tanks rather than mediums and its headquarters section only had two tanks.

Both the medium and light companies were to be self-sufficient as they would routinely be operating away from the battalion. Therefore they each had their own maintenance and administrative sections.

The battalion's largest unit was the service company. The battalion maintenance section was equipped with a few trucks and two M32 ARVs with heavy wreckers. The M32 was essentially a Sherman minus its 75-mm gun and equipped with an A-frame crane, or boom. Their role was to recover disabled vehicles and tow them to a maintenance collection point, where the overall damage would be assessed. Often the maintenance section could repair a tank and have it returned to action within a short period of time. The service company also had a battalion administration and personnel section, a maintenance section, an AM&S section, and a headquarters section. These all consisted of jeeps, light tanks, trucks, and trailers. The battalion supply and transportation platoon, however, consisted of a ¾-ton truck, one jeep, fifteen trailers, thirteen ammunition carriers, and twenty-nine 2½-ton trucks.

The Battalion's Role

By doctrine, the separate tank battalion operated by surprise, fire and maneuver, and concentration of effort. Relying on speed and concealment, it could obtain surprise by striking the enemy at an unexpected time and from an unexpected direction. More specifically, the battalion's role was "to assist the infantry, cavalry, or motorized division to advance by destroying hostile machine guns, personnel, and vital installations."[3] Notably absent from this list is destroying enemy tanks.

Following the arguments of Lieutenant Colonel Swinton and Colonel Fuller from the First World War, American tanks were to deploy in concentrated mass. The tank battalion manual dictated that officers not "disperse the command by making simultaneous attacks on widely dispersed objectives. Such action is ineffective, wastes effort, and usually leads to failure." The tank platoon manual further emphasizes attacking with mass, stating that the platoon should hit targets "with all power that can be mustered. If effort is made on several positions, the enemy may easily destroy you by concentrating successively on each attacking element."[4] While this method would be useful in the open and even in multipronged attacks in the French hedgerows, the terrain of the Vosges Mountains constrained many of the routes available to the tanks, sometimes limiting them to single-lane roads straddled by thick woods or rivers, thus not permitting large concentrations of direct fire.

As noted earlier, the battalion consisted of both light and medium tanks. Utilizing their speed, light tanks were used to seek out weak spots in the enemy's defense, to screen an advance, to attack an enemy's flank or rear, to exploit breakthroughs, or to draw the enemy into prepared traps. The role of the medium tanks was to lead attacks against "known" resistance and provide direct fire support for the infantry or light tanks.

One major blunder concerning tank-battalion operations would reveal itself on the battlefield. While the role of the battalions was to support the foot soldiers, they received no integrated training with either infantry, artillery, or air support. Neither manuals nor training maneuvers had stressed how armor was to work with adjacent units. Furthermore, army leaders had failed to develop any tactics for taking an enemy-occupied town.

Control and Movement

In theory the battalion commander had direct communication with all of his company commanders. He would also coordinate—again, in theory—with infantry commanders. Tactical control of the battalion was carried out primarily by radio but also included the use of messengers and signals. Orders directed keeping radio communication at a minimum in the field and prohibited its use while in bivouac.

Fire control was primarily the responsibility of company commanders, who were free to direct their unit's fire. If a company was in reserve, its role then was to support the leading companies, protect unit flanks, or to cover particular areas of possible threat.

Infantry was essential in reducing enemy antitank threats. While the tank-battalion commander could order tactical support, he did not have the authority to control infantrymen.

During a march, officers would give orders verbally, brief each vehicle on operations, and provide each crew a map of the route. This included furnishing plans concerning the formation, route, phase lines, security, reconnaissance, and supply. The armored battalion manual stated: "A well-trained battalion should be able to move out within ½ hour after receipt of warning orders."[5]

When the battalion was on the move, or "marching" to a new location, regulations advised that the column not exceed seventeen mph for long durations, otherwise such extended fast travel would "cause an exorbitant increase in maintenance needs."[6] Vehicles should maintain separation of at least fifty yards but ideally approximately ninety yards. Circumstance, of course, would determine how closely these regulations were followed, if considered at all.

A staff officer often monitored the column. Riding in a jeep, he would wait at a phase line and watch the vehicles pass by, checking their position and condition. At the halt the officer could then travel to the front of the column and report to the battalion commander on the condition of the unit. During long marches, the column would halt every four hours to refuel, a process lasting from thirty to forty-five minutes. At these breaks the driver and BOG were advised to trade places to reduce fatigue.

When tanks were at a halt, each platoon had a number of responsibilities depending on the duration of the stop and the situation at hand. If under strict observation or in a hazardous area, the crews were to move their tanks off the road, spread out, direct guns to all-around security, keep one man at the ready at the gun, make one man responsible for the platoon leader's radio, arm one or two men with submachine guns to provide flank security, designate others to watch the sky for enemy aircraft, and have one man in a position to see signals from company commanders. If the halt was in a hostile area and lasted for a longer duration, the crews might be ordered to dig slit trenches for their security during air attacks; this became less necessary as the Allies began to dominate the skies.

When the battalion was in bivouac, companies would move into assigned areas and be further divided into platoon sections. Within the platoon, tanks would usually "coil," or form a circular perimeter with guns facing outward in case of any enemy attack. Vehicles also would park in positions that would permit them to move out without having to back up. The crewmen would rest near or under their tank while they rotated security duties.

Often, armor units would form an outpost, "a security detachment to protect a resting command or a defensive position against annoyance, surprise, and observation by [enemy] forces."[7] At other times the platoons would provide a flank guard. While both light and medium tanks would be used for this duty, the light tanks were ideal due to their increased speed and greater mobility.

Problems

In reality, a separate tank battalion's companies rarely worked together. One company might be providing flank security for an infantry battalion, while another, fifteen miles away, supported an artillery battery. Therefore, battalion commanders seldom knew what each of his companies was doing at any given time. This was not negligence but rather a result of flawed organization. Circumstance demanded adaptation. Infantry divisions rarely had a single objective, being elastic organisms that adjusted tactics according to the various strategic aims, which themselves were continually changing. Consequently, the tank-battalion headquarters had little tactical control and often remained limited to administrative and advisory tasks.[8]

Offensive Movement

The tanks could be used to facilitate attacks. They were to "attack through weak spots in an enemy position, break through, and destroy rear installations." Armor could also attack by envelopment, moving "rapidly around the enemy flanks and attack from flank or rear." In case of tank-versus-tank engagements, the crews were to rely on speed, defilade positions and cover, and ambush. The armored battalion manual stated: "When attacked by an enemy whose armament is superior to your own, withdraw and lead him into your own anti-tank defenses. If there are no anti-tank defenses backing you up, place smoke on enemy and maneuver rapidly to approach within effective range."[9] Yet when attacking an enemy mounting *inferior* armament, the tanks were to move rapidly to positions beyond the effective range of the enemy's weapons, take up stationary positions, and fire. If the enemy advanced, the tanks were to keep beyond range of their guns while still keeping them within effective range of their own guns. In either case, US tanks were to rely on their maneuverability first, then armament, when engaged against enemy armor.

Defensive Positions

When in defensive positions, infantry typically would hold the main line while the tanks were held in reserve, thus being able to concentrate their fire fully on the point of enemy contact. During a withdrawal, armor could be used very effectively by making rapid thrusts into pursuing formations and disrupting their organization, thus permitting infantry and other units the opportunity to withdraw.

But as we will see, the tanks were rarely used as instructed by the field manuals.

15

Battalion Operations, October–December 1944

> Operations demonstrated that if infantry closely watches over tanks, and tanks deliver accurate fire in large quantities, operations can be carried out against [a] town with a minimum of tank and infantry losses.
>
> **—"781st Tank Battalion Unit History"**

The 781st Tank Battalion was activated at Fort Knox on 2 January 1943. Initially, it was a light tank battalion under the command of Lt. Col. Harry L. Kinne Jr. Many of the enlisted men had experience, previously serving within the ranks of the 742nd and 191st Tank Battalions, while the majority of the officers had just completed officer-candidate school. But mostly the men who formed the 781st reported directly from the Armored Replacement Training Center.

From its activation until its eventual deployment, the battalion spent most of its time carrying out work for the Armored Force Board. Its most important role was prototype testing that eventually resulted in the M4A3 tank.

The 781st was responsible for the "Million Dollar Tank Test." Armored units complained about the performance of the radial R-975 engines in the field. The cylinders in these aircraft engines had extra "cold clearance" between the pistons and the cylinder walls to allow for expansion in the metals as the temperature increased. Operating at constant high speed in an aircraft, this was a sound design. Tanks, however, are often idling, stopping and going, or cruising at low speeds, far from the operational stresses for which the R-975 was designed. Thus, there remained a gap between the pistons and cylinder walls as the metals stayed below expansion temperatures. Over time this gap allowed excessive oil to pass through into the combustion chamber, fouling the spark plugs and causing the engine to fail.[1] New engines designed for tanks were needed.

The 781st Tank Battalion took forty Shermans and carried out various field tests utilizing and assessing three potential replacement engines and the current R-975: ten tanks were equipped with a new Ford liquid-cooled V-8 model GAA; ten were equipped with the Twin GMC liquid-cooled model 6–71 diesel engine; ten used the R-975; and ten used the complex thirty-cylinder Chrysler multibank liquid-cooled engine. The tankers determined that the 1,100-cubic-inch Ford V-8 GAA was the best engine for the Sherman. Ford had taken the Rolls Royce twelve-cylinder Merlin engine and modified it to eight cylinders. The result was a 550-horsepower engine that was about 25 percent more powerful than the R-975. Shermans that received this engine were officially M4A3s.

The 781st's relationship with the Armored Force Board was interrupted when it was reorganized as a medium tank battalion and in November 1943 set off for Camp Shelby, Mississippi. There the battalion switched from its role as a test unit to a combat unit. The men began work on field problems by exercising at platoon, company, and battalion strength. Prior to an exercise, the battalion commander would assemble all company commanders for a briefing of the situation followed by verbal orders. These officers would return to their platoon leaders and give their orders. Exercises could include everything from moving across terrain while maintaining defilade concealment to carrying out attacks on enemy installations. After each maneuver came a debriefing, during which commanders could critique and reflect on every decision, good and bad, that had been made in the field.

On 7 October 1944 the olive drab–clad men of the 781st Tank Battalion shuffled into their new quarters. Covering nearly 2,000 acres and engulfing Orangetown, New York, Camp Shanks was home to roughly 50,000 American troops on their way to war and the last bit of American soil they would call home for some time (that is, unless they made it thirty miles south into the hustle and bustle of New York City before departure).

Shortly after the 781st arrived, the men received passes. But just as they made ready for their first trip to the Big Apple, they were put on alert; the Stage Door Canteen would have to wait. Instead, the battalion boarded a troop train that took them parallel to the Hudson River into Weehawk, New Jersey. There, the troops ferried over to the 42nd Street Docks in the Port of Manhattan.

Men gazed at all the vessels resting in the harbor, wondering which one would take them to war. For the 781st Tank Battalion, it would be the USS *La Jeunne*. Built by the Germans in 1936 as a luxury liner, the ship eventually went into military service as a supply ship. It had escaped the British fleet in 1939 and made its way to Brazil, where it was interned. The United States purchased the liner in 1943 and went to work converting it into a troopship. Commissioned into service on 12 May 1944, the vessel was designated AP-74.

On 13 October, with "hold numbers chalked on their helmets, and their stomachs filled with Red Cross doughnuts," the men of the 781st paced up the gangplank into the belly of AP-74.[2] The next day USS *La Jeunne* pulled out of port and cruised past the Statue of Liberty. New York faded behind them, and they were soon surrounded by the vast horizons of the Atlantic Ocean.

The troopship passed through the Strait of Gibraltar and into the Mediterranean Sea. Bearing north along longitude 5° east, the *La Jeunne* and the men of the 781st approached their final destination—Marseille, France. After two weeks at sea, the Americans disembarked into the European theater of operations on 27 October 1944.

Upon landing in Marseille, the battalion marched, by foot, eight miles to their first overseas bivouac. The men set up camp on a muddy piece of real state, which they dubbed Goat Hill. There they would wait until all of their supplies and equipment were unloaded. But a major logistics error had occurred. The tanks were late, and worse, the army and navy scratched their heads at the whereabouts of 1,000 crates of cargo belonging to the 781st Tank Battalion. The battalion had arrived in France naked and was without tanks and supplies for nearly a month. Meanwhile, perhaps supply officers in Normandy scrambled through paperwork trying to make sense of the mysterious arrival of 1,000 containers of cargo belonging to the 781st Tank Battalion.

While the battalion waited for its supplies that would never come, the battalion-operations officer (S-3) and the platoon leaders were sent 350 miles to the front in order to observe the 753rd and 756th Tank Battalions, part of the 1st Armored Group, VI Corps, then operating in the vicinity of Epinal.[3] It was important for tank units arriving in Europe to learn from the veterans. Three separate tank battalions, the 191st, 753rd, and 756th, had landed with the Seventh Army on 15 August as part of Operation Dragoon. The Germans had launched two counterattacks beginning a week later. Elements of the 753rd Tank Battalion had engaged panzers on 27 August. Harry Yeide described one of these encounters. The Shermans opened fire on the Germans from a range of eight hundred yards, but their armor-piercing rounds failed to knock any out. A tank destroyer moved in to augment the fire, quickly destroying one of the enemy panzers, but then itself fell victim to incoming fire. Later that same day the Germans moved in again with what were either Mark Vs or VIs. The American tanks disabled one of the panzers by wrecking its track. Two Shermans kept a distance of six hundred yards and fired no less than fourteen rounds into the remaining tank until they saw it begin to burn.[4] It was actions like this that were passed on to the new battalions coming in through southern France. While these lessons had been learned in Normandy months earlier, the Seventh Army, operating hundreds of miles away, had to learn them through their own experience.

After observing the 1st Armored Group, the battalion S-3 made three alterations to the 781st. The headquarters and service companies were formed into forward and rear command posts. The assault and mortar platoons were formed into a single reinforced assault-gun platoon to provide direct and indirect fire support. Lastly, the transportation platoon was dispersed throughout the line companies to facilitate mobility within the units, which would unlikely be operating in tandem.

Once the 781st Tank Battalion was reequipped and up to its authorized strength, it moved out by army trucks and French railcars destined for the Vosges Mountains in the Lorraine region. Lorraine was a very important strategic area bordering Belgium, Luxembourg, and most importantly, Germany. The region is forested and dissected by river valleys and rolling mountains, severely limiting mobility—challenging country for armor operations.

Padoux

The 781st traveled 350 miles to Padoux, France, a small town nine miles northeast of Epinal. The men took over various barns and buildings nearby for sleep. The civilians in the area were welcoming. On 5 December the battalion was attached to XV Corps and further assigned to the 100th Infantry Division. That unit, dubbed the Century Division, had entered combat only a month prior on 1 November. It had moved into the Meurthe-et-Moselle region to relieve the 45th Infantry Division.

American infantry divisions in Europe had roughly 15,000 men typically in three infantry regiments and four artillery battalions. These units were supported by signal, ordnance, and quartermaster companies in addition to reconnaissance, engineer, and medical units. The 100th Infantry Division was made up of the 397th, 398th, and 399th Infantry Regiments. Approximately 3,200 men made up an infantry regiment. Each regiment had three battalions; thus the 397th had battalions one through three, the 398th had battalions four through six, and the 399th had battalions seven through nine. While infantry battalions were further broken down into companies and platoons, a separate tank battalion typically attached its armored companies to infantry regiments. In other words, eighteen Shermans would support one infantry regiment.[5]

In the case of the 781st and the 100th Infantry Division, Company A was attached to the 399th Infantry, Company B to the 398th Infantry, and Company C to the 397th Infantry. The three platoons of Company D (the light tanks) were dispersed one to each regiment. This tank company/infantry regiment relationship became necessary as troops were constantly in need of armor support. This linkage was common due to the fact that infantry regiments, though organic units of a division, did not necessarily operate in conjunction with other divisional units. Often they formed semipermanent relationships with various supporting units of the division, such as artillery, engineer, or armor, forming composite units called "regimental combat teams."

Lemberg

On 5 December the units continued forty-five miles northeast to Hangwiller and then to Zittersheim on the sixth. Simultaneously, elements of the 100th Division attacked north from Wingen toward Lemberg. Through the rain the Americans successfully took Sarreinsberg and Goetzenbruch without firing a shot. The 781st's reconnaissance platoon moved on with its jeeps and M3 halftrack toward Lemberg. The men discovered that the bridge leading into town had been demolished. Surveying the area, they spotted German entrenchments parallel to the road entering town. The platoon opened fire on the entrenchments, which remained silent. Within a few short moments, though, enemy mortar rounds began dropping on their position. Most of the men dropped and flattened themselves against the frozen ground, while some scrambled for cover near their vehicles. Lemberg would have to be taken by force.

Companies L, K, and I of 3rd Battalion, 399th Infantry Regiment (3/399), began their attack on the town directly from the south. As their companies moved in, the Germans opened up with heavy artillery that pounded the area. The infantry came to a halt. The Germans had a battalion of 105s to the southwest of Lemberg. To the north were 75-mm and 88-mm guns, while to the east, on a hill commanding the town, were entrenchments and fortifications with troops from the 953rd Volksgrenadier Regiment.[6]

The 781st was called into action. Lt. William J. Kaiser and his 1st Platoon, Company A, was ordered to the front. His five tanks were connected to 1/399 and ordered to attack on the seventh. Together the tanks and infantry advanced on the western flank of Lemberg. The troops moved in supported by heavy machine-gun fire provided by the 1st Platoon. The tanks also fired high-explosive rounds at targets identified by the infantry. Between these requested shots, the tanks continuously raked the German positions with bursts of machine-gun fire. This allowed the infantry to move up. During their assault, the infantry came under indirect artillery and mortar fire. But the Shermans could do nothing to counter the German artillery, and thus the infantry became pinned down. The attack stalled.

The next day the Americans continued the attack. The 399th's Companies B and C arrived and began to advance along with the tanks under a smokescreen. Immediately two Shermans fell victim to antitank mines. No crewmembers were wounded, but both tanks had thrown a track and were out of action. The assault continued with the remaining armor and infantry.

Finally, with the aid of smoke and close infantry support, the tanks crawled up the road, with Companies A and C on their flanks. As they approached the houses and assorted buildings on the edge of town, the tanks opened up. BOGs eyed every cellar and window, spraying them with machine-gun fire. Gunners also kept a close eye, firing the coaxial machine gun and 75-mm cannon. Commanders gave orders and coordinated their fire as infantrymen signaled potential threats. As the tankers closed their distance, they continued firing, often point-blank, into the buildings.

One way to deal with a stubborn enemy, fighting from a row of houses, was to use a combination of armor-piercing and high-explosive rounds. One tanker recalled: "We would fire one round of 76mm solid shot into the first house on each side of the road. . . . The shot usually penetrated two or more houses; it might go through a picture on one wall, perhaps a desk on another, then on to the next house where it would go through a chair on the first wall and a sofa on the other side. . . . We followed the shot with an HE [high-explosive] round into the same hole. That would really clean house and also rearrange a good sized room."[7]

The fighting continued all night, with the tanks firing into cellars and the infantry lobbing grenades. It was not until 9 December that Lemberg was secured. For his actions against the enemy, Lieutenant Kaiser was awarded the Silver Star.

That day another 781st unit, 2nd Platoon, Company A, under the command of Lt. Donald Crane, was committed to action. The previous night a flakwagon had approached Lemberg from the north, reconnoitering the

Figure 37. A tank from Company A at Lemberg. The original caption indicates that the roadside had caved in along a ditch under the weight of the tank, but the vehicle was recovered "easily." *Courtesy National Archives and Records Administration, Washington DC*

area and quickly withdrawing. On the morning of the ninth, the Germans returned with two flakwagons and infantry support. These forces overran an infantry platoon and annihilated them, firing their 20-mm cannons into their foxholes at point-blank range before withdrawing.

The next day Lieutenant Crane and his platoon attacked north of Lemberg toward Bitche. They came upon and destroyed three flakwagons, two 75-mm field guns, and two howitzers. The 2nd Platoon also lost two tanks as a result of mines, but these were quickly repaired (within twelve hours). Crane was also awarded the Silver Star.

The unit history noted that "these two operations demonstrated to Battalion that if infantry closely watches over tanks, and tanks deliver accurate machine-gun and 75-mm HE fire in large quantities, operations can be carried out against [a] town with a minimum of tank and infantry losses and that tank evacuation can be successfully carried out during operations and under fire."[8]

Mouterhouse

Three and half miles to the east of Lemberg lay the village of Mouterhouse. On 11 December Company B of the 781st assisted the 398th Infantry as they began their drive toward the city of Bitche and beyond to the Maginot Line.

Company D's light tanks advanced with the 397th. At one point the infantry was held up by a flakwagon. When the Germans saw the tanks moving forward, they abandoned their vehicle. One of the tank crews used thermite grenades to put the flakwagon out of action.[9]

Though the 1st Platoon, Company C, had taken twenty-four German prisoners in action north of Mouterhouse, bad communication with supporting troops resulted in the missed opportunity of firing on exposed enemy infantry for fear they might be friendly forces. Following this foul up, as the unit history recorded, "There are two SCR 300 radios in each platoon of tanks, and the importance of making SCR 300s available to any infantry unit, no matter how small, that has a mission with tanks, cannot be [overemphasized]."[10]

Bitche

As the Seventh Army moved north, its divisions worked themselves into the eastern notch of northern France. Only five miles from the German border sits the fortress city of Bitche. Its centrally located citadel commands the surrounding area. At the base of the stronghold and sprinkled along the surrounding hills are buildings and green fields that spread into the forest that surrounds the area. Though the large nineteenth-century fortress dominates, the surrounding forest was littered with Maginot Line bunkers.[11] The Germans planned to use these bunkers to their fullest potential.

The Maginot Line was an immense complex of fortifications, most of which were located underground. The casements had reinforced concrete walls and roofs up to twelve feet thick, capable of withstanding artillery and bombs. Fixed steel turrets housed machine guns and antitank guns, while larger retractable turrets housed large-caliber howitzers. Each fortress had a vast network of underground tunnels connecting various fighting bunkers, or blocks. Small rail systems transported ammunition and equipment thorough these tunnels. Like large naval ships, there were protected underground quarters for hundreds of troops, kitchens and eating halls, medical facilities, and large ammunition magazines.

Within the vicinity of Bitche were a number of these fortifications, defended by the 25th Panzer Grenedier Division and the 361st Voksgremier. Fort Simserhof, comprising ten fighting blocks, was about two miles west of the city, on the north side of the main east–west road. About a mile east was Fort Schiesseck, one of the largest complexes in the area with eleven blocks.

To the west of Bitche was the American 44th Infantry Division, and to the east was the 45th Infantry Division. Between these was the 100th Infantry Division, which had the responsibility of taking the city. The Century Division's plan for would require the occupation of high ground to the left and rear of Bitche and the silencing of the Maginot bunkers in that area. Once the town had been surrounded, the division would make its assault.

All three regiments of the 100th Division were committed in the attack. The 398th would advance along Bitche's west flank, enveloping it around to the north. In the middle the 399th would head to the south of town. The 397th was to move up from Mouterhouse, located south of Bitche, and advance to the east, blocking any Germans trying to escape. Its move also protected the division's right flank, which would be exposed once it moved north away from the 45th Division's line.

On 14 December Company B, along with a three-gun section from the assault-gun platoon, moved on line with the 398th Regiment. Tanks of

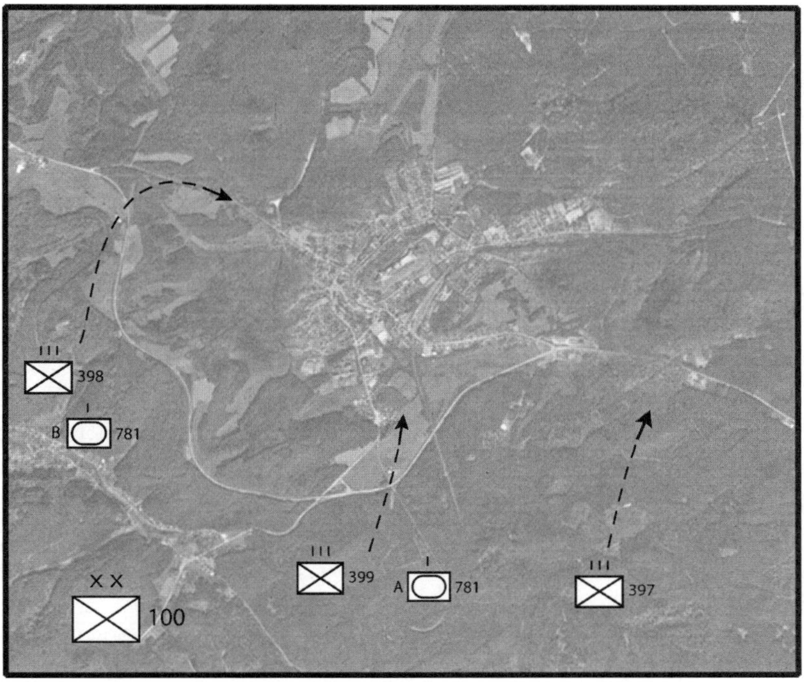

Figure 38. Attack on Bitche, December 1944.

Company A accompanied the 399th and took up firing position along the high ground overlooking Bitche, ready to support the infantry's attack.

That afternoon the Americans began their assault. The 1st Battalion, 398th Regiment, advanced with the tanks of 1st Platoon, Company B, under the command of Lt. Augustus Sitten. The force moved northwest along the road north of Ryeseviller until the infantry came under fire from a roadblock. With the troops pinned down, a Sherman moved up and fired into the enemy positions. A concealed German gun opened up, and an antitank shell screamed passed the tank. The commander looked for the gun while other Shermans moved up. Spotting the weapon, the Americans knocked it out with high-explosive rounds. The force then continued along the road, finally approaching the first Maginot forts.

Tanks and infantry had to learn to work together under fire. They also had to figure out how to jointly attack fortified positions, not having received any training for such engagements. The actions of the 781st at Bitche reflect the common ad-hoc tactics US units used against fortified positions.

Figure 39. The attack on Bitche required all three regiments of the 100th Infantry Division and the entire 781st Tank Battalion. Here, an infantry machine-gun crew prepares to attack. *Courtesy George C. Marshall Foundation, VMI*

Figure 40. A 781st tank crew discuss their attack route. *Courtesy George C. Marshall Foundation, VMI*

The first one engaged was at Freudenberg farm, one mile west of town on the south side of the road. Unable to knock out this lone blockhouse, Companies A and B of the 398th continued northeast toward Fort Schiesseck. This was a massive complex whose works stretched for nearly 875 yards in depth. The 75-mm guns of the Shermans were no match for the reinforced concrete walls—all they could do was provide suppressing fire over the infantrymen's heads to at least keep the Germans down. "The general plan for the employment of tanks against these fortified positions was for close-in, direct, overhead fire by tank elements in support of assault echelons of the infantry."[12] Even so, the infantry came under heavy fire; unable to move forward, they had to dig in.

The next morning, the fifteenth, Company A again moved in against the fort and again withdrew. Yet this time the withdrawal was to avoid being hit by the massive American bombardment about to fall on the German positions. "Now began 36 hours of air and artillery attack on the forts surrounding Bitche," recorded the 100th Division's historian. "Besides its [four] organic artillery battalions, our division had five attached battalions: two of 105mm howitzers, two of 155mm howitzers, and one 4.5-inch gun, or 60 [total] firing pieces. On call, in addition, were a battalion of 155mm rifles, a battalion of 8-inch howitzers, two batteries of 240mm howitzers and one battery of 4.2-inch chemical mortars."[13] Typical artillery battalions had three batteries of four guns each. Therefore, an infantry division with three 105 battalions and one 155 battalion had forty-eight guns. In contrast, 8-inch and 240-mm batteries consisted of only two pieces, giving these battalions only six guns each.

Throughout the fifteenth, the forts around Bitche were pummeled with a constant barrage. The next morning two 240-mm shells plowed into Fort Freudenberg. Fort Schiesseck also received its share of blasting. One 240-mm shell hit the retractable turret on Block 7, jamming it in the up position; another direct hit only aided in jarring the systems back into use. Even after seventy-eight fighter-bombers had dropped twenty-seven tons of 500-pound bombs on the area, the overall damage to the forts was slight at best.

The tank, artillery, and aerial bombardment could not reduce the defenses. It was now up to the infantry to place charges on the bunkers. Equipped with bazookas, grenades, twenty-five-pound satchel charges, and thermite grenades, the troops moved up under the protective fire of the tanks. The Shermans moved in close, spraying gun ports with machine-gun fire and sending in high-explosive rounds to keep the Germans buttoned up. Slowly the infantry units worked their way from block to block, detonating explosive charges on entrances and firing into embrasures.

One tank-dozer crew from the 781st's Headquarters Company went into action, braving direct antitank fire. At least two Shermans in the battalion were equipped with the M1 bulldozer kit. The ten-foot blade was mounted at the front of the tank and was elevated by a hydraulic jack, which was protected by an armor plate and fixed onto the front of the hull. The two support arms stretched back along the side of the tank and were hinged onto the center bogie.

The 100th Division's history noted that Tec 5 Joseph Anderson, from Salt Lake City, was the only man in the 781st willing to take the tank dozer into action. His task was to seal up the blocks, and though under fire, he maneuvered the vehicle to bury one block, fill in the moats and seal the escape passages for a pair of others, and moved earth to block the turrets of two more. His tank dozer finally bogged down as he was working on another position; Anderson and a group of engineers rendered the machine useless and abandoned it. The history of the 781st also named Cpl. George Cote from Company A, who worked a tank dozer to seal up other Maginot forts. He too bogged down and had to destroy his vehicle. By the nineteenth all but two of the eleven blocks of Fort Scheisseck had been silenced.

On December 20 the 1st Section, Assault Gun Platoon, supported the 398th. The M4(105)s fired into the trees, pinning down German defenders there and covering the temporary withdrawal of nearby infantry units.

Platoons of Company D had provided night security for forward infantry elements and supported close security for three self-propelled 155-mm guns. Two of their tanks "hit the dirt" (bottomed out) and had to be abandoned; both were retrieved under fire and returned to their crews.

On the evening of the twentieth, XV Corps ordered all units to consolidate their gains, dig in, and prepare for a German counterattack. But the 781st did not wait around for this attack since it was needed elsewhere. The tankers bid their Century Division brethren farewell. The capture of Bitche would have to wait.

The unit history recorded, "the tank employment in the attack on Bitche was successful in its mission as the close-in direct fire of 76mm and 75mm tanks guns and 105mm HEAT ammunition; although having little effect on fortifications, did cause the enemy to button up and not man automatic weapons emplaced in vicinity of forts."[14] This fire superiority permitted US infantry to move in and take positions to destroy embrasures with explosive charges or at least lay down covering fire while tank dozers moved in to complete the work.

16

Hunting Tanks, Improving Tanks

> If I had millions of them [panzerfausts] in the troops, then eventually a few hundred tanks would not approach a certain point.
>
> **—Adolf Hitler**

As the Allies began to close in on Germany, the Germans began using handheld antitank weapons more frequently. Whereas a 75-mm field gun could be spotted, flanked, and taken under fire, a *Panzerfaust* was as concealed as the individual soldier holding it.

The first of these weapons, called the *Faustpatrone* (or Panzerfaust 30 klein), was produced in 1943. The weapon was an inexpensive solution to infantry tank defense. It consisted of a tube filled with propellant and a warhead attached to its end. Capable of penetrating five and a half inches of armor at its ideal range of thirty yards, the fourteen-ounce projectile was more or less lobbed from the gun tube into its target.

But the velocity did not dictate lethality. Rather, the projectile utilized a shaped charge to achieve penetration. The warhead was designed to channel its explosion through a conical liner in its interior. The explosion was thus narrowed into a small jet that would penetrate armor like a hot needle through butter. The resulting blast wreaked havoc in the tank, annihilating the occupants if they were not lucky enough to be ejected by the blast.

The idea of a lone German soldier hiding in a cellar or ditch with one of these weapons plagued the minds of tankers entering small towns. It did not take long for tank platoons to demand adequate infantry support before entering the close confines of a French village. Hitler himself was aware of the psychological effects of the weapon, stating in early January 1945 that if his troops had millions of them, "eventually a few hundred tanks would not approach a certain point."[1]

The Military Intelligence Division went to work spreading the word of this lethal weapon, including a chapter about it in the October 1944 issue of *Tactical and Technical Trends*, which read in part: "The new German Faustpatrone, a recoilless anti-tank hollow charge grenade with expendable launcher, designed as a basic close-combat antitank weapon, is the latest German development in close-combat antitank material. The tables of issue give 36 to each rifle company, and a total of 2,000 to the infantry division. . . . Their dependence on these methods is now increased by United Nations supremacy in the air and superiority in fire power which interdict effective employment of German antitank guns, forcing them to be sited with more consideration for cover than would normally be the case."[2]

The panzerfaust was improved upon throughout the war. The early model, called the Gretchen, had a warhead that measured 14.25 inches (including stabilizing fins) and was capable of penetrating 5.5 inches of armor. The upgraded version of this model was the Panzerfaust 60. Its 19.5-inch warhead was recorded by the Germans as having the capability to penetrate nearly 8 inches of armor. It had a larger launching tube that held more propellant than its predecessor, increasing its effective range to sixty yards. In November 1944 German troops were issued the Panzerfaust 100, which had a nominal range of 100 yards and capable of penetrating about 8.75 inches of armor.

Hitler was very interested in the weapon and its logistical potential. During a meeting he was informed: "Using a different head, we've managed to achieve the same penetration effect with half the explosives. At the same time, [we] can reach a range of 150 m because the head is lighter. [We] save 0.9 kg per round. That's exactly the explosive content of one field howitzer round. That's an enormous gain." Hitler was pleased, replying: "The Panzerfaust goes 100 m further, has greater penetration, and takes half the explosives. That gets me a million field howitzer shells."[3]

While Patton forbade his Third Army tankers to add additional protection to their vehicles, such as mounting sandbags to the hull and turret, many armored units, including the 781st, took to welding on metal baskets large enough to hold sandbags. This would reduce the risk of penetration from panzerfausts since they would detonate on the sandbags and their explosive charge would be expelled on the exterior of the tank, thus preventing the fiery jet from penetrating the armor.

Tanks and Infantry

During the film *To Hell and Back*, the story of Audie Murphy, an infantry squad boards a Sherman. One of the infantrymen turns toward the tank commander and says: "You tankers have really got it soft. Man this is the way to travel with a couple hundred thousand dollars' worth of machinery under ya." The tank commander challenges the idea, claiming: "If we run into German Tigers you won't think so. This thing's only got about four inches of armor." "Oh yeah," the rifleman smiles before continuing, "Say, how thick do you think this GI shirt is?"[4]

The exposed foot soldier had a difficult time trying to understand why the tanks were not consistently up front, slamming shells into every German position. In their eyes the tankers were not only heavily protected but also had at their disposal thousands of rounds of machine-gun ammunition and plenty of 75-mm rounds. An infantryman hunkered down in a ditch, smashing his body as low as he could while bullets snapped over his head, cursed his tanks squatting in the rear. It was common for an infantry lieutenant to lose his cool, demanding that armor be brought forward only to be told it was too risky.

While all infantrymen feared death, many could still fantasize about those million-dollar wounds in the arms or legs that would send them home. But to a tanker it was all or nothing. Rolling up to a village in a thirty-ton tank was an *all-in* wager. If wounded, an infantryman was typically in the open, could at least see his own men around him, and hopefully would be attended to by a medic if not crawl out of harm's way on his own. But being hit while inside a tank rang an entirely different kind of bell. Gruesome details of violent death rested in the back of a tanker's mind—a deafening blast, being trapped, consuming darkness, dismemberment, decapitation, and incineration. An antitank round slamming into a hull would spray the interior with bits of steel, shredding flesh and igniting ammunition fires. Knocked-out tanks often emitted a stench of burnt flesh. Many learned not to gaze too long at the charred remains hanging out of turrets or the bullet-riddled bodies lying next to immobile vehicles.

One ordnance liaison officer (who was responsible for receiving and analyzing knocked-out tanks) recalled his difficult task, "as the tanks and other armored vehicles were brought into the VCP [Vehicle Collecting Point] with broken and twisted bodies still inside, the horror of war began to settle into my being." He noted that his job required him to "deliberately" not look at the bodies. But sometimes that would be impossible: if the "tanker . . . received the full effect of penetration, sometimes the body, particularly the head, exploded and scattered blood, gore, and brains throughout the entire compartment. It was a horrible sight. The maintenance crews had to get inside and clean up the remains. They tried to keep the body parts together in a shelter half and turn them over to the grave registration people. With strong detergent, disinfectant, and water they cleaned the interior of the tank as best they could so the men could get inside and repair it."[5] Obviously the clean-up men could not get to every nook and cranny. This was evident to the next crew when increased interior temperatures brought with them the faint odor of death.

Another advantage the infantryman had over tankers was the natural ability to see anywhere he wished. Crewmen were restricted to limited fields of view from within their machine. Only the commander, exposing himself out of the turret, could have a 360-degree view. Even then, his head was ten feet above the ground, and enemy soldiers were more likely to see him than he was to see them.

Despite these differing perceptions of one another, it was mutually important to establish a working tanker-infantry relationship. Many units conducted exercises designed to build team relationships between the different servicemen. A battalion commander from the 175th Infantry recorded that in order to make his men "realize the limited vision and field of fire and the closed-off feeling of the tankers, every infantryman should be given a ride in a buttoned-up tank. One such ride does a lot to counteract the infantryman's dread of a tank attack and to increase his faith in his own ability to resist tanks."[6]

The hope was that an appreciation for each other's abilities would help dissolve any tactical confrontations between the infantry and tank commanders. One report stated: "At certain times the burden of carrying the attack must, because of the terrain and the situation, fall on the infantry.

At other times, the tanks are best qualified to bear the brunt of the attack. Both units must know this and learn to recognize the situations in which one or the other unit should lead."

Many infantrymen received a taste of tank life when instructed to load up on a Sherman. According to Lieutenant Colonel Kinne of the 781st Tank Battalion, a maximum load of ten infantrymen could be carried on a tank. It was also "imperative that before mounting the infantry, thorough plans are made by the infantry commanders and tank commanders, who are to ride together. It is the duty of the infantry commander to mount infantry personnel in such manner as to preserve unit tactical integrity. This insures [*sic*] that no time is lost in organizing for combat after dismounting." Once reaching an objective, the infantry would dismount, disperse, and leave "a small number of men for tank protection; the remainder [would] proceed with reconnaissance. When contact [was] made, the tanks prepared to support the infantry on call." All of this coordination relied on communication between tanker and infantryman.

Without a team dynamic, infantrymen cursed tankers for their apparent timidity, while tankers cursed the lack of armor knowledge displayed by infantry leaders, who committed many errors when commanding supporting tanks. For example, foot commanders frequently failed to communicate to crewmen the exact locations of enemy strongpoints. At other times they ordered in tanks without proper reconnaissance. The use of piecemeal armor attacks reduced their overall effectiveness, depriving both infantry and tanks of mutual support.

During the first weeks in Normandy, most communication between the infantry and the tankers was face to face. This required the foot commander to first make himself visible to the crewmen, often by leaving cover and mounting the tank to talk with the commander. Suffice to say, if under heavy fire, such discussions were brief and generally ineffective.

One of the best means of communication was the use of the EE8A telephone. One War Department publication about tank-infantry contact recommended their use: "An EE8A telephone is placed inside the tank turret. Also in the turret, at a place easily visible to the tank commander, is strapped a regulation flashlight. A 20-foot length of four-strand electric cable is laid from the telephone box inside the turret and extended down in rear of the tank. An EE8A telephone handset is connected to the end of the cable. The butterfly switch on the handset is modified so that, when pressed, it completes a circuit through one channel of the cable, lights the flashlight, and attracts the attention of the tank commander. Telephone conversation is then held over another channel of the cable, the telephones being wired for that effect. With this telephone setup, the squad leader has only to carry the handset to be able to communicate readily with the tank commander."

Second-Generation Shermans

The original M4s that came off the production lines in 1942 are referred to as the first-generation models, whereas those produced later, featuring new design elements, are second-generation models. These many modifications began with reengineering the front glacis plate. On first-generation models this part was inclined at a fifty-six-degree angle, which resulted in the undesired protrusion of the driver's and BOG's hatches. Newer models reduced this angle to forty-seven degrees and increased the armor's thickness to compensate. In addition, the hull's crew hatches were reoriented. As mentioned earlier, these hatches were narrow and originally positioned in a way that required a crewman to twist his body to enter or exit the tank. The new placement of the hatches now made entering and exiting the hull much easier.

Next came improvements to the tank commander's hatch. The rotating split hatch from earlier models was removed in favor of a single-piece rotating hatch equipped with a rotating periscope. The new cupola also featured six vision ports housing bulletproof glass. This allowed the commander to view his surroundings without exposing himself to enemy fire.

A third modification introduced a loader's hatch. This crewmember finally had a direct way to enter or exit the tank, with the door located above his seat on the left side of the gun.

Another improvement was the relocation of ammunition storage. Early-model crews had packed away their rounds into storage bins located in the sponsons, the turret walls and floor, and behind the BOG. After it became apparent that most of the interior fires after damage resulted from the ammunition igniting, designers decided to move much of the ammunition into the turret subfloor. This required changing the layout of the turret-basket floor so as to give the loader access to these new containers. While the first-generation design had a complete circular floor fixed to the turret, the second-generation turret basket featured only a partial floor. Traversing the turret would give access to the subfloor panels and the ammunition supply underneath.

The new storage containers featured what were called "ammudamp cans." These were liquid-filled inserts that would help extinguish any flames resulting from penetration of the ammunition bins, called "wet" storage. A postwar study indicated that this addition reduced the chances of a tank burning after being penetrated from 80 percent to 10 percent.

The fifth, and most apparent, modification was the new 76-mm gun. Plans for this weapon went back to early 1942, but the army moved forward with only one design dubbed the M1A1. Production was slow due to the weight of the barrel. Engineers went to work designing a new gun mount, solving weight ratios, working with counterbalances, and designing a new turret for the weapon. Although by December 1942 no modified turret was ready, the Ordnance Department had been busy working on new medium-tank designs featuring larger turrets for the 76-mm gun. While the new medium tanks were ultimately rejected, the turret from the T23 design was adopted for the new Shermans housing the M1A1 gun.[7]

Unfortunately, the new gun came as a tradeoff. While the 75-mm high-explosive round weighed 14.6 pounds, with an explosive charge of about 1.5 pounds, the new 76-mm high-explosive shell weighed 12.37 pounds, but with an explosive charge of only 0.86 pounds. Though lighter, the shells were shot from the barrel at a much higher velocity, for the new 76-mm ammunition used 3.6 pounds of propellant versus the 75-mm's 1-pound charge. Again, though, there was a cost. Due to the larger charge and the barrel's overhang, the gun produced a violent muzzle blast. Lacking a muzzle break, the blast would erupt a cloud of dust from dry terrain that would not clear for up to thirty seconds in calm conditions. This would completely obscure the gunner's and tank commander's view of the shell's trajectory, not to mention revealing to the enemy the tank's location.

The first 76-mm guns mounted on M4A1 tanks arrived in England in April 1944. But due to tank officers' frustrations with the blast, the army decided to hold off on deploying the new model until muzzle breaks were mounted. This decision might not be judged as rash, for up to this point the Sherman's primary role was still that of eliminating infantry strongpoints and rear installations. As for taking on enemy tanks, the 75-mm gun had proved adequate to take on the Mark IVs that had made up the majority of panzer units to that time. Though Tiger tanks had been encountered, their numbers were few and had only appeared on rare occasion.

Shermans thus landed in Normandy mounting 75-mm guns. But to the shock of the tankers, their primary counterparts were no longer the Mark IVs. In the following days British and American tanks began being knocked out by the long 75-mm guns of the new Mark V Panthers. By June 1944 the numbers of Panthers in France had increased to 46 percent of panzer forces, with the remaining 54 percent being older tanks.[8]

Commanders soon decided that the 76-mm guns were a necessity regardless of their drawbacks. The 2nd and 3rd Armored Divisions received around one hundred M4A1 (76-mm) tanks just as they began Operation Cobra in July 1944. In September the army would receive M4 and M4A3 tanks equipped with the 76-mm gun.

Again, disappointment and frustration filled the ranks of the armored units. Even the new 76-mm gun, with its higher velocity, could not penetrate the Panthers' armor. The standard armor-piercing round for the M1A1 was the M62 APC-T. On paper it could penetrate four and a half inches of armor at about 550 yards. As the Panther had up to nearly five inches of armor, closing in to within 550 yards was dangerously close for a Sherman. As a result, tankers had to use tactics, maneuverability, and their own skills to knock out a Panther.

The Ordnance Department went back to work developing new armor-piercing ammunition. The resulting new round was the T4 High-Velocity Armor-Piercing (HVAP) projectile. The T4 featured a tungsten-carbide core encased in an aluminum-alloy shell with a ballistic cap. The tungsten-carbide core was one and a half inches in diameter and weighed four pounds, making the round relatively lightweight and thus providing an increased velocity of 3,400 fps.[9] Even after traveling 2,000 yards, the projectile had a velocity of approximately 2,300 fps and capable of penetrating nearly five inches of armor.[10] When the round struck an enemy tank, the aluminum shell would virtually disintegrate while the core achieved penetration. The T4 thus was capable of penetrating a Panther's mantlet at 800 yards versus the M62's 200 yards.

Unfortunately, production of the T4 was very slow due to the limited sources of tungsten. These highly valued rounds thus were divided between antitank and armor units. As a result, a single tank may only have had two or three of these HVAP rounds in their ammunition racks from the fall of 1944 through the winter of 1944–45.

Shermans were eventually equipped with muzzle breaks. This equipment would channel the muzzle blast out laterally, away from the ground, and thus reduce the chance of visual obstruction from dust kicked up by the blast. As many of the panzers had muzzle breaks already, it was very important to display these modified Shermans to Allied infantry units during brief recognition presentations to minimize friendly fire losses.

It is worth noting that, according to Twelfth Army Group figures, in September 1944 13.4 percent of its armor units had the 76-mm gun; by December that number had risen to 30 percent. It would not be until April 1945 that the figure would reach above 40 percent, its wartime peak being 52.3 percent at the beginning of May.[11]

A final second-generation modification was new suspension. Into the fall and winter of 1944, tank crews had been increasingly agitated with the Sherman's performance on soft terrain. Its tracks were just more than sixteen and a half inches wide. In order to improve on this, a type of extension was produced for fastening to the outside of the tracks, thus distributing more of the vehicle's weight over the soft ground. These extenders, commonly referred to as "duckbills," were issued at the onset of winter. Many crews installed them onto their tracks, decreasing their tank's ground pressure from 14.5 to 12.4 psi (pounds per square inch).

While tankers utilized these field modifications, the Ordnance Department continued working on a new suspension for the Sherman. During the latter part of 1943, designs appeared for a new system based on a 23-inch, center-guided track. The larger tracks required a bulkier suspension, which developed around a horizontal volute-spring system (HVSS). Each bogie had two pairs of road wheels, distributing the wear more evenly and thus increasing track life. Also, the addition of shock absorbers gave the crew a more comfortable ride. The new track system reduced ground pressure from 14.5 to 10 psi, increasing floatation. Tanks coming out of production with this new suspension had "E8" added to their designation (for example, M4A1E8).[12] The first models entered combat in December 1944.

17

Battalion Operations, January 1945

Tank losses . . . demonstrated [the] results of committing tanks without prior coordination with supported infantry elements and lack of reconnaissance and orientation of tank personnel.

—"781st Tank Battalion Unit History"

On 16 December 1944 the Germans unleashed their massive counterattack through the Ardennes Forest. Walther Model's Army Group B, consisting of the Fifth Panzer, Sixth Panzer, and Seventh Armies, crashed into Bradley's Twelfth Army Group in Luxembourg. By 20 December the Germans had pushed back Allied lines twenty miles. As a result, many of the US Third Army units located south of the counteroffensive shifted north to try and stabilize the American line. The Seventh Army, immediately south of the Third, had to stretch itself to cover the area previously held by that command. This required many units to fall back, relinquishing territory to straighten and strengthen the line.

On New Year's Day 1945, the 781st, minus Company A, was attached to the 79th Infantry Division. The 79th had held a defensive position along the Lauter River from Wissembourg to Lauterbourg but was at that time in the process of withdrawing to an alternate main line of resistance running along the Maginot forts in the area. The tanks of Companies B and C supported the 314th and the 315th Regiments, respectively. Company D was held in division reserve with the division's reconnaissance troop.

The reinforced assault-gun platoon, consisting of six medium tanks with 105-mm guns, provided fire support alongside the 79th Division's artillery. As the M4 105s were more mobile than the artillery, they maintained their position until the last of the infantry units had withdrawn; the platoon was the last unit to pull out. "As we withdrew, the people stood in groups on street corners and looked scared. French flags weren't hanging from the windows any more and no little kids waved. Moving back was a new and unwelcome experience."[1]

This began a new campaign in a region the Germans called Elassas and Lothrinnen but that the French called Alsace and Lorraine. The French had lost this territory following the Franco-Prussian War (1870–71), yet regained it after World War I. It changed hands again in 1940, and Hitler attempted to Germanize it by renaming the towns. The Americans planned to take this region back again.

Company B at Wingen

On 3 January the 361st Volksgrenadier Division attacked Reipertswiller. Ten miles to the southwest, two battalions of the 6th SS Mountain Division struck at the village of Wingen. That night German troops infiltrated behind the main line of resistance of the 45th Division's 179th Regiment. The next morning they attacked the 70th Division's 276th Regiment in Wingen.

Located within the Vosges Mountains, Wingen stretches along an east–west railroad line. The track rested on a high embankment that ran along the north side of the village, separating it from a large hill. The village was surrounded, as most villages in the area, by wooded hills.

German author and veteran of the Battle of Wingen Wolf T. Zoepf explained that Wingen was vital territory, "a transportation nexus amid heavily wooded, snow-covered mountains. Besides the district road, there was a more significant one that led from the Saar Valley in the west to the Alsatian Plain in the east. It connected the important cities of Sarre-Union, Ingwiller, Haguenau, and ultimately, Strasbourg. Also, there was another road, which entered Wingen from the south, from Saverne, the greatest gateway to the Rhine Valley."[2]

The Germans had attacked from the north and headed toward the railroad station and a large church. After a brief firefight and some house-to-house fighting, they secured the village and began digging in.[3]

US commanders ordered a task force assembled with the mission of "driving the enemy north and reducing the enemy concentration behind the MLR [main line of resistance] of the 45th Infantry Division." A G-2 report had indicated "a large concentration of enemy troops held in reserve to the north, in a position to exploit a successful breakthrough." If the Germans could hold Wingen, they planned to send the 21st and 25th Panzer Divisions through the town to reinforce their units at Bitche.[4]

The 781st Tank Battalion received orders from VI Corps to move up to La Petite Pierre as part of Task Force Herren, whose mission was to retake Wingen.[5] Icy roads delayed the battalion. Tanks, trucks, jeeps, and halftracks inched their way through Miderbetschdorf. The column encountered a traffic jam as it moved through Haguenau, further delaying the march. On 3 January at 10:00 p.m. the unit finally arrived in La Petite Pierre, which Hitler had renamed Lutzelstein in 1940. Amusingly, a 781st report claimed that "more than one man drove through Lutzelstein with a French map looking for La Petite Pierre."[6]

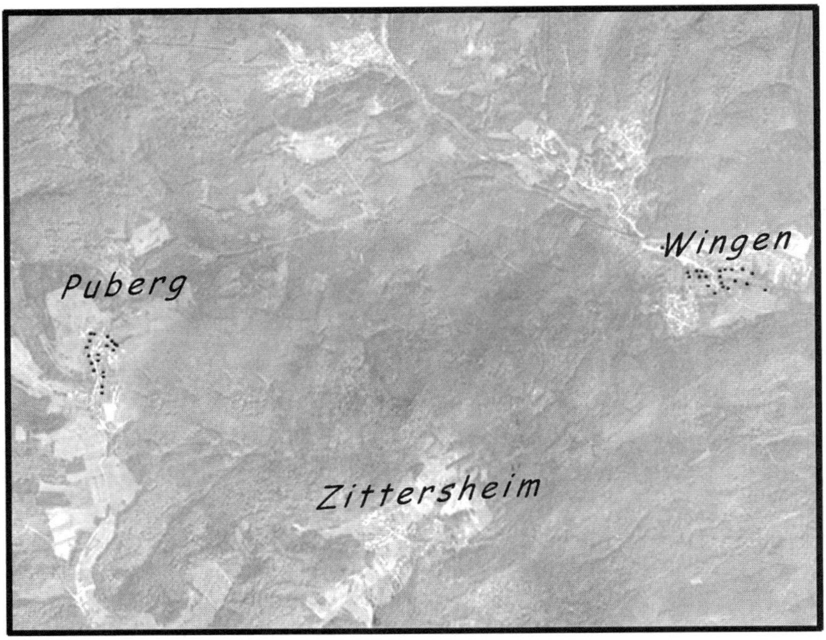

Figure 41. Vicinity of Wingen, France.

Task Force Herren comprised elements from the 274th and 276th Infantry Regiments of the 70th Division, the 781st Tank Battalion, and a medical company; the 45th Division and 69th Artillery Battalion were held in reserve. Company B of the 781st was attached to the 276th Regiment and moved up to Zittersheim. Company C was held in reserve, Company D provided guard for La Petite Pierre, and the assault-gun platoon reinforced the 69th Artillery.

The 3rd Battalion, 276th Regiment (3/276), received orders to attack Wingen from the west, "generally astride the railroad. The 1st Battalion was to support this move by fire from the south and east to permit the attackers to clean out the town. One platoon of medium tanks was attached to the 3d Battalion units. The 3d Battalion companies were to reorganize after accomplishing their mission."[7]

The counterattack began on 4 January. Tanks from Company B, commanded by Capt. John E. Simkins, moved out from La Petite Pierre toward Puberg, located roughly two miles west of Wingen. There they linked up with the two companies of infantry from 3/276 and advanced along a road running parallel to the railroad embankment into Wingen. The road and

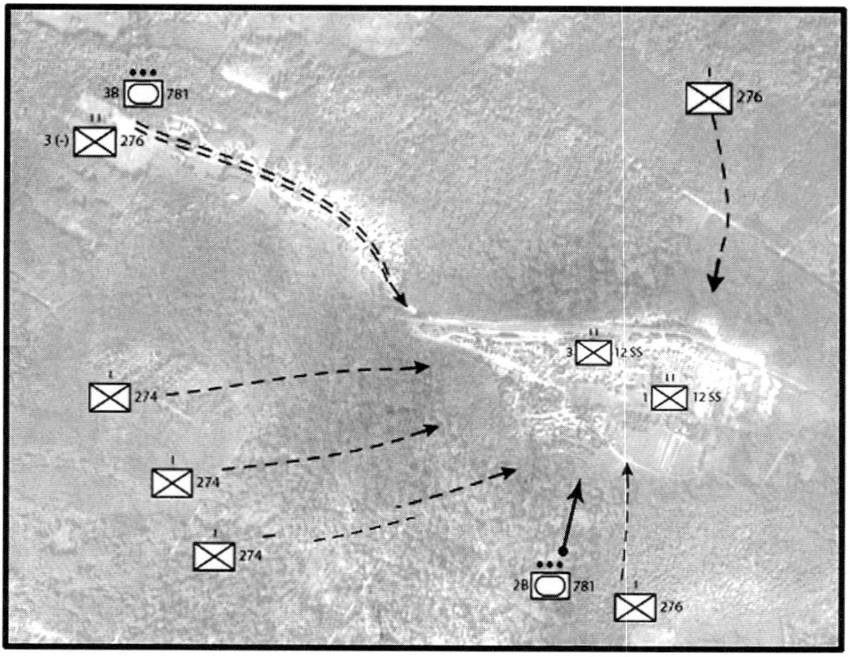

Figure 42. Battle of Wingen, January 1945.

rails were separated by approximately 200 yards before the road veered south and passed under the tracks and into town. As infantry cleared the woods up to the western edge of Wingen, the 3rd Battalion, 276th Regiment; Company C, 276 Regiment; and Company B prepared to attack.

Through the snow and freezing temperatures, the attack began. Infantry took the high ground north of Wingen as tanks from 2nd Platoon, Company B, covered the area from there to the south.

While 2nd Platoon stood by as fire support, two infantry companies from the 276th and the tanks of 3rd Platoon, Company B, advanced down the road. Things were running according to plan until the infantry and tanks approached the western underpass. As they passed through, the infantry came under heavy small-arms fire. Some men dropped dead, while others scurried for cover behind the tanks or in ditches. The tankers buttoned up and tried to locate targets through their periscopes. Infantrymen kept their heads down as bullets snapped overhead and chewed up the icy ground around them. The tanks first directed their fire into the hills and surrounding houses. Infantrymen signaled them to cease fire at once since that ground was supposed to be held by friendly infantry. The crewmen

Figure 43. The railroad overpass where the Shermans emerged only to be knocked out. *Courtesy 70th Infantry Division Association* (trailblazersww2.org)

were therefore restricted from using their 75-mm and 76-mm guns "due to insufficient information to which houses were occupied by the enemy or friendly troops."[8]

At about noon the Germans went to work on the American infantry, unleashing "particular havoc on Company L, enfilading them from positions in the western edge of the forest." This was a prime opportunity to fire at American armor with infantry antitank weapons. One of the Shermans had lost its infantry support, which allowed a German to fire a panzerfaust from behind a house at approximately thirty yards. The projectile slammed into the tank, spraying the interior with lethal bits of steel. It came from precisely where the infantry had told the tankers not to fire, the high ground to the north, assumed to have been taken and now controlled by Company C troops. This obviously was not the case.[9]

Two more Shermans moved out from the underpass. German lookouts monitored the vehicles' movements, relaying their location and actions to other troops. One of them turned off the main road, but the other continued on its way. A German appeared from an attic window and fired his panzerfaust from a distance of only eight yards.[10] The warhead crashed into the tank, killing two of its crewmen. Out of the ten men from the two tanks, four were killed, three were seriously wounded, and the remaining three were captured by the SS. Another Sherman tried to go around the disabled tanks but bogged down in the mud—as did the overall attack on Wingen, lacking adequate armor protection.

While the push from the west had groaned to a halt, infantry from the 276th managed to secure the eastern edge of the village. It was not until later in the day that troops from the 274th managed to secure part of western Wingen.

That night the remaining Shermans pulled back, infuriating the infantry commander. Here is yet another example of the infantry's misunderstanding of armor. It was common practice for tanks to pull back from combat at night for a number of reasons. First and foremost, maintenance was part of every tankman's duties. While the infantryman was responsible for his rifle, pack, helmet, ammunition, and anything else he carried, the tanker was responsible for maintaining a thirty-ton machine that needed gas, oil, lubrication, readjustments, ammunition resupply, gun barrels cleaned and other resupply and care. So as the sun went down, tank units would pull away to a relatively removed location, assemble to create a secure perimeter, and take care of those things (not to mention feeding and resting the crews).

One can imagine an infantryman who has sat in his foxhole with the rumbling tank commanding the area no more than a few yards from him. Its engine idles and the 75-mm gun points in the direction of the enemy. The infantryman might have a smoke. But at night he watches as this protective beast rumbles away, and he now feels naked and alone. No longer does the engine rumble at his side. It is now quiet and the crickets can be heard. He imagines the tankers back in some prepared quarters like the Army Air Forces has. "They're probably listening to a record, smoking cigarettes, reading Yank, and have a nice mess kit full of warm grub." Unknown to the infantryman, the tankers have climbed out of the tank, in which they have been cooped up all day. Once they arrived back at their bivouac area, they had to assemble in a fashion so as to provide all-round security. Now begins their night of work. They carry ammunition to the tanks, including armor-piercing and high-explosive rounds as well as hundreds of rounds of machine-gun ammunition; clean the guns; grease the road wheels; fix the engine leak; stock the shells in the tank; check the fluids; and top off their gas. All the while members take turns providing security. Hopefully they get everything done soon so they can catch some sleep.

The next day, 5 January, infantry elements continued to hold the east end of town. They tried to mount another attack, but their attempts were fruitless. On the sixth new attacks were made in the east. The 1st Platoon, Company B, was committed to an assault in the east, while 2nd Platoon continued to provide fire from the south.

To the west a vicious, close-quarters fight raged among the houses. Concealed MG-42s opened up at close range, Americans hurled grenades into windows, BARs (Browning automatic rifles) fired into cellars, while Germans flung "potato mashers" (grenades) into groups of US troops. Casualties were high on both sides. The infantry demanded that armor come forward again to deal with the area around the underpass. Shermans from Simkins's 1st Platoon moved up but hesitated to move in. Zoepf recorded: "Simkins was hesitant in the employment of his tanks. During the last two days of combat he had supported 2/276 and had lost two [Shermans]."[11] The tankers knew that the infantry would hesitate to leave cover to provide close support, and only after both tankers and infantry made promises and guarantees to provide mutual support did the tanks begin to move forward.

As darkness began to close in, Captain Simkins requested to withdraw and was flat-out refused by the infantry commander, who believed that the tankers were going back to relax—in fact they needed more gas and ammunition. Simkins went to higher authority in the task force and received approval to pull back.

Finally on 7 January the 274th cleared out the remaining German units in Wingen. Nearly a hundred American POWs being kept in the village church were liberated, three of whom were the members of the 3rd Platoon captured during the first day of fighting.

In a review of this action, "tank losses in the 3rd platoon occurring [on] 4 January 1945 demonstrated [the] results of committing tanks without prior coordination with supported infantry elements and lack of reconnaissance and orientation of tank personnel." The Company B's casualties were four killed in action and three seriously wounded. The "uncoordinated tank-infantry attacks [during the fourth and sixth] with tanks firing large amounts of ammunition, with their fire restricted due to incomplete information as to location of friendly troops [resulted in] unsuccessful attacks" against an enemy that lacked any firepower other than small arms. The SS units in Wingen had no antitank guns or artillery support; mortars were useless due to the close proximity of the fighting. In summary, it was the "proper coordination with advance of infantry . . . so as to allow maximum tank fire power with proper close-in security furnished tanks by infantry" that resulted in the retaking of Wingen.[12]

While Company B was fighting in and around the village of Wingen, Company A was busy slugging it out with the Germans thirty miles southeast along the Rhine River.

Figure 44. Wrecked buildings and fires attest to the heavy fighting in Wingen. *Courtesy 70th Infantry Division Association* (trailblazersww2.org)

Figure 45. An M4A3 belonging to the 781st crawls through Wingen. Note the open split hatch for the tank commander. *Courtesy 70th Infantry Division Association* (trailblazersww2.org)

Figure 46. A second-generation M4A3, mounting the larger 76-mm main gun. The markings on the rear of the tank indicate this Sherman belongs to the 781st Tank Battalion, Seventh Army. This tank is almost certainly from Company B. *Courtesy 70th Infantry Division Association* (trailblazersww2.org)

Figure 47. In the close confines of the village, much of the fighting was done house to house. Here a 70th Division soldier breaks in a door with his rifle. Interestingly, he has two cartridge belts. *Courtesy 70th Infantry Division Association* (trailblazersww2.org)

Figure 48. A 781st tank, likely the same in figure 46, engages the Germans with supporting infantry. Note the soldier standing on the Sherman, talking with the tank commander. *Courtesy 70th Infantry Division Association* (trailblazersww2.org)

Figure 49. Troops in Wingen plan their next move. A Sherman's open pistol port is visible in the background. *Courtesy 70th Infantry Division Association* (trailblazer sww2.org)

Figure 50. Moving through Wingen, this photo, apparently taken from the turret of a tank, demonstrates the tight quarters of the village, a good example of where tankers dreaded to fight. These tanks maintain a considerable distance between each other here as they would in other urban combat areas. *Courtesy 70th Infantry Division Association* (trailblazersww2.org)

Figure 51. A church in Wingen, possibly where American POWs had been held. *Courtesy 70th Infantry Division Association* (trailblazersww2.org)

Figure 52. Damage from the battle is evident. Note the stretchers leaning up against the wall. *Courtesy 70th Infantry Division Association* (trailblazersww2.org)

Company A at Gambsheim

The new year found Company A attached to Task Force Linden, serving as supplemental batteries in an area around Lingolsheim. On 6 January the tankers were informed that the Germans had made a breakthrough at Gambsheim. With the ultimate objective of stopping this offensive, the company divided, with 1st Platoon heading to Wantzenau, 3rd Platoon going to Weyersheim, and 2nd Platoon remaining in the area around Hoerdt to continue fire missions for the task force.

At 2:45 p.m. that day the 3rd Platoon and supporting infantry attacked Gambsheim from Weyersheim. After crossing a canal on the outskirts of town, the infantry fell behind and the armor recalled to establish a defensive line for the night. The attack was renewed at dawn on the seventh. This time the assault was met with heavy fire. Just as 3rd Platoon entered the town, platoon leader Lt. James Barrickman's tank was hit. The round penetrated the turret, disabling the vehicle and killing Barrickman. Three of the remaining Shermans were then disabled by mines but later retrieved and repaired overnight.

The 1st and 2nd Platoons also launched an attack on Gambsheim from the south. This was a hit-and-run operation, with only seven infantrymen supporting them.

The Americans soon saw white flags as Germans came out from their cover, not able to withstand the Shermans' 75- and 76-mm guns. Eleven smiling soldiers also came out of a pillbox and began approaching the tanks, Americans who had been cut off and had been holding off the Germans for the last two days. Before withdrawing with nearly sixty prisoners of war, one Sherman was knocked out by antitank fire, wounding three crewmembers. The platoons and their prisoners moved back to Kilstett. On 8 January the two platoons were relieved by the French and withdrew to Watzenan. The casualties for Company A were six killed in action and three seriously wounded. For the next week, the company remained behind the lines to do maintenance and repair work.

Company A at Sessenheim

On 16 January, 1st Platoon, Company A, supported a company of infantry raiding the town of Dengolsheim and provided cover as engineers demolished a bridge over the Moder River, located in the woods west of town.

The next day the Germans attacked and encircled the town of Sessenheim, sealing in Company B, 232nd Infantry Regiment. At 11:30 a.m. a small Allied task force moved in to check the enemy advance. Tanks from the 2nd Platoon descended on the town with infantry from 1st Battalion, 232nd Regiment, as the 1st Platoon's tanks dug in to protect the town from further enemy assault. As the task force moved in, they came under attack from the 75-mm guns of multiple Mark IVs. Second Platoon engaged these panzers, knocking out two of them. The American tanks and infantry linked up with B/232 and secured the town.

The next morning the Germans attacked again with a much stronger force, forcing the infantry and the tanks to withdraw. Quickly the Americans again assembled a strike force to take back Sessenheim. Moving out from the woods south of Schirroffen, 1st Battalion, 411th Infantry. moved forward with the tanks of 1st and 2nd Platoons. Covering the right flank of the attack were elements of the 232nd Infantry supported by the Shermans of 3rd Platoon.

As the force moved in, the Germans attacked the right flank and its covering force. The Shermans of the 3rd Platoon fired all of their ammunition into the enemy, inflicting heavy casualties. Only after exhausting its supplies did the platoon withdraw to Schirroffen. The German attack eventually lost its momentum and came to a stop around 2:00 p.m., though only after successfully retaking the town.

At 2:00 a.m. on the nineteenth, the commander of the 411th Infantry drew up orders for a final strike against Sessenheim. Eight Shermans of Company A would provide support to the soldiers of Companies I and L.

At 6:00 a.m. Company A started their engines, their exhaust clearing the heavy mist that had settled around them and began to move forward to their line of departure. The tanks were in column formation on the narrow blacktop road with the soldiers of Companies I and L, waiting to advance. The plan was for Company I to move along the left side of the road and Company L along the right. There would be no artillery barrage as they hoped to achieve surprise and thus be too close for the enemy to use their mortars against them. The tanks would move in behind the infantry, giving them a ten-minute head start. This tactic was based on the notion that armor advancing at the speed of a man on foot would require them to remain in the open too long. It was better, planners believed, for the tanks to move up fast and join the infantry at the moment they anticipated contact with the enemy.

The assault began at 6:30 a.m. Sessenheim was surrounded by woods to the west, south, and east, with roughly six hundred yards of open space between the trees (from which the Americans would come) and the town. As the morning darkness began to fade, the infantry moved over the frozen ground toward their objective. Just as they were closing within a few hundred yards of Sessenheim, eight Shermans from Company A rumbled up the road from the rear. Closing in on the forward units, the tanks split off to the left and right of the road to join the infantry. All was moving according to plan.

As the tanks rolled through the foot of snow blanketing the area, their drivers kept the throttle forward while their BOGs manned the .30-caliber machine guns and the gunners were at the ready to throw high-explosive rounds into any enemy strongpoints. The infantry and tanks continued to crawl forward. It was almost 7:00 a.m.

In an instant an enemy shell streaked dangerously close to one of the tanks. Sgt. Hobert Sexton's eyes found a cloud of smoke from where the shot had come. A second later the radios of Company A all received his astonished voice, report: "My God! It's as big as a house!" It was one of four Jagdtiger tanks the Germans had advanced into Sessenheim under the cover of darkness, dug in to position, and waiting for the attack.[13] Intelligence had no idea that the Germans had these heavy panzers in the area. Painted snow white, they brought their monster 128-mm guns to bear on the Shermans.

Immediately the US tank commanders guided their gunners to the Jagdtigers. The gunners in turn called for armor-piercing rounds, which the loaders quickly threw into the gun breeches. They then lined up their shots and fired. Commanders watched in horror as the 75- and 76-mm shells streaked through the air only to glance off the German tanks, had up to ten inches of armor, deflecting skyward or into the ground. Sgt. Berger Johnson recalled the shells bounced off the panzers like tennis balls.

Almost simultaneously, the infantry began taking small-arms and mortar fire. Meanwhile, the tanks fought in vain for survival. As the American gunners continued to fire away, their tanks soon began receiving heavy fire from all four panzers. Tec 5 Joseph Huya recalled, "one shell hit to the right of [Sergeant] Johnson's tank, then the left, then one left a trail of sparks as it scraped harmlessly along the belly of the tank." Harmless shelling did not last, and soon the Shermans started to get rocked by armor-piercing rounds. One by one the tanks were knocked out as the German fire tore through hulls and turrets. In less than ten minutes, all eight Shermans of Company A were wrecked. Of the forty tankers committed to the attack, twenty became casualties, ten of whom were killed or missing.[14]

Due to the presence of four heavy panzers and the resulting total loss of armor support, the infantry attack failed to reclaim Sessenheim. While elements of Companies I and L did reach the outskirts of town, without direct-fire support, they could not advance any farther. The 781st's unit history of the inferiority of the 75-mm and 76-mm guns was "further proof of inability of present medium tanks to successfully fight the German" heavy tanks. Though the results of this armor battle were disastrous for Company A, the initial advance "was an excellent coordination between tanks and infantry." Had it not been for the failure of intelligence concerning the panzers, the unit historian believed that the attack "would have been highly successful."[15] On the contrary, if intelligence had discovered the Jagdtigers, the attack probably would have been completely reorganized, if not called off altogether.

By January 1945, the 747th Tank Battalion had developed a different approach to crossing open terrain to attack a defended town. Its theory recommended that "tanks should habitually lead the attack. . . . [T]he plan for supporting fire should be carefully laid on, the battlefield should be isolated, and the tank[s], used in company strength or greater, should move against the town, take full advantage of their speed to move into the edge of town under artillery fire, and silence the outlying enemy machine guns around the perimeter enabling the infantry to move quickly into the town and commence clearing it up systematically." It also discouraged sending armor and infantry in together as "the tanks will be slowed down and the artillery fire that will fall on the tanks [will] cause casualties, [or] the infantry may be able to approach the objective from a direction unsuitable for tanks to take advantage of defilade."[16] The 781st would develop its own tactics the following month. It is worth emphasizing that these theories and practices were being tested only in the latter months of the war. As this demonstrates, the tank-infantry team had to learn on the job.

Now consisting of only three tanks, Company A was attached to the 79th Division's 813th Tank Destroyer Battalion until 25 January. That day, though, would bring further losses to the company. As the battalion's history noted, "s/Sgt. Kelly's section, previously ordered to a road block position," was directed to support the 1/314's attack on German penetrations north of Schweighaussen. During this strike, "infantry support fell behind advancing tanks allowing one tank to be hit by bazooka fire. Other tank stuck while trying to pass first tank. All but two of tank crews either killed or captured."[17] For the remainder of the month, the survivors of the company were attached to reserve units and began reorganizing, equipping, and training replacements. Company A had lost nearly all of its line tanks.

The Events of Company D

During January 1945, Company D was attached to the 79th Division's reconnaissance troop, its platoons being rotated on the assignment. (Reconnaissance platoons consisted of three M8 armored cars). At the same time the Germans moved on Wingen and Gambsheim, they also took Stattmatten. During this time, the company had been in Schirrhoffen. First Platoon, under the command of a Lieutenant Pais, was ordered forward with three reconnaissance platoons from the 79th Division. They passed through Sessenheim and took up positions six hundred yards west of Stattmatten in preparation for an attack.

On 6 January the M8s and the M5s of 1st Platoon began their strike. The M8s established positions to the west so they could establish a base of fire with their .50-caliber and 37-mm guns. One section of Company D, supported by less than a platoon of "cooks, clerks, and KPs," attacked to the north of Stattmatten while another section attacked to the south. Once the town was encircled, all units attacked and caught the defenders by complete surprise.[18] After the skirmish, sixty Germans were dead and thirty were taken prisoner. Not only was the mission a strategic success, but the attack force also had bagged the German battalion commander and his staff.

First Platoon had four casualties resulting from a freak occurrence. Whether luck or an unbelievable shot, a German infantryman had managed to shoot a rifle grenade precisely through the open turret hatch of one M5. The blast killed three and wounded another.

After the successful attack on Stattmatten, 1st Platoon returned to Company D, which was held in reserve through the twelfth. On the thirteenth the tankers were still in reserve when they had a taste of the future of warfare. As the men went about their daily duties, rested, worked on their tanks, shaved, and such, a peculiar noise came from the sky. To some it may have sounded like steam whining out of a large kettle. As a few looked skyward, all guesses were shattered when 30-mm rounds came pouring into the area, chewing up the street and disintegrating walls. Men dove for cover or scrambled underneath tanks, dropping whatever they had been doing. Just as quickly as it began, the firing stopped. The Americans were not under attack from tanks or artillery, but rather the Luftwaffe. As the aircraft banked and climbed into the sky, the men could see the flames from the jet engines under their wings. They had just been strafed by a handful of German Me 262s.

During one operation, the 2nd Platoon had a peculiar situation unfold before them. Its leader, a Lieutenant Shartel, was ordered to a "particular place on a map as indicated by the now famous 'Big Finger' method" in hopes of finding some infantry to link up with.[19] The tanks were on their way when they passed a few hundred soldiers in white snowsuits who were busy digging in. Searching and finding no other infantry, the 2nd Platoon returned, again passing the snow-suited troops. After returning, the platoon was receiving another briefing when information clarified that the snow-suited infantry were in fact Germans. At once the tankers loaded up and set off with supporting infantry. Upon reaching the dug-in troops, a firefight broke out, the result being 300 Germans killed.

Companies B and C at Schillersdorf

During the latter part of the month, the Germans took Muhlhausen and pushed through the Schillersdorf. On 25 January 1st Battalion, 410th Infantry Regiment, supported by Shermans from 1st Platoon, Company B, attacked Schillersdorf at 9:00 a.m. Tanks fired high-explosive shells into all houses that could have potentially held enemy panzerfaust teams. As the tanks crept through town, a lurking panzerfaust fired from the cellar of a destroyed house and struck one of them. The blast killed one crewman and wounded two others.

Simultaneous to this American attack, 2nd Battalion, 410th Regiment and 2nd Platoon, Company B, surprised a German column advancing from the north. Firing into the column inflicted several casualties and caused the enemy to retreat.

The 1st and 2nd Platoons joined together to support 1/410 as they cleared out Schillersdorf on the twenty-sixth. The 1st Platoon provided direct-fire missions, while 2nd Platoon moved in with the infantry. While Company B focused on direct support, Company C set up on the high ground west of the village to prevent any German units from escaping.

During January, the 781st Tank Battalion was not attached to the 100th Infantry Division, with which they had spent all of December 1944. It may not be coincidental that the tanks suffered heavy losses in January after being attached to a new infantry unit. Some have argued that maintaining a tank-infantry relationship between the same two units only strengthened the effectiveness of both. The soldiers and tankers build mutual respect, mold tactics, and learn each other's appropriate roles, capitalizing on their strengths. Both learn when armor should lead and when infantry should.

Again, training did not include joint operations. The only joint "training" the tankers had received was on the line, under fire, in Normandy—it was trial and error all the way. Infantrymen unwittingly guided tanks into fields where they bogged down or told them to advance down roads where they were knocked out by a panzerfaust. Tanks held their fire against enemy positions since no one had told them if they were in fact enemy positions. The combat history of the 743rd Tank Battalion recorded this snafu: "By the time [the] dirt-grimed tankers . . . had gone out to report that the[y] had arrived as ordered, the XIX Corps had already planned an attack for the 30th Infantry Division"; the corps commanders had totally failed to consider the tankers in their plan.[20]

Infantrymen and tankers agreed that they should be training together. Some urged that armor should be organic units within the infantry division. Since that would be impossible to organize overnight, most at least argued that long-term relationships between infantry and armor units were the best answer. The commander of the 745th Tank Battalion, Lt. Col. Wallace J. Nichols, noted in July 1944 that "through the practice of attaching each company of this battalion to one infantry regiment continuously, a more thorough understanding and closer cooperation has developed between infantry and tank personnel."[21] This sums up what most knew would be the best method for the tank-infantry team at that time.

18

Battalion Operations, February–March 1945

Great numbers of freed Russian, Greek, French, and Polish slave laborers appeared along the highway. Most of the displaced persons seemed bewildered by their sudden liberation from bondage by the onrushing Americans.

—Story of the Century

January had been a costly month for the 781st. February would provide a break from action but no opportunity for real rest. For the time being, the battalion was held in reserve, fulfilling a defensive role in a quiet area along the Seventh Army's front.

February 1945

While the remnants of Company A limped back from the front, some of the battalion's other companies had a few more tasks to perform before they took a break. On 2 February 2nd Platoon, Company B, again supported 2nd Battalion, 410th Infantry Regiment, on their small raid on Bischoltz, firing on enemy concentrations to the north of town.

The 781st was primarily attached to the 103rd Infantry Division for much of this month. Due to the fact that many infantry raids were not intended to hold ground, it was not viable to send in tanks. Even the smallest "mechanical failure . . . or bogging down due to soft terrain would have necessitated destruction [or] abandonment of valuable mechanized equipment."[1]

Because Company A had suffered such heavy losses in personnel and equipment, it was moved to the division's rear. In Steinbourg the unit focused on rehabilitation and the training of replacements. Its February report stated: "Tank replacements and personnel reinforcements were received in sufficient quantities to bring the company up to T/O&E strength during the period 1–23 February 1945, the company under battalion control conducted intensive training in tank gunnery, radio security and transmission, destruction of ordnance materiel, tank driving and many tactical field problems as a reconstitution program to bring company up to prescribed combat efficiency."

During this time, the battalion tested the idea of using tanks to tow 57-mm guns into close indirect-fire positions. Light tanks proved to be most practical "due to their quietness and maneuverability." As a result, a team composing one light platoon from Company D was used to tow one section of antitank guns. Ammunition for the guns was carried in trailers, while the antitank-gun commander rode in the platoon leader's tank.

During the second week of February, the battalion, working with division engineers, devised methods of preparing dug-in positions for armor. Tests included using bulldozers to clear a position with an appropriate parapet. In addition, engineers used TNT to simply blow large holes for the tanks to move into. Each method proved disappointing. The bulldozer took too much time, while the TNT did not provide the best cover or line of sight for fire; in addition, the fire positions created by the TNT acted more as a tank trap since the vehicles had trouble leaving them. Best results were obtained when both methods were combined. Engineers would blow a hole with TNT first, then bring in the bulldozer to finish it out and prepare an adequate parapet.

Company A was busy training its new men as well as developing new tactics for attacking (along with infantry) a defended town. The 781st dubbed this new fire-support technique "zone firing." Its method was as follows:

1. Tank platoon to establish base of fire moves into position approximately 45° to long axis of town.

2. Platoon laid reciprocally and base piece laid on some prominent building in town such as church steeple etc.

3. Using the mil formula, base piece is deflected either left or right through necessary number of mils to correspond to 100 yard intervals in the town.
4. These readings are then given to all guns of platoon allowing platoon to fire at any 100 yd sector desired or on call by use of azimuth indicator rather than indistinct target recognition. Smoking of town does not hinder gunners in this method of fire.
5. Infantry company commander establishes phase lines in town in 100 yd sectors for infantry advance. Phase lines conforming with those zones laid off by tank platoon.

> Proposed method has base platoon fire zone 1 & 2 prior to assault of infantry, shifting to zone 3 as infantry enters zone [1]. Length of time and zone to be fired, can be controlled by ground commander by either flares or use of SCR 300 radio. This allows tanks to continue pressure fire with a minimum time lag prior to arrival of infantry on objectives and its simplicity effects maximum control by infantry commander of supporting direct fire.

While the battalion replaced its lost tanks, Company A adopted two tanks, one M4A3 from Headquarters Company and one M4A3 from Company B. On January 27 Company A also received the battalion's first M4A3E8s.

March 1945

During the first two weeks of March, the battalion remained in reserve. No offensive missions were carried out, although the line companies assisted the 374th Artillery Battalion extensively with indirect-fire missions. When not throwing shells into German positions, the crews busied themselves with training and maintenance. Tanks that had been camouflaged with white paint during the winter received a fresh layer of olive drab as the men focused on preparing their machines and themselves for additional combat. "The Germans had thrown their Sunday punch, now we were going to throw ours."[2]

Field Maintenance

All crewmembers contributed to the maintenance of their tank. When the time was appropriate, the men would inspect the vehicle before and after movements, checking everything from the engine to their seatbelts. The jobs were divided among the crew, with each member responsible for a number of items.

The tank commander inspected all of his men's field equipment. After inspecting the crew, he would check the tracks and bogie systems of the tank. Mounting the vehicle, he would help the gunner with any necessary adjustments to the gunsight. Next, the commander was to swab all machine guns and the 75-mm gun. Moving to the rear of the tank, he checked the engine for leaks and the condition of the exhaust system. After checking his own personal equipment, including binoculars, safety belt, flag set, and submachine gun, he would dismount and instruct the driver to slowly move the tank forward one length, simultaneously observing the return wheels, suspension, and tracks of one side while the BOG inspected the other. The commander would then mount the tank again and check the workings of the radio and interphone system.

The gunner was responsible for the 75-mm gun. He manually traversed the turret 360 degrees and then made any necessary sight adjustments. He was also required to check numerous fluid levels, including the power-traverse and hydraulic oil, engine oil, and the gyrostabilizer oil and all of its connections. After this he would check the automatic and manual fire controls for the 75-mm gun and the coaxial machine gun. The gunner would then check his personal equipment, including submachine gun, elevation quadrant, periscope, and seatbelt. Lastly he would check the recoil mechanism and clean the chamber and breech of the 75-mm gun.

Primary responsibility for the engine fell to the BOG. After manually turning the engine over, which required fifty revolutions of the hand crank, he would inspect the ground under the tank, looking for any drips or puddles from fuel or oil leaks. Mounting the tank, the BOG then inspected the engine compartment for leaks, then checked drain valves and air cleaners. Afterward he would ask the driver to start the engine so he could observe its operation. With the engine checked out, the BOG would return to his position in the hull and look over his personal equipment, the .30-caliber machine gun and mount, his submachine gun, and each 75-mm round located beneath the turret. After inspecting his compartment, the BOG exited the tank and assisted the commander with examining the tracks and suspension.

The driver more or less stayed in his seat during inspection and maintenance. Before starting the engine, he would check his steering levers, the parking brake, and the clutch as well as a number of gauges in his direct vicinity, including the transmission and fuel gauge. He would then start the engine and hold it at 800 rpm, listening to it and checking the smoothness of operation. This was followed by examining his personal items, including manuals and his submachine gun. Then at the order of the commander, he would slowly move the tank forward for the inspection of the suspension and tracks.

The loader checked all equipment secured to the outside of the tank, including entrenching and mechanic's tools, tow cable, and camouflage netting. He then entered the turret and looked over every 75-mm round in the turret and in the sponsons. After inspecting the auxiliary generator, he checked the hull drain valves and fire extinguishers. Like the others, he examined his personal equipment, including the coaxial machine gun, personal submachine gun, radio, and seatbelt.

Two Weeks in March

During the beginning of March, the 100th Division held a line that ran from Petite Rederching to Goetzenbruck. The 781st had its companies in

Figure 53. A captain examines the firing mechanism for the flamethrower. *Courtesy National Archives and Records Administration, Washington DC*

Figure 54. A Sherman demonstrates its flame-throwing capability. While tactically limited, the flamethrower's psychological effect was arguably demoralizing to the enemy. *Courtesy National Archives and Records Administration, Washington DC*

Enchenberg, Soucht, Petite Rederching, and Montbron. With the exception of providing indirect-fire missions, the battalion continued maintenance and also worked on radio procedures.

On 6 March men gathered around to witness a demonstration by Headquarters Company. A Sherman rolled into the area approaching a mock enemy position. The tankers watched with anticipation, arms crossed. A jet of flame shot from the Sherman's bow, engulfing the target.

The tank's bow machine gun had been replaced with the E4–5 flamethrower. In approximately one minute the BOG could remove the flamethrower and reinsert his machine gun. The Sherman was equipped with a twenty-five-gallon tank that held a congealed-gasoline fuel, similar to napalm. This provided the gunner with approximately fifteen two-second bursts.

The tank-mounted flamethrower's effective range was listed at eighty yards but was more like twenty-five. As its targets were outlined as trenches, foxholes, and embrasures of bunkers, the E4–5 was an antipersonnel weapon. Shermans with flamethrowers were to lead the way during attacks to clear out enemy infantry. While flames would no doubt incinerate any soldier, it was not designed to target troops , but rather to encourage them to abandon their position. It was hoped to simply demoralize the enemy and cause him to retreat before he was consumed.

The flamethrower also offered the tankers “around the corner” firing possibilities. A gunner could potentially trigger a burst into an area behind or next to an enemy position, hoping the heat and smoke would drive him out. The problem for American armor was that the average effective range of the flamethrower was within that of panzerfausts, which made tankers hesitant to actually use the device. Furthermore, the installation of the E4–5 required the removal of the main-armament storage bins behind the BOG. The combined result was that these flamethrowers were not used extensively.

On 10 March the battalion worked on tank-infantry operations. During an exercise against the town of Ratzwiller, Headquarters Company’s tank section moved in with their E4–5s while a platoon from Company D towed 3-inch guns belonging to the 824th Tank Destroyer Battalion.

The 781st soon received word that VI Corps was going to mount an attack, and the 100th Division was again ordered to take the city of Bitche, a mission which had been abandoned in December 1944. The battalion’s companies were again attached to infantry regiments: Company A to the 399th, B to the 398th, and C to the 397th. The platoons were distributed to the infantry battalions as follows:

1/A–1/399	1/B–1/398	1/C–1/397
2/A–2/399	2/B–2/398	2/C–1/397
3/A–3/399	3/B–398 rsv.	3/C–3/397

The 2nd Platoon of Company D was attached to the 925th Field Artillery Battalion to provide security for the large 155-mm self-propelled howitzers.

Shortly after midnight on 14 March, “the whole Seventh Army front was one continuous flash and roar made by the thousands of pieces of artillery that started the Battle for Germany.”[3]

Bitche Revisited

During the early hours of 15 March, US infantrymen waited in their foxholes. In the darkness Shermans moved up to their line of departure. Infantry squads mounted the tanks as other troops filed in behind.

In order to secure the high ground north of Bitche, the 397th, with

Company C of the 781st, was ordered to move northeast toward Hotviller, 3.5 miles northwest of the fortified town. The force bypassed that village and continued east to the town of Schorbach, only 1.5 miles north of Bitche. Moving out at 5:00 a.m., the force reached the high ground north of Schorbach. At approximately noon Companies I and L of 3/397, assisted by tanks of 3/C, entered Schorbach. Simultaneously Companies A and B of the 1/397th continued east with ten tanks from the 1st and 2nd Platoons of Company C. This force moved east along the road for nearly 1.5 miles until it secured the junction with the Bitche–Hanviller road. The 397th had received little resistance from small arms but did take heavy fire from artillery, mortars, and rockets in the area. Due to lack of enemy small-arms support, many of the mortar and rocket positions were captured. The area north of Bitche was secure.

The 398th, with two platoons from Company B, moved in to secure the west end of Bitche. Second Battalion of the 398th, along with tanks from the 2nd Platoon, moved from Legeret. The infantry came under heavy

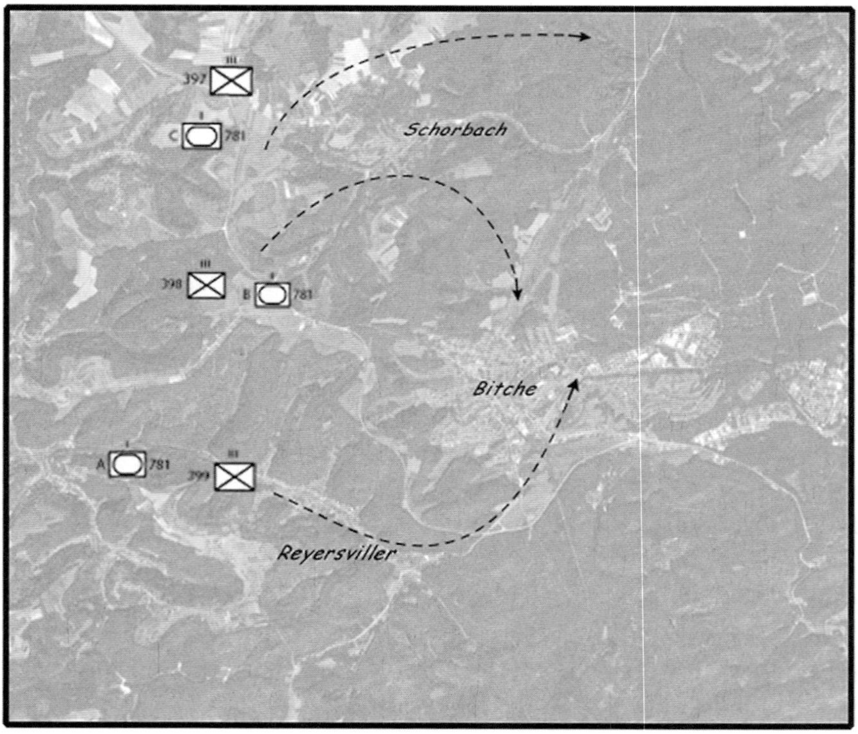

Figure 55. US attack on Bitche, March 1945.

small-arms fire, and mines hindered further advance by the armor. The 1st Battalion and Shermans from the 1st Platoon swung north into the hills commanding the area, bypassing the resistance. Antitank mines claimed two of the tanks, but the force continued until southeast of Schorbach and north of Bitche. After clearing mines and slowly pushing back pockets of German resistance, the 2nd Battalion pushed its way through to the old forts of Schiesseck and Freudenberg, which the Americans discovered had not been reoccupied due to the actions of the infantry engineers and tank dozers of the 781st months earlier.[4]

The 399th, with tanks from the three platoons of Company A supporting, was ordered to protect the division's right, or southern, flank. The 3rd Battalion took the area north of Reyersviller, which was situated in a valley that ran east–west on the southern doorstep of Bitche. While the 3rd Battalion had taken the commanding hills of the north side, the 2nd Battalion, along with tanks from the 2nd Platoon of Company A, moved in to take the south side of Bitche. The main assault force consisted of Company F and three tanks. This open area was heavily mined, resulting in casualties among the infantry. So while many of the troops climbed onto the Shermans, those who followed on foot were careful to stick to the ground that bore tank tracks.

Infantryman John C. Angier III recounted this attack years later. At 6:00 a.m. he was crouched behind the lead tank. Taking the field phone secured to its aft, he gave the order, "O.K. Let's go." After moving only twenty-five yards from the line of departure, the lead tank threw its tread. "Of all the fucking luck," Angier recalled thinking. He then ordered another tank up to his position. But the presence of armor was now bringing in heavy enemy fire. German shells began landing in the area, spraying some of the infantry with shell fragments, the men buckling and falling off the tanks. Others had the misfortune of being blown off a tank by the concussion only to land on mines a few feet away. As the two remaining Shermans pressed forward, both struck antitank mines. Their crews remained inside and fired through their ammunition before clambering out of the disabled vehicles and heading to the rear on foot. Angier remembered that "two [of these tankers] didn't make it because of the mines." Another tank from 2nd Platoon moved up to continue providing support as the infantry pressed on. It took the company nearly six hours to cross a distance of a thousand yards, reaching the edge of the hill to the south of Reyersviller.[5]

As companies from the 3/399 secured the surrounding hills, the battalion's executive officer "led a platoon of tanks into bypassed Reyersviller at 1300 [1:00 p.m.] and met no resistance."[6] The southern edge of Bitche was secure.

With the areas north and south under American control, the 398th Infantry entered Bitche at 6:20 a.m., encountering only four German rifleman. The 2/397 passed through 1/397 and moved east along the road that met the Bitche–Hanviller road in order to secure any northern escape route and to protect against possible counterattack.

At 7:00 a.m. 1st Platoon, Company A, attacked northeast into Bitche, entering the town after waiting for mines to be cleared. The infantrymen then spread out to mop up any resistance, though there was virtually none. Company A of the 399th passed through and started along the Bitche–Camp de Bitche road with Shermans of the 1st Section of 1st Platoon, Company A. The 2nd Section of 1st Platoon fell in with Company B of the 399th and moved down a road heading to the southeast.

As Company B headed out, its men dismounted the tanks and took cover as mortar shells began to come in. As the infantry spread out, they were fired upon by machine guns. Forward scouts radioed back the positions of two pillboxes, one with an armored turret, on a slope on the north side of the road. Two platoons of infantry fell in with the two Shermans on the south side to engage these strongpoints with a frontal assault.

The tanks moved in, firing high-explosive shells into the pillboxes and providing cover fire for the infantry. The real attack was coming from the 3rd Platoon maneuvering in from the north around the enemy. As the Shermans maintained their fire, troops moved in close enough to take out one of the positions with a well-placed bazooka shot. One German from the remaining pillbox came out at the threat of a grenade attack and was subsequently captured. This brought the remaining defenders out. The entire enemy force consisted of seventy men, all of whom were taken prisoner. The Americans had also captured the commander of 2nd Battalion, 225th Volksgrenadier Regiment.

While Company B organized its prisoners, roadblocks slowed Company A as it approached Camp de Bitche. The unit encountered little resistance until it reached the eastern edge of the settlement. There, four Tiger tanks and a number of self-propelled guns attacked from the northeast. Thankfully the commander of Company A knew the Shermans were of no use

Figure 56. Men of the 100th Infantry Division having passed through a dismantled roadblock on their way to Bitche. *Courtesy George C. Marshall Foundation*, *VMI*

Figure 57. A 781st tank rolls through Bitche. This Sherman was one of the battalion's M4A3E8(76)s. Its crew had welded brackets onto the sides and filled them with sandbags for extra protection. It also appears to be painted in camouflage. *Courtesy George C. Marshall Foundation*, *VMI*

against the panzers and ordered them to withdraw. As the Tigers came in, one infantryman scored a hit with a bazooka, blowing off a tread. Without adequate infantry support, the German armor declined to engage and continued off to the southeast, bypassing the Americans. This was the close of action around Bitche. Within the city, things were strangely quiet. Infantrymen checked houses while tanks and military police set up defensive positions at road junctions. Troops made their way into the commanding citadel to find it void of enemy positions. It appeared the Americans had taken Bitche—and they had. Angier recorded the troop's reaction: "How come we fight our asses off for four cold months and then we march through it and out the other side in ten minutes?" The reply—"Das ist der Krieg."[7]

On 18 March the 781st established its forward-command post in Bitche. The battalion staff, company commanders, and platoon leaders discussed the river crossings they might soon make.

Concerning Tanks

On 19 March Maj. Gen. Isaac D. White, commander of the 2nd Armored Division, received a letter from Supreme Allied Headquarters. It began:

> Dear General White:
>
> From time to time I find short stories where some reporter is purportedly quoting non-commissioned officers on our tank formation to the effect that our men, in general, consider our tanks very inferior in quality to those of the Germans.[8]

Signed by General Eisenhower himself, the full letter laid out his own viewpoint of armor as he had gathered from his "casual" conversations with junior officers and enlisted men. What he wanted from White were firsthand opinions of the tanks from "tank commanders, drivers, gunners, and so on." The fact that Eisenhower asked White to mark his reply "personal" emphasizes the supreme Allied commander's concern.

White was punctual with his reply, having his report ready the next day. After brief formalities, the division commander wrote: "I have also included a large number of the actual statements made by [the soldiers]. Allowing for the traditional enthusiasm displayed by the American soldier when he is given (or takes!) the opportunity to express himself in regard to any possible shortcomings in his rations, clothing, and equipment, I think they are sincere, reasonably factual, indicate considerable thought and knowledge of the subject, and above all they are most refreshing."

The general felt that much of the disapproval would not have surfaced had armor units been equipped with a larger percentage of M4A3E8s. By the time of his report, White stated that only "two or three" of his E8s had seen combat. Regarding the M4A3s, only 29 percent of them were equipped with 76-mm guns. Furthermore, only four rounds of the HVAP ammunition were allotted to each of those tanks. Worst of all, the 76-mm gun "even with the HVAP" ammunition was not effective against enemy armor at the typical ranges they were encountered. White personally felt that the Easy Eights were as good as the German tanks in terms of speed and maneuverability.

As per request from White, Brig. Gen. J. H. Collier, then commanding Combat Command A, wrote a report concerning the consensus of opinion from members of the 66th Armored Regiment. He forwarded their messages to the major general, stating that German tanks had

Better flotation
Greater mobility
Higher muzzle velocity with no muzzle flash
Better sights
Better sloped armor
Better silhouettes

Collier concluded, writing candidly, "the fact that our equipment must be shipped over long distances does not, in the opinion of our tankers, justify our inferiority. The M4 [had] proven inferior to the [Tiger] in Africa before the invasion of Sicily." He took advantage of this analysis assignment by closing, "press reports of statements by high-ranking officers to the effect that we have the best equipment in the world do much to discourage the soldier who is using equipment that he knows to be inferior to that of the enemy."

The commander of Combat Command B, Col. S. R. Hinds, made a similar report, though it teetered on the edge of fiction. He declared that the successful engagements against the enemy were "not due to any means of a superior tank, but to our superior numbers of tanks . . . and the willingness of our tankers to take their losses while maneuvering to a position from which a penetrating shot can be put through a weak spot of the enemy tank." Yet it is difficult to imagine a tanker "willing" to take casualties—the fact that these grievances had reached the concerned ears of the supreme Allied commander attests to this.

Other commanding officers in response to White added that while the Shermans were, by doctrine, not to engage enemy armor, they felt that almost every offensive action thus far had resulted in their encountering panzers.

Lt. Col. Wilson Hawkins of the 67th Armored Regiment remembered his experience in Tunisia. Upon examining American tanks there, he found that nearly every one was lacking gouges in its armor, indicating that all hits had penetrated the steel. Therefore, he felt that a new tank should be designed to meet new standards of firepower and armor protection. These suggestions, after all, "were told to representatives of the War Department and Ordnance representatives almost two years ago." The tankers were impatient.

In contrast, on the same day that White received his letter from Eisenhower, Lieutenant General Patton recorded his own observations concerning the Sherman:

> Since 1 August 1944 when the Third Army became operational, our total tank casualties have amounted to 1,136 tanks. During the same period we have accounted for 2,287 German tanks, of which 808 were the Tiger or Panther variety, and 851 on our side were the M4. These figures themselves refute any inferiority of our tanks, but let me add that the Third Army has always attacked, and therefore better than 70 percent of our tank casualties have occurred from dug-in AT gun and not enemy tanks, whereas a majority of the enemy tanks have been put out by our tanks.
>
> In the current operation had the 4th Armored Division been equipped with Tiger and Panther tanks, and been required to make the move, from Sarreguemines to Arlon then through to Bastogne, from Bastogne to the Rhine, and now to Mainz, it would have been necessary to re-armor it twice; and furthermore, it would have had, if not insurmountable, difficulty in crossing rivers.
>
> Finally, we must remember that all our tanks have to be transported on steamers, and the difference in 40 tons and 70 tons is very marked. The 70-ton tank could never have been brought ashore in landing boats as many of our medium tanks were. Nor could they

> have marched from the Contentin Peninsula to the Rhine as practically all of our tanks have been required to do.[9]

Both perspectives on the Sherman are valid, so the question expands into a matter of the cost in human lives. From a bird's-eye view (strategic), as Patton stressed, it is clear that the American tank was worthy of praise. But from the worm's-eye view (to use Ernie Pyle's term)—the driver, the gunner, and other crewmembers—the Sherman was lacking in various tactical necessities, including armor and firepower.

The Sherman's worthiness as a weapon has been questioned since it first arrived in North Africa. But as shown above, there is no easy answer. What is often overlooked during the scrutiny of the Sherman is its strategic and tactical role. Too often tanks are compared simply by their firepower, armor, and mobility. But these arguments neglect context, not only of intended purpose but also of the larger military operations in which they are used. In theory the Shermans were not to engage enemy armor. Yet the Allies were on the offensive—attacking—and encountering enemy tanks operating defensively (or counterattacking) was unavoidable. So one must consider the role that the Allies' military situation played in the Sherman's perceived shortcomings.

First one must recognize the advantages of a defender, which includes selection of position, which usually provides an advantage in both cover and visibility. These components allow for the third and most significant advantage, which is the increased potential of initiating the engagement—that is, achieving the "First to Fire" (FF) advantage. In this regard, the Ballistic Research Laboratories (BRL) of Aberdeen Proving Ground issued a study of tank engagements involving the 3rd or 4th Armored Divisions.[10]

This report examined the beneficial effects of FF. Using data collected from fifty-seven engagements in which the *defenders* achieved FF, they lost 22 weapons out of 238—a loss rate of 9.2 percent.[11] Yet data collected from sixty-eight engagements in which they did not achieve FF, they lost 154 of 397 weapons—a loss rate of 38.8 percent. This variance of 29.6 percent between the two cases provides a strong correlation between FF and a lower loss rate.

Similarly, the report also investigated the effects of the *attackers* achieving FF. In the engagements examined, offensive units that failed to achieve FF experienced a 46.9 percent loss rate. In contrast, those that did achieve FF experienced a loss rate of only 13.6 percent. So even when attacking, a unit that fired on its enemy first statistically reduced its loss rate by 33.3 percent. To this extent, while Patton argued that his force's lower loss rates were a result of their constantly attacking, it may also be that they were achieving FF with their offensive movements—hitting the enemy before they had a chance to regroup and dig in. Rommel also noted this advantage in 1940 within the first few days of the invasion of France. In a letter to his wife, he explained that typically "the day goes to the side that is the first to plaster it[s] opponent with fire. . . . Observation of this rule, in my experience, substantially reduces one's own casualties."[12]

Another variable in the armor-combat study is the range in which the fighting took place. While the scope of the data in the BRL report is limited to averages, it is interesting to note the similarity in ranges at which Allied and German tanks were knocked out. While many of the American vehicles were lost from enemy fire beyond a range of 1,000 yards, the *average* range of the 199 recorded losses was 946 yards. Surprisingly, the 140 German panzers lost were knocked out at an *average* range of 893 yards.[13]

Arguably, the FF advantage can be found within the experience of the 781st Tank Battalion. The most obvious example was at Sessenheim, where four German heavy tanks attained FF against eight Shermans. The fact that these panzers were classified as "heavy" presents another variable in the case. Regardless, the smaller German force opened fire on the larger American force, suffering no losses while inflicting 100 percent losses on the attacking tanks. Another example occurred at Heilbronn, Germany (discussed in chapter 19), when 781st tanks achieve FF against four Mark IVs, knocking out one and causing the remaining three to withdraw. Again, Rommel wrote about this tactic, claiming that his experience "showed that in tank attacks especially, the action of opening fire immediately into the area which the enemy is believed to be holding, instead of waiting until several of one's own tanks have been hit, usually decides the issue."[14]

In most cases the 781st Battalion's losses were the results of mines or panzerfausts. While panzerfausts were infantry weapons and therefore not considered in the BRL report on armor engagements, they do fit within the scope of the FF discussion. The ability to conceal these weapons permitted the soldier to go undetected and therefore open fire at his discretion. It would be nearly impossible for a tank crew to locate and eliminate such a concealed threat. But supporting infantry and prophylactic cannon and machine-gun fire from the tank, targeting conspicuous foliage or buildings, would deny most soldiers with an antitank weapon the FF advantage. In basic terms, the more likely a force can achieve FF, the more likely it can maintain its active control of the engagement. Similarly, the force that fails to do so is more likely to be forced into a reactive role and thus less likely to attain control.

Germany

After the fall of Bitche, the tank platoons were sent out on reconnaissance missions to link up with units of the 3rd Infantry Division, which had broken through the Siegfried Line at Zwebrüken, fifteen miles to the north. Some platoons advanced into Germany between 18 and 21 March, but it was on the twenty-first that Service Company became the first company-sized unit to set up headquarters on German soil in the city of Brenchelbach. The unit history recorded that on 22 March, "Battalion forward CP established first headquarters in Germany at [Thaleischweiler]," roughly ten miles east of Zwebrüken.[15]

As the tanks rumbled through the country and into Zwebrüken, which "was a pile of smoldering ruins," the men of the 781st saw "table cloths, sheets, underwear—anything that looked like a white flag—hung out the windows." One of the most memorable sights was "the streams of men and women moving down the roads toward France. They were French, Dutch, Belgian, Polish, and Russian. They had been brought from all over Europe to work as slaves of the mighty war machine. Like slaves they wore little tags to show which was a Pole, a Russian or a Belgian. They seemed never to grow tired of telling of the three, four, or five years of being pushed around by German soldiers and civilians, of not being able to go to church or the movies, or buy new clothes, or have a vacation; of four or five years wondering where their families were; or remember how their homes had been burned and their children murdered by the conquering Wehrmacht."[16]

The official story of the 100th Division painted a similar picture with greater detail: "Great numbers of freed Russian, Greek, French and Polish slave laborers appeared along the highway. Most of the DPs [displaced persons] seemed bewildered by their sudden liberation from bondage by the onrushing Americans. . . . A Stocky Russian girl with a bright red bandana covering her head and carrying an infant in her arms, paused to rest against an embankment. . . . From around a bend in the road came the sound of a horn blowing a clarion call of victory and a confiscated

German truck loaded with French men and women and with the Tricolor dancing on a rough, wooden staff lashed to the bumper, careened down the road toward France and freedom." Sights such as these only helped drive the liberating army. The 100th Division writer closed the scene, noting that watching the refugees "made the cold and the blood and the death and the inhuman hardships we had suffered seem worthwhile." And so—the tanks rolled on.[17]

On 22 March the 100th Division, along with the 781st, was attached to XXI Corps. On the twenty-third the armor convoy raced through the country toward the Rhine. The only impediments to the tanks as they sped from Zwebrüken to Ludwigshafen were blown bogie wheels, a testament to the rapidity of the advance, otherwise they were well fueled and well oiled. By midafternoon Ludwigshafen became visible. The battalion had outrun its supply dumps (now far to the rear), but Service Company drove day and night up to the line companies, keeping the tanks fueled and the men fed.

As the 100th Division closed in around Ludwigshafen, the 399th Regiment ran in to elements of the 94th Infantry Division coming down from the north. The 94th had moved in to clear the city. Then in the early hours of 24 March, tanks of 1st Platoon, Company A, entered with the 399th Infantry to help mop up any resistance. Light tanks from 1st Platoon, Company D, arrived as well, driving all the way to the Rhine. For the next few days, the 781st was dispersed among the units of the 100th Division to run patrols, harassed only by some sniper fire and occasional artillery.

On 25 March the 100th and the 781st passed to control of VI Corps and were held in reserve. For the next few days, the battalion focused on maintenance, training, and recreation. Though in reserve, the infantrymen and tankers were to be ready to move on twenty-four-hour's notice. And on 31 March—they moved.

The tanks were fired up, and the men were indifferent to the cool air. Commanders stood in huddles, pouring over maps in a casual fashion, as gunners and loaders waited, looking on from their vehicles. The commanders soon trotted back and climbed aboard. The tanks were put into gear and crawled through the streets of shattered Ludwigshafen. The columns made their way through the rubble toward the Rhine. Flying low in the overcast sky were P-47s, providing an umbrella of protection. While the drivers watched the military police and followed their signals and directions, other crewmembers looked out at the murky river. A steady stream of traffic moved across the pontoon bridge through clouds of artificial fog that hovered over the water. Eight hundred feet on the other side lay another shattered city—Mannheim. Drivers focused, and men who could not swim prayed, as trucks, tanks, jeeps, and vehicles of all kinds crossed the river on a floating bridge that strained under the weight.

Passing through Mannheim, the 100th and the 781st turned south to relieve elements of the 63rd Infantry Division.

19

Battalion Operations, April–May 1945

I hope that's the last damned time I get into a tank that's got a life preserver on it.

—Tank commander, Company A, 781st Tank Battalion

There was no hunting for eggs on Easter Sunday, 1 April 1945—at least not in Mannheim, Germany. Chaplains set up where they could, be it in the surrounding woods or the fragile, burned-out churches of the city. To most of the men, however, it was simply another day of war. While many GIs took communion, most made sure they had a full magazine, locked and loaded, as they prepared to press against an enemy beginning to buckle under the weight of the US Army.

The 100th Division and the 781st attacked south from Mannheim. The 63rd Division guarded their left while the Rhine protected their right. Spearheading the attack was the 10th Armored Division. Speed was essential as to "prevent the reorganization of the defeated German forces."[1]

Company A's 1st and 3rd Platoons were attached to the 1st and 2nd Battalions of the 399th Infantry Regiment, which attacked south. The combined force moved toward Hockenheim, meeting no resistance.

Company C's 1st Platoon supported the 1st Battalion of the 397th Regiment, on the 399th's left flank, in pushed south toward Walldorf. They too met no opposition.

On the left side of the attack, heading southeast from Eppelheim, was the 2nd Battalion of the 397th Infantry, supported by the 2nd and 3rd Platoons of Company C. As this group moved south, they were hit by a "terrific artillery barrage." The two platoons engaged the enemy positions, each platoon expending approximately one hundred rounds of 75-mm high explosive. Two of the ten tanks were immobilized by mud, and one was knocked out by a mine. Light tanks from Company D moved up to assist in the attack. With the remaining seven medium tanks, they advanced with the infantry to take the towns of Sandhausen, Nussloch, Saint Ilgen, and Weisloch. Meanwhile, 1/397 advanced nearly ten miles with 1st Platoon, Company C. Encountering only limited small-arms fire, they continued into Walldorf at 11:45 a.m. There they captured 337 prisoners, two hospitals, a battery of howitzers, three buildings of weapons and ammunition, a searchlight and radar unit, and a gestapo headquarters.

Ten miles south, the light tanks of 1st Platoon, Company D, were given the mission of linking up with French units working down the west bank of the Rhine. The 399th Infantry, along with Company D tanks, finally made contact with them opposite the French beachhead near Speyer. This meeting was the first link between American and French forces on the east side of the Rhine.

Heilbronn

As the 100th Division and the 781st rolled up to Heilbronn, the Germans dug in their heels. Before reaching the city, 1/399 with tanks from Company A ran up against stiff resistance on the outskirts of Gemmingen, ten miles west of Heilbronn. The Germans had set up defensive positions in the woods and on the hills commanding the area and brought heavy mortar and artillery fire on the battalion. The infantry dismounted their vehicles and tanks and proceeded on foot, advancing slowly over the open ground as supporting armor provided covering fire. But they faced stubborn defenders, whose positions controlled the road from Gemmingen to Heilbronn. Nevertheless, the Americans closed in, and as the 100th Division recorded, the "coordinated tank-infantry attack proved too much for the enemy."[2]

The other battalions of the regiment moved in with their armor support and cleared out the other towns leading to Heilbronn. That city provided the Germans a perfect place for a last-ditch defense, with the Neckar River to the west and higher ground overlooking the city from the east. They had blown up the four bridges leading into town.

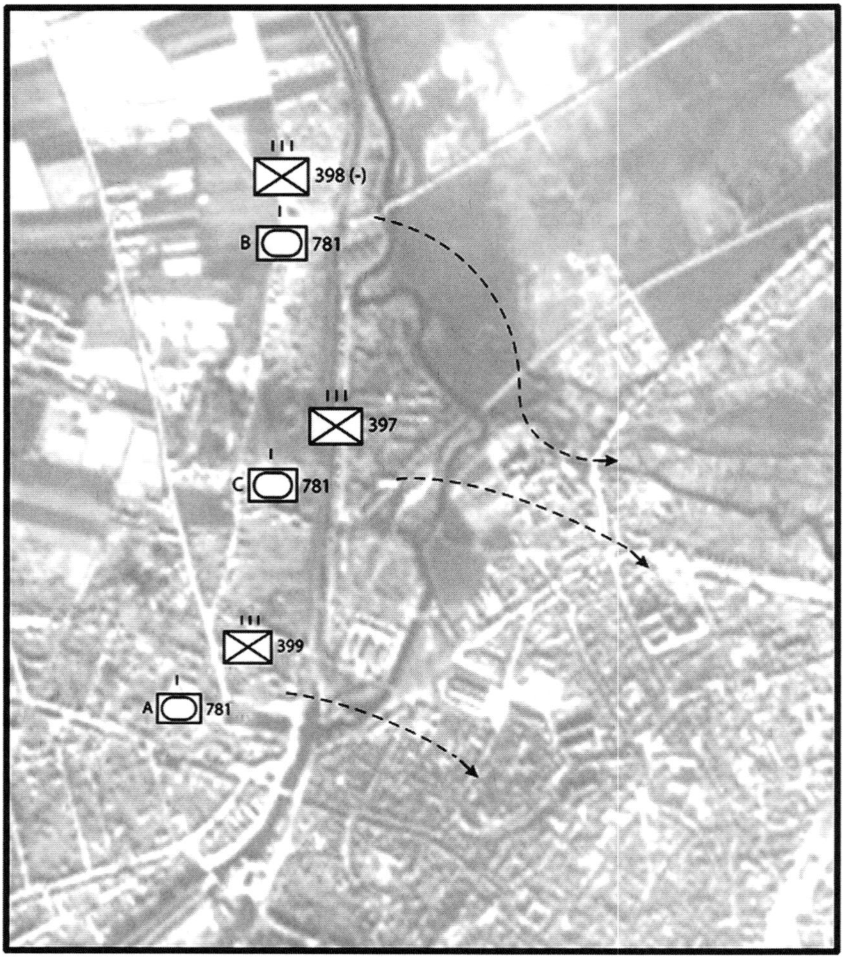

Figure 58. US attack on Heilbronn, April 1945.

Maj. Gen. Withers A. Burress, commander of the 100th Infantry Division, had a tough nut to crack. His orders were to protect the right flank of the advancing Seventh Army. His own right flank was supposed to be protected by the French units, but they were lagging behind. This exposure of his right prevented Burress from enveloping Heilbronn with wide attacks around the city. As he made plans to cross the river farther north, he was interrupted by VI Corps orders to send in an infantry battalion to assist the 10th Armored Division, which had moved in against Heilbronn from the north.

That night Burress sent in 3/398 with tanks from Company B. Temporarily detached to the 10th Armored, this force took up positions in Neckargartach, located on the north side of the city. There the infantry and armor looked across the river for signs of enemy activity. A soft rain combined with a silent city housing a lurking enemy nagged at the minds of the Americans, who knew they would have to cross the river.

At 3:00 a.m. on 4 April, Company K of 3/398 crept into fourteen assault boats along with engineers from the 10th Armored Division. Silently they paddled, having three hundred feet to cross until they reached the east bank, which was commanded by a large power plant. Only after landing did a sniper's shot ring out. The entire company took refuge in the power plant as Companies L and I made their way across the river. The entire battalion completed the crossing in one hour.

At dawn the soldiers began to move out to take up positions in the hills in the northeast of the city. As the force advanced, they were met by a German counterattack. The situation deteriorated as the Germans threw everything against 3rd Battalion, using underground tunnels to take up positions behind (and within) the American positions. The battalion was soon cut off and taking heavy casualties. To make matters worse, the 10th Armored Division was relieved of its mission against Heilbronn and ordered to move north.

With the Germans in position between the 3rd Battalion and the river, Burress knew that any attempt at withdrawing them would be met with disaster. Furthermore, he knew that giving ground to the enemy now would make any future attempts at the city much more difficult. He decided to send in help.

At 2:00 p.m. 2/397 began to cross the river in the assault boats. By 5:40 p.m. the battalion was across. As the infantry took stock of the situation, they began to call in fire support. The tanks of Company C moved in and provided direct fire support against German positions across the river.

On the fifth all attempts made by the engineers to build pontoon bridges were met with precise enemy artillery fire, inflicting many casualties. The tanks, stuck on the west side of the river, could only provide limited direct fire. To furnish artillery support, two tanks from Headquarters Company maneuvered to a position northwest of Heilbronn. They would not be firing 75-mm high-explosive shells. Instead they had nearly a hundred rockets to send into the city.

Figure 59. A T34-equipped Sherman of Headquarters Company, 781st Tank Battalion, prepares to move into position. *Courtesy George C. Marshall Foundation, VMI*

T34 Rocket Launchers

The T34 rocket launcher was a multibarreled platform mounted above the turret of a Sherman. Nicknamed the Calliope, the T34 was held on by two support arms fastened onto the turret. An elevation rod for the launcher connected to the tank's gun tube. This allowed the gunner to use his existing controls in the turret to control elevation and lateral movement for the rockets.

Sixty firing tubes held 4.5-inch high-explosive rockets.[3] The electric firing mechanism allowed for these to be launched at about two rounds per second either in one long volley or individually. The launchers were not accurate but were still psychologically effective, firing sixty large-caliber rockets in thirty seconds.

Once the two T34-equipped Shermans were in position, they unleashed ninety-six rockets into Heilbronn. This barrage, combined with division field artillery, gave effective support to the infantry hanging on to their positions on the east side of the river.

That night, engineers constructed a pontoon ferry concealed by a riverside house, with the plans of taking armor across the river. Early in the morning on 6 April, Company C attempted to use the ferry. The first tank from 2nd Platoon loaded up, slowly moved across the river, and successfully reached the opposite side. There the acting ferrymen ran into

Figure 60. The Sherman provided the army with a single fighting platform that served many different roles, including bombardment with the T34 Calliope rocket launcher. *Courtesy National Archives and Records Administration, Washington DC*

trouble, however, when they were unable to secure the ferry's ramps onto the riverbank. The tank commander then had his Sherman drive off the ramps and at first managed to begin climbing the soft embankment. But the treads could not gain traction. At this point "the ferry, unbalanced, listed and gave way, plunging the tank into the river."[4] Maybe in an effort to try again, the engineers pulled the ferry back. Before it returned to the west bank, though a German artillery shell scored a direct hit and obliterated it. Engineers could only watch as pieces of the ferry floated downstream.

There were no more armor-crossing attempts at the river that day. Most of the tanks could only provide fire support as it was called in by the infantry. The platoons of Company B fired a combined total of 160 rounds of high explosives while the two Calliope tanks launched an additional 105 rockets into the city.

Meanwhile, on 6 April the Germans who had infiltrated behind the Americans in Heilbronn began firing on the engineers and infantry crossing the Neckar in the small assault boats. Tanks of 1st Platoon, Company C, were brought down to the river's edge to provide direct fire into these enemy positions on the other side. As the tankers focused on the houses across the river, a German self-propelled gun moved up. Before the Shermans could pull back, the gun found their range and sent a shell through one of them. The four remaining tanks pulled back.

At this time, Company A was moved to a small city fifteen miles northwest of Heilbronn to receive new equipment—ten Duplex Drive tanks.

Duplex Drive Tanks

In preparation for the landings in Normandy, planners had looked to the ongoing development of amphibious armor. They hoped that these tanks could land with the first waves and provide immediate artillery support. Since the landings, the Duplex Drive (DD) tanks had been used in many amphibious operations in Europe, whether beach assaults or river crossings.

The DD tanks were the final product of British engineer Nicholas Straussler, who started working on the idea as far back as 1927. After the war began in 1939, he and others carried out experiments with a number of models. Designs were eventually limited to using Shermans due to their standardization and available numbers.

Progress was made by welding a deck onto the hull just above the tracks. A heavy rubberized canvas skirt was fastened to a collapsible frame built out from the decking. Attached to this were thirty-six vertical rubber tubes that, when inflated by air tanks, would raise the canvas up beyond the height of the turret. Once in the water, the tank held nearly three feet of freeboard.[5] Propulsion was attained by attaching a gear mechanism to the idler wheels that would spin two propellers, driving the tank slowly through the water.

The crews of the 1st and 3rd Platoons of Company A had less than twenty-four hours to work with their new swimming Shermans before being called to action. On 7 April the DD tanks made their way down to the Neckar. At the bank the crews inflated their canvas hulls and engaged the propellers. Slowly the tanks approached the river's edge. The first eased its way into the water and began its slow approach to the opposite bank. Successfully reaching the other side, it then struggled to gain traction. While the riverbanks were not necessarily steep, the grade below the surface had been dredged to permit shipping traffic. The angle of the submerged bank was too steep for the Sherman, and during the struggle

Figure 61. A Duplex Drive tank makes its way into a river with its canvas up. *Courtesy George C. Marshall Foundation, VMI*

Figure 62. A crew from A Company, 781st Tank Battalion, becomes familiar and frustrated with the Duplex Drive tank. *Courtesy George C. Marshall Foundation, VMI*

it faltered and sank. After two more DD tanks suffered similar fates, the operation was called off. A Lieutenant Sloggatt, commanding one of the Shermans, declared, "I hope that's the last damned time I get into a tank that's got a life preserver on it." It would be the last time anyone had to climb into a swimming tank as this small operation was the last time DDs were used in the war.[6]

Company D had been patrolling along the west side of the river. During one of these patrols, the tanks ran into heavy small-arms fire that had an infantry unit pinned down. Shermans from Company C were ordered into the action. Rushing forward, five medium tanks passed through the American infantry, who in turn were reluctant to get up and support the tanks—that is until one infantryman jumped up from his position and shouted for the others to follow. At first, only a few did so, but eventually his whole company filed in behind the armor. The infantryman who rallied his troops was Pfc. Mike Colalillo, who opened up with his M3 grease gun until it was hit by shell fragments. Not to be stopped, he then boarded one of the light M5s and asked the commander for permission to use the .30-caliber machine gun on the turret. Permission granted, he began firing at the enemy positions. He knocked out a few machine guns and

Figure 63. Members of the 31st Engineer Combat Battalion construct a pontoon bridge across the Neckar River. *Courtesy George C. Marshall Foundation, VMI*

wounded or killed more than a dozen Germans. When the machine gun jammed, Colalillo borrowed a submachine gun from the tank and took charge on foot. The M5s fired at least two hundred rounds of high explosive and five thousand rounds of machine-gun ammunition and, having expended all of their ammunition, began to pull back. Private Colalillo decided to accompany them. On his way he spotted one of his squad leaders, who had been severely wounded. Risking his life under heavy mortar and artillery fire, he aided the NCO and brought him back to safety. For his actions, Colalillo was awarded the Medal of Honor—one of only 198 recipients from World War II who lived.[7]

During a lull in the fighting, the engineers went to work constructing a pontoon bridge. When they were nearly finished, tanks began to assemble along the bank in preparation to cross. But German artillery observers, patiently waiting while peering through field glasses, must have grinned at the engineers' vain endeavor. Just before the span's completion, artillery shells rained in and obliterated the bridge.

Meanwhile, the 100th Division's men remained under constant attack. Though most of their artillery zeroed in on the riverbanks to prevent further US crossings, the Germans used their heavy machine guns and panzers to attack the small foothold on the eastern side of the Neckar.

During the night of 7–8 April, with heavy overcast, the engineers again went to work to build a bridge across the river. Finally succeeding in this task, during the early morning hours all three platoons of Company C, 781st, crossed the bridge and entered Heilbronn. But as before, the German shells poured in beginning at 11:30 a.m., again destroying the pontoon bridge. As one man put it, "Now you see it, now you don't!"[8] But the US infantry in Heilbronn now had an armor company to provide close support.

Company C moved into the rubble of the city and linked up with the infantry. The troops were sheltered in cellars and in the ruins. Gaping holes had been blown in walls, roofs had collapsed, and bricks, stones, and twisted metal littered the streets. Everywhere German and American troops dashed in and out of the skeletons of buildings. Shermans rolled up to spray structures with machine-gun fire and pummel them with high-explosive rounds. All of the debris of destruction provided the defenders, Americans and Germans alike, excellent cover. One Company C tank was inching forward, providing cover for the infantry, when it was knocked out by a well-placed panzerfaust shot.

The bridgehead in the city was eventually widened as the infantry and supporting tanks moved through. Fighting block by block, clearing out small pockets of resistance, they pressed east. Doing so, they eventually pushed out the German artillery observers, which hampered and finally denied enemy artillery the eyes necessary for effective shelling along the river. Another pontoon bridge was completed, and Companies A and B of the 781st joined Company C in Heilbronn.

Company A supported the 399th Infantry, Company B supported the 398th, and Company C moved in with the 397th. On 9 April Headquarters Company fired approximately 100 rounds of 75-mm high explosive, 150 rounds of 105-mm high explosive, and ten rounds of smoke. Combined with the fires of the divisional and attached artillery units, the 781st's fires prevented many German counterattacks from gaining ground. The main

Figure 64. A crew from the 781st relaxes on the west side of the Neckar River, across from Heilbronn, after the pontoon bridges had once again been destroyed. Note the 76-mm gun on the Sherman and its sandbag protection. Also visible are the "duckbills" connected to the tracks. *Courtesy George C. Marshall Foundation, VMI*

Figure 65. A Sherman from the 781st among the ruins of Heilbronn. This tank is also fitted with sandbags. Note the commander's split hatch and the 75-mm gun. *Courtesy George C. Marshall Foundation, VMI*

Figure 66. Engineers operate a ferry across the Neckar River. *Courtesy George C. Marshall Foundation, VMI*

Figure 67. Heilbronn had suffered heavily from aerial bombing. *Courtesy George C. Marshall Foundation, VMI*

guns were also responsible for razing buildings housing enemy machine guns. Often a Sherman would send 75-mm rounds into a structure, causing the Germans inside to dash out, only to be cut down by infantry mortars and machine guns.

One method for dealing with strong enemy resistance among this street fighting was for the tanks to send rounds into the lower quarters of a building, blasting holes big enough for infantry to move in. Tankers could also use their machine guns to spray through windows while supporting troops closed in to clear out a position.

On 11 April the battalion continued to support the infantry with close fire support. The day before the Germans had brought in three or four Mark IVs, which were soon taken on by divisional artillery and the 75-mm and 76-mm guns of the Shermans. The panzers pulled back, though not before one of them was struck and caught fire.

Company A was pulled off the line and spent three days practicing for future amphibious operations with the DD tanks. Heilbronn was now securely in Allied hands, as were 1,500 German prisoners of war.

Landsberg

Through the month of April, the 781st Tank Battalion supported the advance of the infantry as the Seventh Army continued to press through Germany.

On 23 April the 781st was detached from the 100th Infantry Division and attached to the 103rd Infantry Division. The next day Company B was attached to the 410th Infantry Regiment, while both Companies A and C supported the 411th Infantry Regiment. Company D was attached to the 409th Infantry Regiment.

On 26 April the advance of the 103rd and 781st brought them the Danube River in the vicinity of Ulm. Having to wait for the construction of a bridge in order to cross, the crewmen busied themselves attending to much-needed service on their tanks. The following day the infantry and supporting armor crossed the Danube and headed southeast.

As generals and officers poured over maps to plan their routes, the soldiers of the 103rd Infantry Division noted the city about twenty-five miles west of Munich—Landsberg. After Adolf Hitler had been arrested following his unsuccessful "Beer Hall Putsch" in Munich in the 1920s, he was sentenced to five years for high treason and sent to Landsberg Prison. He would only serve nine months, but during that time he composed much of his manifesto, *Mein Kampf*. Many of the men anticipated entering the city that had such close ties to Hitler. It would be a personal as much as a strategic victory to them, further pushing the führer's reign into the annals of history. But as the Americans moved in, word began to spread of something else, "something more important than Hitler's clink," recalled the 781st's unit history.[9]

When the 103rd Infantry Division entered Landsberg, they approached the prison only to discover a new element of the war—in its courtyard were stacks of dead bodies. Soldiers, covering their noses at the odor and cringing at the sight, noticed that these were not uniformed men, nor were they civilians killed in the fighting. These were different. They were the emaciated remains of hundreds of people who had withered to little more than skin and bones. Landsberg Prison had been a concentration camp.

The battalion's official history recorded that Company C (attached to the 411th Infantry Regiment) bore witness to the atrocity: "Many of the inmates were so weak with hunger they couldn't get out of their bunks. Some who were able to walk went to a medic's jeep and started to eat packages of three-inch bandages thinking they were food."[10]

The end of April brought all units of the 781st and the 103rd Infantry Division to Garmisch and Partenkirchen. Over the following days, contact with the enemy had been constant, though it was usually initiated by white flags waving out of windows or white handkerchiefs being dangled from behind a street corner. Nazi Germany was collapsing.

During the month of April, Company D turned in five of its light M5A1s in exchange for five of the new M24 tanks. The era of the 37-mm gun was officially over.

Light M24

The light tank had taken a backseat in favor of the medium tank in both role and numbers. As the army came up against German armor in North Africa and Europe, the light tank was all but obsolete. Its most significant deficiency was lack of firepower.

What was to become the M24 light tank retained the twin V-9 Cadillac engine that had been in the light M5, but most every other part of the M5 series was left on the shelf.

Initial plans called for a 75-mm gun in the turret of the M5A1. After unsuccessful attempts at this, designs shifted to a new tank altogether. Cadillac went to work on producing a light tank to weigh under twenty tons that would be outfitted with a 75-mm gun. Initially looking to use the existing M3 gun (as mounted in the Sherman), to save weight production moved ahead with a lighter 75-mm originally designed for the H model of the B-25 Mitchell bomber. In contrast to that of the M5A1, the new turret was wider, providing the crew more space. The armor of the M24 was sloped, presenting a sleek, low profile offering better protection to the crew.

While the M5A1 used 11.5-inch outside-guide tracks, the M24 used 16-inch center-guide tracks that provided much better off-road mobility. The suspension was also improved. Whereas the M4 and M5s were using the volute systems, the M24 featured a much more durable torsion-bar system with five medium-sized road wheels, similar to what had also been adapted on the M18 motor carriage.

The pilot model of the M24 was delivered in October 1943, and production began in 1944. The first of these new tanks arrived in Europe that November. But the numbers were slow since only the Cadillac and Massey-Harris production lines made M24s; many units, including divisions, would not receive them until after the war. Company D's tankers were happy to switch to the M24 as it gave them a tremendous jump in firepower and at least a small chance against enemy armor.

On 1 May the 781st, with a platoon from the 107th Cavalry Squadron and one squad of the 328th Engineer Battalion, moved against the towns of Krunn and Wallgau, less than ten miles from the Austrian border. There they were ordered to establish roadblocks north and east of Wallgua and east of Krunn in order to prevent enemy probes against the 103rd Infantry Division's northern flank.

The Americans entered Krunn without incident. But as the force approached Wallgau, they were greeted with hostile fire. Infantry dismounted tanks and took cover as the Germans opened up with small arms from within the town and the surrounding hills. Men and machines moved to positions to engage the enemy, who had established defensive positions on the northern edge Wallgau. At this point the mortar/antitank platoon, assault platoon, and Company D moved in. More than one panzerfaust streaked through the air, just missing the tanks. They soon reduced the enemy positions, and the Americans succeeded in establishing the roadblocks. This action resulted in a haul of two hundred enemy soldiers (including high-ranking officers, SS troops, and the commandant of the German Infantry School and Staff from Mittenwald).

The 781st's command post moved south to Innsbruck, Austria; Germany was now behind. Soon the entire battalion and the regiments to which they were attached moved into the Austrian city.

Before the Seventh Army lay the Alps, separating them from the Fifth Army, which had worked its way north through Italy. The forests strained up the steep mountains—so steep in fact that the trees seemed stacked on top of one another, reaching into the low clouds. In other areas, collections of large rocks protruded from the mountainsides. Near the peaks were sloped pastures, glazed at this time with snow in the freezing weather. At lower altitudes the snow was melting, revealing the brilliant greenness of the Alps. The view struck the Americans who entered this quiet domain as something of the land of fairytales.

Brenner Pass

The Brenner Pass stretches along the Italian-Austrian border. Mussolini and Hitler often met here, and where they had forged their "Pact of Steel" in 1940. Now it was to be the location of the historic linkup between two American armies hoping to close their chapters of the war in Europe.

The assignment landed in the laps of the 1st and 2nd Platoons of Company C. Maj. Gen. Anthony McAuliffe, commander of the 103rd Infantry Division, told the tankmen, "I want you men to reach the Fifth even if you have to go to Rome to do it."[11] Joined by elements of the 411th Infantry Regiment, the tanks made their way along the road at the bottom of the pass.

As the small force cruised along the wet roads, driving with lights on through the early morning darkness of 4 May, a red light appeared in the road near a bridge. As the drivers reduced speed, the light danced toward them, revealing itself to be a lantern held by a soldier. But as the man came into the headlights, the tankers were surprised to see that he was an armed German, "complete with potato masher grenades and a burp gun." The company commander got out to talk to the German, who politely informed him, "your 32-ton tank will be able to get across this bridge but you'll have to drive slowly." Taking his advice, the column pressed on.[12]

The American force crept along the road, up slopes and around sharp turns, as daylight began to break over the mountains. Finally at 10:51 a.m., two vehicles rounded a bend and approached the tanks. They were American jeeps with the markings of the Fifth Army. All of the men jumped

Figure 68. German prisoners of war pass through a roadblock, guarded by men from the 781st. *Courtesy Davis Memorial Library, Patton Museum, Fort Knox*

Figure 69. The crew from Company C credited with driving the first tank in history through the Brenner Pass. (Pictured: driver, Sgt. Jim Kee; gunner, Sgt. Samuel Hicks; loader, Pfc. John Thomas; BOG, Cpl. Donald Vermett; and commander, Sgt. Carl Hertlein.) Of interest too is the steel brackets on their tank, which the men had yet to fill with sandbags. Perhaps they saw no reason to do so in the final days of the war. *Courtesy Davis Memorial Library, Patton Museum, Fort Knox*

out of their vehicles and approached each other on foot with smiles in the quietness of the mountains. Finally the European and Mediterranean theaters of operations came together as this small band of soldiers shook hands and patted each other on the backs. And just like that, without fanfare, the job was done.

On 6 May all armor companies were relieved of their attachments to the 103rd Infantry Division and returned to the control of the battalion. The 781st was assigned an area to police along the Inn River. At 1:00 p.m. that day the battalion command post opened in Telfs, while Company A moved to Obsteig, Company B to Unter Meiming, Company C to Telfs, Company D to Wildermieming, and Service Company to Ober Meiming.

Victory in Europe

Three days later, at 2:41 a.m. on 7 May, Gen. Alfred Jodl signed the unconditional surrender for all German forces at Supreme Headquarters, Allied Expeditionary Forces, in Reims, France. On the morning of 8 May,

Americans awoke in their homes to their radios and neighbors declaring that the war was over in Europe—the Germans were finished.

For the next week and a half, the 781st Tank Battalion served as an occupation force, responsible for the security of the towns it held and running continuous patrols. Many of the men relaxed near their tanks while manning roadblocks. Those not on guard duty were back to training and maintenance. But work did not come without play. The men stayed fit with more-agreeable methods of physical activity. Many took to the mountains to climb the beautiful Alps. Others found quiet spots along the rivers to fish, to take in sounds and smells they had almost forgotten. Others stalked the forests with their rifles, looking for game. They could not shoot at Germans any longer, so they might as well go after some deer.

On the seventeenth the 781st was relieved of its occupational duties and assembled by company in Telfs, Obermeiming, and Wildermeiming. The men continued their "vacationing," though, hoping the generals might forget about them. They had tried not to think about the other war that still raged on the other side of the world, hoping Gen. Douglas MacArthur and other army commanders there did not need additional tank units.

20

Postwar and Review

It is often said, and it may be true in the abstract, that the principles of war do not change. It is, nevertheless, absolutely true, that methods do change and are constantly changing.

—Maj. Gen. Adna R. Chaffee Jr.

The first day of June 1945 found the battalion still assembled in Austria, awaiting orders for redeployment. The men were busy practicing gunnery and maintaining their vehicles. On the eleventh the battalion received orders from the Seventh Army to move to Camp Lucky Strike in Le Havre, France. From there the unit was to sail home, back to the United States. The same order also instructed that all tanks be turned in to the Ordnance Department at Aubing, Germany. The men had to say goodbye to their armored battlewagons—it would be trucks and trains on the way back to the States.

The next day the battalion's officers boarded trucks and jeeps and set out for their long trip home. For the first time in nearly seven months, the men were heading in a new direction—west.

On the thirteenth and fourteenth, the majority of the battalion loaded up into trucks and started the journey to Camp Lucky Strike. Company D and 1st Platoon, Company C, were fortunate to depart from Garmisch-Partenkirhcen on a train. Everyone else traveled by road.

The motor convoy arrived at Camp Lucky Strike on the sixteenth, followed two days later by Company D and elements of Company C. After spending twelve days there, the men made way for the ships that would take them back to the States. Headquarters Company, Service Company, and Company B boarded the SS *Alfred Moore*, while Companies A, C, and D loaded into the SS *Leland Stanford*.

On 4 July a presentation of awards ceremonies was held aboard each ship. Awards, including Silver Stars, Purple Hearts, and Bronze Stars, were presented to officers and enlisted men.

A week later the SS *Alfred Moore* arrived in New York Harbor. The men moved out to Camp Kilmer, New Jersey, for transport to their respective reception stations on 12 July. That same date the SS *Leland Stanford* docked at Hampton Roads, Virginia. The troops unloaded there headed to Camp Patrick Henry, Virginia, for processing and departure to their reception stations. Beginning on 13 July, the battalion began its thirty-day recuperative leave.

On 14 July Major General Burress, commander of the 100th Infantry Division, wrote the following letter, addressed to the commanding general, US Forces, European Theater—General Eisenhower:

> During a large part of the combat activities of this Division, the 781st Tank Battalion was attached to it. I consider this battalion a superior combat unit. Its conduct was such that it gained the respect and admiration of the entire Division, and I have it from the Commanding Officer of that unit that it felt the same way towards this Division. I therefore request, in the interests of the combat efficiency of this unit, that, if feasible, the 781st Tank Battalion be attached to the 100th Infantry Division for any combat operations it may be called on to conduct.[1]

On 6 August 1945, returning from the Potsdam Conference aboard the USS *Augusta*, Pres. Harry Truman received word that the first atomic bomb had been dropped on Hiroshima, Japan. Three days later another bomb was dropped on Nagasaki. The author of the 781st Unit History recorded, "the same bomb that vaporized steel buildings in Japan was to step up the point system and dissolve, if not the tank battalion itself, at least the old gang of the 781st at Camp Campbell, Kentucky."[2]

On 11 August the first handful of 781st troops returned from their leave to Camp Campbell and began preparations for the arrival of the rest of the battalion.

Points

The Advanced Service Rating Score was a system that distributed "points" to determine which soldiers were sent home first. A total of at least eighty-five points would qualify an enlisted man for discharge. He acquired these points in a number of ways:

1 point per month of active service
1 point per month spent overseas
3 points per month spent in a combat zone
6 points per Purple Heart
12 points per child or dependent under the age of eighteen
5 points for each medal
5 points for each campaign star

Since the 781st took part in the linkup between the Seventh and Fifth Armies, each man received an extra five points on their scores.

On 18 August the rest of the men started to return from their leaves. By the end of the month, most members of the 781st had returned, and training resumed, with emphasis on tank-crew gunnery and range firing. On 8 September the entire battalion was reassembled. At the end of the month, the unit began sending all enlisted men on an additional forty-five days of furloughs as ordered by the army. All officers and men eligible for discharge under the points system were processed and prepared for separation centers.

Amid this activity, the commanding officer of the battalion wrote to his unit and its men:

> At the time this record of the 781st Tank Battalion goes to press, I still have no indication as to whether or not it will be officially deactivated. Certainly it is clear to all of us that the eagerly awaited discharge of the "old timers," both officer and enlisted, will so change the unit that it can truly be said the outfit as we have all known it for long, will soon cease to exist.
>
> As I look back on the period of the life of the battalion, a period lacking but a very short time of being three full years, it is with a feeling of intense pride. Very few commanders have had the good fortune to activate, train, fight and, I hope, deactivate his unit. While I find a number of situations in my memory that might have been

> modified if they were to be done again, I am confident every one of us realized that the distinction the battalion has earned has resulted from sincerity of purpose of every last member of the organization. Mistakes, if made, were honest mistakes and were not repeated. That is important. This inherent sincerity of purpose has made the 781st a unit of which we can all be justifiably proud.
>
> I want to take this last opportunity to thank every member of the command for his part in making our record possible. I only wish I could thank each one of you personally. No single individual or group could have accomplished alone what we have done together. It is my fervent hope that we can all leave the 781st with a full measure of pleasant memories. I personally have made many friends I shall never forget. In the days to come I hope we will meet again as civilians enjoying the success we all so richly deserve. May God Bless you.[3]

The combat awards earned by the battalion and its members were:

> 152 Bronze Stars with 11 oak leaf clusters
> 9 Silver Stars with 1 oak leaf cluster
> 30 Presidential Citations
> 81 Purple Hearts with 6 oak leaf clusters
> 32 men killed or died of wounds
> 1 recommendation for Distinguished Service Cross.

The 781st Tank Battalion was inactivated on 19 February 1946 at Camp Campbell, Kentucky.

Review

Possibly reflecting on the growing pains of the Armored Force, Major General Chaffee noted: "It is often said, and it may be true in the abstract, that the *principles* of war do not change. It is, nevertheless, absolutely true, that *methods* do change and are constantly changing. We may study the great captain of the past to learn of their principles and, above all, of their character, but do not let us be tied too much to their methods. For methods change with every change of armament and equipment."[4]

The tank had become an integral part of the US Army during the Second World War. Yet combat had demonstrated the weakness in American tank design up to the end of the conflict. Within the separate tank battalions, their drawbacks were compounded by tactical mismanagement. Furthermore, they had been mostly neglected when it came to administration, supply, and training. This was often the case with many nondivision units, such as medical, engineer, and antiaircraft. The separate tank battalions called themselves "bastard battalions," while the army would refer to them and other nondivision units as "spare parts."[5] For armor advocates, the 1941 maneuvers had demonstrated that tanks must train with infantry and be permanently assigned to infantry units. Both the Army Ground Forces and the Armored Force discarded this idea. As a result, tank battalions had to learn under fire and often paid a heavy price in men and material. Most of the Armored Force's attention was centered on the larger armored divisions, whose tankers received joint training with their organic infantry units. In 1943 and 1944, field manuals for the separate tank battalions stressed that such units should be deployed en masse, rather than broken up and dispersed on independent missions. But this theory never fully materialized in the field, where geography and infantry commanders dictated otherwise.

Battalions were constantly reattached to different infantry divisions. Units belonging to the 781st Tank Battalion had been attached to the 45th, 70th, 100th, 101st, and 103rd Infantry Divisions during its eight months in action. The 781st was fortunate that much of its service was in support of the 100th Infantry Division. Many tank battalions, especially those in the Mediterranean, were consistently detached and reattached to various infantry units. This impeded both tankers and infantrymen's efforts to build efficient combined-arms teams.

The tankers were not the only ones who stood to benefit from a long-term relationship. Once infantrymen understood how to use armor, and tankers understood how to support foot soldiers, both benefited. In the case of the 100th Infantry Division, they relished the 781st's armor support, as evidenced by the Major General Burress's letter to Eisenhower at the end of European operations.

After the war, Armored School thought maintained that the armored division should be deployed en masse and must be used to exploit initial gains by the infantry. From there it should attack with combined forces, such as artillery and tactical air support, in order to seek and destroy the enemy's rear installations, namely artillery, reserves, and communications. In essence, the primary function of armor was to overwhelm the enemy, paralyze him by denying the opportunity to reorganize his forces, and finally annihilate him.

Contrary to official doctrine from 1940 to 1945, a new secondary mission for American tanks in the field was the destruction of enemy armor. Commanders recognized that armor was now an established element on battlefields and that enemy tanks must be eliminated before the infantry could advance.

A third function, established by 1955, was that the infantry's survivability relies on the tank so that infantry divisions should have organic armor battalions whose companies would support the infantry regiments. These organic tank battalions had three roles: to add depth to antitank protection; to add firepower to the infantry attack through direct fire support, mobility, and shock; and finally to exploit success from the attack. While this seems like the role of the separate tank battalion, the fact that they would be organic and trained with the infantry improved their effectiveness in the field. Furthermore, new tanks, capable of engaging enemy armor, would become part of the US arsenal. An Armored School publication of 1955 directly contradicts the old armor doctrine, stating: "In the offensive, enemy tanks can be destroyed most effectively by our own tanks; it takes tanks to defeat tanks. . . . *The tank must be able to live in the element in which it fights*."[6] Within this statement is what the original authors of US tank doctrine in 1940 had failed to recognize. In contrast, the Germans had recognized this well before 1944.

The Shermans were slowly phased out by the new M26 Pershings, which arrived in very small numbers in the spring and summer of 1945. The M26 was the final result of the T20 project. Utilizing the new Ford V-8 GAN engine, the T20 housed the transmission and drive sprockets at the rear of the tank, which eliminated the need of running the driveshaft to the front. It was fitted with the new M1A1 76-mm gun and used the horizontal volute-spring suspension (HVSS). The design went through many stages, bringing in a new transmission, a new turret, and finally a new 90-mm gun. In the end it was officially christened the M26. The tank was twenty feet, nine inches long; eleven feet, six inches wide; and just over nine feet tall. Its wide turret housed an M3 90-mm gun. It was driven by a 1,100-cubic inch Ford V-8 Model GAF that was rated at 2,600 rpm with 500 hp. Unfortunately, the engine was decided on when the tank was planned to carry the lighter 76-mm gun; as it was ultimately armed with the 90-mm gun, adding additional weight, the Pershing proved to be underpowered. Though early designs had the HVSS system, this was eventually dropped in favor of a torsion-bar system like that of the M24.

In 1947 the armored division was reorganized. The new division called for four tank battalions, four armored-infantry battalions, and four armored field-artillery battalions. As the United States entered the Cold War era, the Armored Force argued that tanks were "the ideal ground medium for [the] waging of atomic warfare. Of the component parts of the corps team, the armored division is best able to gain passive protection from the heat, blast, and radiation of enemy atomic weapons by spreading its units widely; yet, its communications, flexibility, and mobility still give it the capability of massing effort quickly at the decisive time and place."[7] To echo the words of MacArthur, too often organization is attempted from the standpoint of equipment rather than of the missions assigned. Therefore it has been the adaptation of the tank as a tool of war, and the evolution of its tactical flexibility, that has maintained its necessity on the battlefield.

The postwar Armored Force emphasized to its commanders that they "must be motivated by flexibility of mind, a progressiveness in thought, and a liberal imagination so that they may fully realize in action the full effectiveness of armor characteristics." In recognition of the complications that occurred during the formation of the armored corps, these officers were further instructed "to transcend the petty jealousies which at times have hindered the progress of our forces in the past. We must be capable of formulating and accepting a team of combined arms, where each arm is used in its most favorable role . . . , a team of combined arms capable of accomplishing decisive missions, utilizing to the fullest extent the outstanding characteristics of mobility, shock action, and firepower."[8]

▪ ▪ ▪

Today we sometimes see a Sherman on static display in a park or a city center. Though regarded as tactically inefficient against their enemy counterparts, these tanks spearheaded the strategic offensive, and ultimately victory, against the Axis powers of World War II. They had performed well for their designed missions. Unfortunately, they were often faced with other tasks. The modernizing battlefield of the 1940s demanded better weapons, and by the time the Shermans arrived, they were outgunned and outarmored. The American soldiers were also at the mercy of their nation's support and production capabilities. Uninterrupted war production, churning out B-24s, LSTs, and M1 Garands, gave the United States a tremendous advantage over its enemies. Yet the story of American tank theory and practice during World War II is bittersweet. Infantry officers, ignorant of armor's capabilities and doctrine, often controlled the tanks of the separate tank battalions. This mismanagement resulted in many losses. The momentum of American war production also made it difficult for tank advocates to make their cases for new armor. The men of the Armored Force were tasked with maintaining the offensive with obsolete machinery. Regardless, they and their machines pressed on—and they pressed hard. Their sacrifice will always be controversial, especially to those who were buttoned up in the steel beasts of the bastard battalions.

Notes

Chapter 2

1. Keegan, *History of Warfare*, 216.

2. Black, *Tools of War*, 1.

3. Chainmail proved to be an effective defense, for it was death from bleeding out or infection that killed the vast majority of those receiving major lacerations in pre-antiseptic times.

4. Francis Bacon, *The New Organon*; *or*, *True Directions Concerning the Interpretation of Nature* (1620), bk. 1, sec. 129. Available online at the University of Adelaide Library, updated 17 Dec. 2014, https://ebooks.adelaide.edu.au/b/bacon/francis/organon/index.html.

5. Black, *European Warfare*, 61.

6. Bert Chaney, "A Lad Goes to War," in Moynihan, *People at War*, 122–23.

7. Fuller, *Armament & History*, 138.

Chapter 3

1. Hart, *Real War*, 253.

2. Because its roots were laid down by the Admiralty, tank anatomy reads like that of a naval vessel: e.g., hull, bow, starboard, etc.

3. Hart, *Real War*, 255.

4. Ibid., 245.

5. Wheldon, *Machine Age Armies*, 13.

6. Fuller, *Conduct of War*, 243.

7. Yockelson, "United States Armed Forces and the Mexican Punitive Expedition," http://www.archives.gov/publications/prologue/1997/winter/mexican-punitive-expedition-2.html (accessed Apr. 2015).

8. Wilson, *Treat 'Em Rough!*, 12.

9. In March 1916 Patton had led a small party against some of Poncho Villa's men they had happened upon in a small town in Mexico. He organized an impromptu attack on a ranch, using three cars at their disposal, to rush the ranch where Villa's men had been seen.

10. Blumenson and Hymel, *Patton, Legendary World War II Commander*, 31.

11. Ibid., 15–16.

12. Blumenson, *Patton Papers*, 527.

13. Ibid., 552.
14. Ambrose, *Eisenhower*, 33–34.
15. Wilson, *Treat 'Em Rough!*, 56–58.
16. Quote from Blumenson, *Patton Papers*, 602.
17. Wilson, *Treat 'Em Rough!*, 96.
18. Blumenson, *Patton Papers*, 612.
19. Wilson, *Treat 'Em Rough!*, 100.
20. Patton had ordered his men to press on with the infantry if their tanks became inoperable. Rochenbach, however, later instructed Patton that in the future any man who abandoned his tank would be court-martialed. See Blumenson, *Patton Papers*, 648.
21. Ibid., 109.
22. Keegan, *First World War*, 411.
23. Quote from Blumenson, *Patton Papers*, 647.
24. Wilson, *Treat 'Em Rough!*, 191.
25. Ibid., 204.

Chapter 4

1. Keegan, *History of Warfare*, 188.
2. Parker, *Final Report of United States Liquidation Commission*, 48.
3. "Development of Combat Vehicles, Tank Doctrine, and Policy Statements," in Greenfield, *United States Army in World War II: The Technical Services*.
4. Eisenhower, "Tank Discussion," 454, 456.
5. House Document 863, "Report of the Chief of the Tank Corps," 30 June 1920, 1892.
6. From Greenfield, *United States Army in World War II: The Technical Services*, 190–91.
7. Ibid.
8. For more discussion on this study and the Armored Corps, see chapter 9.
9. Blumenson, *Patton Papers*, 964.
10. Jarymowycz, *Tank Tactics*, 28–29.
11. Cameron, "Fort Knox," 28.
12. Icks, *Famous Tank Battles*, 25.
13. Wheldon, *Machine Age Armies*, 41.
14. Quoted from Macksey, *Tank Warfare*, 131.
15. Hoffmann, *Through Mobility We Conquer*, 99.
16. Fischer, *Washington's Crossing*, 36.
17. Blumenson, *Patton Papers*, 823–24.
18. Jarymowycz, *Tank Tactics*, 15.
19. Hoffschmidt and Tantum, *Tank Data 2*, 43. See also "Light Tanks," in Greenfield, *United States Army in World War II: The Technical Services*, 196–98.
20. B. Cooper, *Death Traps*, 99.
21. Powerplant document, n.d., Armored Force School Papers, Patton Museum Archives, Fort Knox, KY, 2.

22. Quoted from Greenfield, *United States Army in World War II: The Technical Services*, 290.

23. Eiler, *Mobilizing America*, 114–15, 122.

24. Benson had been a cavalryman but had served as an officer with the light tanks under Patton during the First World War.

25. Greene, *Infantry Journal Reader*, 36–39.

26. Cameron, *Mobility, Shock, and Firepower*, 252.

27. Gen. Robert Merrill Lee Papers, Patton Museum Library, Fort Knox, KY.

Chapter 5

1. Guderian, *Panzer Leader*, 20.

2. Ibid.

3. Ibid., 21.

4. Ibid., 25.

5. Ibid., 45.

6. Guderian, *Militar Wissenschaftiche Runschau*, 10.

7. Guderian, *Panzer Leader*, 39.

8. US tankers would refer to the panzerkampfwagen models as "Mark"—e.g., a Panzer IV was to the Americans a Mark IV. For this reason, "Mark" is used hereafter when referring to a specific type of German tank. These specific designations often were followed by the term "Ausf" (short for *Ausfuhrung*, the German word for "model"), which preceded an alphabetic designation—e.g., Panzerkampfwagen III Ausf G. The letter increased with each change or upgrade to the type—e.g., when the Mark III Ausf F received its improved engine, it was redesignated Ausf G.

9. There were two different suspension systems for the Mark I models. The Mark I Ausf A had four road wheels, with the idler wheel trailing flush on the ground. Three support, or return, wheels guided the eighty-four track sections back to the drive sprocket. The Mark I Ausf B, however, had five road wheels, with the idler wheel elevated off the ground; there were four support wheels. Road wheels are designated either by the total number or by just those per track. In this work the number of road wheels mentioned are per track.

10. M. Cooper, *German Army*, 155.

11. Blumberg, "Czech-Designed 38(t) Armored Vehicle," 12.

12. Ibid.

13. Guderian, *Panzer Leader*, 68, 70.

14. Ibid., 73.

15. Dinardo, *Mechanized Juggernaut or Military Anachronism?*, 22.

16. Keegan, *History of Warfare*, 369.

17. Churchill, *Second World War*.

Chapter 6

1. Stokesbury, *Short History of World War II*, 93.

2. Guderian, *Panzer Leader*, App. III.

3. Guderian, *Panzer Leader*, 92.

4. Rommel, *Rommel Papers*, 19–20.

5. M. Cooper, *German Army*, 223.

6. The Matilda I was armed with a single machine gun, while the Matilda II had a 2-pounder (40-mm) cannon and one machine gun. The Somua (Char de Cavalerie 35S) had one 47-mm gun and one machine gun.

7. Harman, *Dunkirk*, 85.

8. Military Intelligence Division, *Tentative Lessons from the Recent Active Campaign in Europe*, 3.

9. Hart, *History of the Second World War*, 60.

Chapter 7

1. Blumenson, *Patton Papers*, 1044.

2. Kennett, *G.I.*, 43. See chapter 3 for more on the camps.

3. Memorandum to Lt. Col. Stephen G. Henry, 27 July 1940, Armored Force School Papers, Patton Museum Archives, Fort Knox, KY.

4. This idea is promoted in *The Tanks Are Coming* (1941). The main character, played by George Tobias, is a taxi driver from Brooklyn—presumably a man qualified to drive a tank.

5. Kennett, *G.I.*, 37.

6. *Practice for the Army Tests*, 3–9.

7. Untitled document, Folder 3, Box 1, Armored Force School History Collection, Patton Museum Archives, 2.

8. *The Tanks Are Coming* (1941).

9. Untitled document, Folder 3, Box 1, Armored Force School History Collection, Patton Museum Archives, 3.

10. Ibid.

11. Staff of the *Infantry Journal*, *Armored Forces of the United States Army*.

12. Cameron, *Mobility, Shock, and Firepower*, 256–57.

Chapter 8

1. Churchill, *Second World War*, 173.

2. Van Creveld, *Supplying War*, 185.

3. Churchill, *Second World War*, 174.

4. Davies, *Great Campaigns of World War II*, 145.

5. Churchill, *Second World War*, 176.

6. To the British, this was designated the Light Stuart Mark 1 and unofficially referred to as "Honey." To avoid confusion, the text will only refer to its American designation, Light M3.

7. M. Cooper, *German Army*, 374.

8. The German high command supplied the forces in Africa conservatively due to the necessity of forces needed for operations in eastern Europe. When reinforcements *were* sent across the Mediterranean, they were in great danger of being sunk by the Royal Navy.

9. To be in a defilade position means to be concealed by an artificial or natural

barrier, such as a wall or a hill. Hull-down defilade means that only the tank's turret is exposed in order to engage the enemy. Turret-down defilade means the entire tank is hidden and thus cannot engage a target.

10. Military Intelligence Service, *Artillery in the Desert*, 58.

11. M. Cooper, *German Army*, 375.

12. Quote from Heckmann, *Rommel's War in Africa*, 231.

13. Quote from Military Intelligence Service, *Artillery in the Desert*, 13.

14. Heckmann, *Rommel's War in Africa*, 231.

15. Cameron, *Mobility, Shock, and Firepower*, 278–79.

Chapter 9

1. Cameron, *Mobility, Shock, and Firepower*, 263.

2. Williamson, *General Patton's Principles for Life and Leadership*, 78.

3. The word "corps" has two meanings. First, there is the "corps" that is the operational command above divisions. There are also the "corps" that are the combative arms of the army, which included the infantry, cavalry, signal, artillery, engineer, and eventually air corps. These were commanded by branch chiefs, who could direct their corps with a high level of autonomy.

4. Cameron, *Mobility, Shock, and Firepower*, 287–88 (Chaffee quote, 287); George F. Hoffmann, "Combatant Arms vs. Combined Arms: The US Army's Quest for Deep Offensive Operations and an Operational Level of Warfare," *Armor*, Jan. 1997, 12.

5. Peterson, *Round Shot and Rammers*, 36.

6. Ibid., 113.

7. Military Intelligence Division, *Tentative Lessons from the Recent Active Campaign in Europe*, 2.

8. *History and Role of Armor*, 52.

9. Heller and Stofft, *America's First Battles*, 235.

10. A table of organization (T/O) outlines the structure of a given military agency or unit. A table of organization and equipment (TO&E) is similar to a T/O but also prescribes the equipment, staffing, and organization of a military unit.

11. Yeide, *Steel Victory*, 7–8.

12. The term "Sherman" originated from the British, who named most of their tanks. They had dubbed the Light M3 the Stuart and the Medium M3 the Grant after American Civil War generals. The M4 family of tanks included the M4 and seven variants: the M4A1, M4A2, and so on. Although many authors use "M4 broadly to include all these versions as a single family, I will use "Sherman" for that purpose and reserve "M4 for that specific model.

13. Greenfield, *United States Army in World War II: The Technical Services*, 484.

14. The Pressed Steel Car Company also built Shermans with the GM diesel engine, but these tanks were equipped with a 76-mm gun and had a different storage arrangement for the main ammunition. These were therefore designated M4A2(76)W.

15. Green, *M4 Sherman at War*, 70.

16. *Tank Gunnery Manual*, 62.

17. The fuse described is the M48 Point Detonation, Selective, Superquick or Short Delay. This "selective" fuse combined the preexisting roles of the instantaneous M46 fuse and the short-delay M47 fuse into a single device.

18. War Department, *Ammunition Inspection Guide*, Technical Manual TM 9–1904 (Mar. 1944), 388.

19. *Tank Platoon Manual*, 31.

20. Since there were no driving controls located in the assistant driver's position, that crewman essentially served as the bow gunner. For the rest of the text, I will refer to the assistant driver/bow gunner as simply the BOG.

21. *Tank Platoon Manual*, 31. In 1944, tanks began receiving the AM radio AN-VRC-3, which was basically a vehicle version of the infantry SCR-300 radio.

22. "HBT" stands for "herring-bone twill," the pattern used in the uniform. These green jumpsuits were made of lightweight cotton and were comfortable in the heat generated within the tanks. Though there were a few variations, the typical HBT coveralls consisted of an adjustable belt that was attached at the back, adjustable cuffs, and large pockets on the chest and/or waist.

23. Greene, *Infantry Journal Reader*, 70–84.

24. Quote from Weeks, *Men against Tanks*, 92.

25. As a testament to this flawed doctrine, one of the great coups de theatre in the armor narrative is General Patton's 2nd Armored Division tanks penetrating deep into "enemy" lines during the 1941 Carolina maneuvers and capturing General Drum and his headquarters on the first day.

26. Other successful tank destroyers were the M18 Hellcat, armed with a 76-mm gun, and the M36, armed with a 90-mm gun.

Chapter 10

1. Davies, *Great Campaigns of World War II*, 172. Allegedly some Germans fled at the sight of the flail tanks, seeing them as a macabre instrument of warfare designed to literally chew up infantry.

Chapter 11

1. Stoler, "George C. Marshall and the Europe-First Strategy," 294–95.

2. In order to meet standard railway regulations, the initial tracks installed on the tanks were 20 inches wide. Once in the field the tanks were refitted with the 28.5-inch tracks.

3. Notable is the fact that much of the armor, specifically on the turret and the side hull, was set at nearly 90 degrees, relying simply on its sheer thickness to withstand enemy fire.

4. Kershaw, *Tank Men*, 235–36.

5. Hart, *Rommel Papers*, 397.

6. B. Cooper, *Death Traps*, 20.

7. Forty, *Tank Warfare in World War II*, 118–19.
8. Hart, *Rommel Papers*, 398.

Chapter 12

1. Quote from Green, *M4 Sherman at War*, 94.
2. Forty, *Tank Warfare in World War II*, 118.
3. The quote here and those in the following paragraphs are from Scott, *Tankers in Tunisia.*
4. Kershaw, *Tank Men*, 236.
5. Greenfield, *United States Army in World War II: The Technical Services*, 236–37.

Chapter 13

1. LCT stands for "Landing Craft, Tank"; LST stands for "Landing Ship, Tank." There were different models of LCTs, but they were roughly 115 feet in length and could carry between 130 and 150 tons—up to five tanks. The LSTs were 328 feet long and could carry 2,000 tons of men and equipment, such as eighteen tanks.
2. Jensen, *Strike Swiftly!*, 82–83.
3. Fazendin, *756th Tank Battalion in the Battle of Cassino*, 63–64.
4. Ibid., 72.
5. The M8 Motor Carriage was basically an M5 light tank with an open turret and mounting a 75-mm howitzer.
6. Eisenhower, *Crusade in Europe*, 202.
7. Lt. Gen. Lesley McNair was killed during this action by friendly fire. Dozens of the planes dropped their bombs well short of their target, killing more than a hundred Americans and wounding hundreds more. McNair was one of the two highest-ranking US officers killed in action during the war, the other being Lt. Gen. Simon Bolivar Buckner Jr., who was killed by enemy fire on Okinawa. In addition, Lt. Gen. Frank Maxwell Andrews was killed when his plane struck a mountain in southwest Iceland, and Lt Gen. Millard Harmon's transport plane disappeared on his flight from the Marshal Islands to Hawaii.
8. The decision to invade southern France was complex and outside the scope of this work. For further information, see Martin Blumenson and Kent Roberts Greenfield, *Command Decisions* (Washington, DC: Office of the Chief of Military History, Dept. of the Army, 1960).
9. While national security and the security and survival of US allies were paramount, the destruction of Germany's and Japan's capacity to wage war would permit international stability capable of a healthy global economy.
10. As far as Eisenhower and the Americans were concerned, a sudden concentrated strike was not an option since the Germans still had enough strength to cut off any deep penetrations through their lines, as demonstrated during Operation Market Garden. Furthermore, aggressive operations also require a concentration of resources, of which the rest of the divisions along the front were in desperate need.

Chapter 14

1. Quote from Palmer, *Reorganization of Ground Troops for Combat*, 36.
2. Yeide, *Weapons of the Tankers*, 93.
3. *Tank Platoon Manual*, 3.
4. *Armored Battalion*, 4.
5. Ibid. A phase line was a specific terrain feature, such as a river or group of hills, used as a means to control the speed and organization of the march. Lead vehicles in columns would be ordered to arrive at phase lines at predesignated times.
6. Ibid., 21.
7. Ibid., 49.
8. *Organization, Equipment, and Tactical Employment of Separate Tank Battalions*, 4.
9. *Armored Battalion*, 107.

Chapter 15

1. B. Cooper, *Death Traps*, 40.
2. *Up from Marseille*, 7.
3. The S-3, or battalion-operations officer, is responsible for planning unit operations that support the execution of policies and strategy; overseeing unit organization, including preparing and modifying the TO&E; and training the unit.
4. Yeide, *Steel Victory*, 119.
5. Each company had three platoons of five tanks each, in addition to the three tanks belonging to the headquarters section. Assuming that all of these were attached to the same unit and were all in working order, an infantry regiment theoretically had eighteen tanks supporting it.
6. The 953rd was part of the 361st Volksgrenadier Division. Organized in the latter part of 1944 in response to diminishing manpower in Germany, Volksgrenadiers came from destroyed infantry divisions, the Luftwaffe, and the Kriegsmarine. These divisions had three regiments of only two battalions each for a total strength of roughly 8,000 poorly trained men.
7. Forty, *Tank Warfare in World War II*, 214.
8. "781st Tank Battalion Unit History."
9. Thermite grenades were incendiary devices used to render equipment, such as artillery guns, inoperable. The weapon does not explode, but rather burns intensely so that molten metal from its shell fuses any moving parts it contacts, such as a gun breech or traversing mechanism.
10. "781st Tank Battalion Unit History."
11. Many of these bunkers have survived into the twenty-first century.
12. "781st Tank Battalion Unit History."
13. Bass, *Story of the Century*, 82.
14. "781st Tank Battalion Unit History."

Chapter 16

1. Heiber, *Hitler and His Generals*, 594.

2. Military Intelligence Division, *Tactical and Technical Trends*, 14.

3. Heiber, *Hitler and His Generals*, 692.

4. *To Hell and Back*, directed by Jesse Hibbs (1955; Universal City, CA: 2004), DVD.

5. B. Cooper, *Death Traps*, 21.

6. The quotes here and in the following paragraphs come from *Combat Lessons No. 9*, 6–19. The *Combat Lessons* booklets covered various opinions and feedback from the combat zone and were published by direction of the army chief of staff by the Operations Division in collaboration with other divisions of the War Department General Staff, Army Ground Forces, Army Air Forces, and Army Service Forces.

7. Some of the features of the new turret were important enough to be included in the tank's official designations. For example, the designation M4A1 indicates that the Sherman has the welded hull and a Wright engine. But a second generation M4A1 might be listed as an M4A1E8(76)W: the "E8" for the suspension, "(76)" for the new 76-mm gun, and "W" for wet storage.

8. Zaloga, *M4 (76mm) Sherman Medium Tank*, 14.

9. Ballistic Research Laboratories, *Ballistic and Engineering Data for Shot, HVAP, 76-mm, M93 with Tracer*.

10. Ballistic Research Laboratories, *Penetration of Armor by 76- and 90-mm HVAP Projectiles*.

11. Zaloga, *M4 (76mm) Sherman Medium Tank*, 22.

12. E8 Shermans were often referred to as "Easy Eights."

Chapter 17

1. *Up from Marseille*, 12.

2. Zoepf, *Seven Days in January*, 99.

3. The Germans' initial success in Wingen was frustrated as their radio vehicle became lost and was captured by US forces. Therefore they could not report their success. As a result, the attacking force would not receive the armor or artillery support that they had planned to move up to the town.

4. Zoepf, *Seven Days in January*, 138.

5. A task force was a temporary conglomerate of units with a specific mission. These varied in size, depending on the mission, and were named after the commanding officer.

6. *Up from Marseille*, 12.

7. "Narrative Report of 276th Infantry," 31 Jan. 1945, in 276th AAR (19 Nov. 1944–31 Jan. 1945), 16 Feb. 1945, 276th Infantry: Documents, 70th Infantry Division Association, http://trailblazersww2.0rg/pdf/276_AAR_Nov44_Jan45.pdf. A transcript of only this narrative report is also available on the site at "AAR of the 276th Infantry Regiment covering the period January 1945," http://trailblazersww2.0rg/units_276_documents_AARJan45.htm.

8. "Battle of Wingen," "781st Tank Battalion Unit History."
9. Zoepf, *Seven Days in January*, 164, 197.
10. Ibid., 197.
11. Ibid., 230.
12. Ibid.
13. These tanks belonged to the 653rd Heavy Tank Destroyer Battalion.
14. *Up from Marseille*, 15.
15. "781st Tank Battalion Unit History."
16. *Combat Lessons No. 9*, 6–16.
17. Record of Events, 25 Jan. 1945, "781st Tank Battalion Unit History."
18. Elements of the 553rd Volksgrenadier Division.
19. *Up from Marseille*, 15. The "Big Finger" method was probably an expression to indicate a place with no name that could only be designated by placing a finger on a map.
20. Quoted from Yeide, *Steel Victory*, 1.
21. Quoted from ibid., 82.

Chapter 18

1. Quotations in this section are from February summary of events, pt. 3, "781st Tank Battalion Unit History."
2. *Up from Marseilles*, 18.
3. Ibid.
4. Bass, *Story of the Century*, 125.
5. Angier, *4f Goes to War*, 67–68.
6. Bass, *Story of the Century*, 127.
7. Angier, *4f Goes to War*, 69. The replay translates as, "That is war."
8. Unless otherwise indicated, all quotes in this section come from White, *United States vs. German Equipment.*
9. Green, *M4 Sherman at War*, 95.
10. Hardison, *Data on WWII Tank Engagements*, 13. This report was unclassified on 29 August 1972 and first published by Merriam Press in 1988. The following discussion of FF is informed by data from ibid., 17–28.
11. Ibid., 22. The data collected includes antitank guns, tanks, and tank destroyers.
12. Rommel, *Rommel Papers*, 7.
13. Hardison, *Data on WWII Tank Engagements*, 23. These figures are taken from combat after Normandy and focus on engagements in or around Stollberg, the Roer to the Rhein, Belgium, Arracourt, Sarre, and Bastogne.
14. Rommel, *Rommel Papers*, 7.
15. "781st Tank Battalion Unit History."
16. *Up from Marseilles*, 19–20.
17. Bass, *Story of the Century*, 131–32.

Chapter 19

1. Bass, *Story of the Century*, 134.

2. Ibid., 136.

3. These rockets had originally been designed for air-to-ground use. The M8 HE was a fin-stabilized rocket. This was replaced later in the war by the M16, which was spin stabilized.

4. Bass, *Story of the Century*, 148.

5. "Freeboard," a nautical term, refers to the part of the hull that is above the surface of the water.

6. Yeide, *Weapons of the Tankers*, 77.

7. The Medal of Honor citation stated, "By his intrepidity and inspiring courage Pfc. Colallilo gave tremendous impetus to his company's attack, killed or wounded 25 of the enemy in bitter fighting, and assisted a wounded soldier in reaching the American lines at great risk of his own life." "Colalillo, Michael," Congressional Medal of Honor Association, accessed 6 Jan. 2011, http://themedalofhonor.com/medal-of-honor-recipients/recipients/colalillo-michael-world-war-two.

8. *Up from Marseilles*, 22.

9. Ibid., 24.

10. Ibid.

11. Clipping from *Wichita Eagle*, n.d., Brenner Pass Letters, 781st Tank Battalion File, Fort Knox Library. See also clipping from *Lubbock Evening Journal*, 11 June 1945, ibid. This was the famed General McAuliffe who was acting commander of the 101st Airborne Division when he gave the Germans the now-famous response "Nuts!" during the Battle of the Bulge. He took command of the 103rd Infantry Division in January 1945.

12. *Up from Marseilles*, 25.

Chapter 20

1. H. L. Kinne Jr. to Commanding General, United States Forces, European Theater (Main), Frankfort, Ger., "Commendable Official Reference to the 781st Tank Battalion," 6 Sept. 1945, copy in author's possession.

2. *Up from Marseilles*, 26.

3. "A Message from the C. O.," ibid., n.p.

4. "Introduction," *History and Role of Armor*.

5. Historical Section, Army Ground Service, "Introduction," *Problems of Nondivisional Training*.

6. *History and Role of Armor*, 26 (author's emphasis).

7. Ibid.

8. *History and Role of Armor*, 41.

Bibliography

Primary Sources

276th Infantry: Documents. 70th Infantry Division Association. http://trailblazers ww2.0rg/units_276_documents.htm.

"781st Tank Battalion Unit History." N.d. Copy in possession of the author.

The Armored Battalion, Light and Medium. Armored Force FM 17–33. 18 September 1943.

Armored Force School Papers. Patton Museum Archives, The Armored Force School, Fort Knox, KY.

Ballistic Research Laboratories. *Ballistic and Engineering Data for Shot, HVAP, 76-mm, M93 with Tracer*. Handbook of Ballistic and Engineering Data for Ammunition, no. 76–1-93. Washington, DC, 1949.

———. *Penetration of Armor by 76- and 90-mm HVAP Projectile*. Report 533. July 1950.

Bass, Michael A., ed. *Story of the Century*. New York: Century Association, 1946.

Combat Lessons No. 9, Rank and File in Combat: What They Are Doing, How They Do It. Washington, DC: Government Printing Office, 1944.

Kinne, H. L., Jr. to Commanding General, United States Forces, European Theater (Main), Frankfort, Ger. "Commendable Official Reference to the 781st Tank Battalion." 6 September 1945. Copy in author's possession.

Eisenhower, Dwight. "A Tank Discussion." *Infantry Journal* 27 (1920).

Greene, Joseph I. *The Infantry Journal Reader*. Garden City, NY: Doubleday, Doran, 1943.

Guderian, Heinz. *Militar Wissenschaftiche Runschau*. 1936.

———. *Panzer Leader*. Cambridge, MA: Da Capo, 2002.

Hardison, David C. *Data on WWII Tank Engagements Involving the U.S. Third and Fourth Armored Divisions*. BRL Memorandum Report 798. Aberdeen Proving Ground, MD: Ballistic Research Laboratories, 1954. Reprint. New York: Merriam, 1988. Sixth ed., 2008.

Historical Section, Army Ground Service. *Problems of Nondivisional Training in the Army Ground Forces*. Study 14, AD-A954 907. 1946.

History and Role of Armor. Fort Knox, KY: Armored School, 1955.

Lee, Gen. Robert Merrill. Papers, Patton Museum Library, Fort Knox, KY.

Military Intelligence Division, War Department. *Tactical and Technical Trends.* Number 51. Washington, DC: Government Printing Office, October 1944.

———. *Tentative Lessons from the Recent Active Campaign in Europe.* Bulletin 13, G-2/2675–235. July 12, 1940.

Military Intelligence Service, War Department. *Artillery in the Desert.* November 25, 1942.

Organization, Equipment, and Tactical Employment of Separate Tank Battalions. Bad Nauheim, Ger.: General Board, USFET, 1945.

Palmer, R. R. *Reorganization of Ground Troops for Combat.* Washington, DC: Historical Section, Army Ground Forces, 1946.

Parker, Edwin B. *Final Report of United States Liquidation Commission.* Washington, DC: War Department, Government Printing Office, 1920.

Patton Museum Archives. The Armored Force School, Fort Knox, KY.

Practice for the Army Tests. New York: ARC Publishing, 1942.

Rommel, Erwin. *The Rommel Papers.* Translated by Paul Findlay. Edited by Basil Henry Liddell Hart et al. 1953. Reprint. New York: Da Capo, 2003.

Scott, C. L., comp. *Tankers in Tunisia.* Fort Knox, KY: Headquarters, Armor Replacement Training Center, 1943.

Staff of the *Infantry Journal. The Armored Forces of the United States Army.* Chicago: Rand McNally, 1943.

Tank Gunnery Manual. FM 17–12. 10 July 1944.

Tank Platoon Manual. FM 17–30. 8 July 1944.

The Tanks Are Coming. Directed by B. Reeves Eason. Warner Brothers Pictures and the Vitaphone Corporation, in cooperation with the US Army, 1941.

Up from Marseille: The History of the 781st Battalion. [Camp Campbell, KY: The Battalion, 1945].

White, Isaac D. *United States vs. German Equipment: As Prepared for the Supreme Commander, Allied Expeditionary Force.* 1945. Reprint, Military Monograph 240. Bennington, VT: Merriam, 1988.

Secondary Sources

Ambrose, Stephen. *Eisenhower, Soldier and President.* New York: Touchstone, 1991.

Angier, John C. *A 4f Goes to War.* Bennington, VT: Merriam, 2008.

Black, Jeremy. *European Warfare, 1660–1815.* London: UCL Press, 1994.

———. *Tools of War: Weapons that Changed the World.* London: Quercus, 2007.

Blumberg, Arnold. "The Czech-Designed 38(t) Armored Vehicle Was Used Extensively by the German Panzer Divisions." *WWII History* (July 2004).

Blumenson, Martin. *The Patton Papers, 1885–1940.* Boston: Houghton Mifflin, 1972.

Blumenson, Martin, and Kevin M. Hymel. *Patton, Legendary World War II Commander.* Washington DC: Potomac, 2008.

Cameron, Robert S. "Fort Knox: Birthplace of Today's Armor Branch." *Armor* (November–December 2006).

———. *Mobility, Shock, and Firepower: The Emergence of the US Army's Armor Branch, 1917–1945.* Washington DC: Center of Military History, 2008.

Churchill, Winston. *The Second World War.* Edited by Norman P. Ross. Vol. 1. New York: Time, 1960.

Cooper, Belton Y. *Death Traps: The Survival of an American Armored Division in World War II.* New York: Presidio, 1998.

Cooper, Matthew. *The German Army, 1939–1945.* Lanham: Scarborough House, 1990.

Davies, J. B. *Great Campaigns of World War II.* 1985. Reprint. Leicester, UK: Silverdale Books, 2002.

Dinardo, R. L. *Mechanized Juggernaut or Military Anachronism?* Mechanicsburg, PA: Stackpole Books, 1991.

Eiler, Keith E. *Mobilizing America: Robert P. Patterson and the War Effort, 1940–1945.* Ithaca, NY: Cornell University Press, 1997.

Eisenhower, Dwight. *Crusade in Europe.* Garden City: Doubleday, 1948.

Fazendin, Roger. *The 756th Tank Battalion in the Battle of Cassino, 1944.* New York: iUniverse, 1991.

Fischer, David Hacker. *Washington's Crossing.* New York: Oxford University Press, 2004.

Forty, George. *Tank Warfare in World War II: First-Hand Accounts from Allied and Axis Soldiers.* London: Magpie Books, 2004.

Fuller, J. F. C. *Armament & History.* New York: Da Capo, 1998.

———. *The Conduct of War.* London: Eyre Methuem, 1972.

Green, Michael. *M4 Sherman at War.* St. Paul, MN: Zenith, 2007.

Greenfield, Kent Roberts, ed. *The United States Army in World War II: The Technical Services, the Ordnance Department Planning Munitions for War.* Washington, DC: Center of Military History, 1955.

Greenfield, Kent Roberts; Robert R. Palmer; and Bell I. Wiley. *United States Army in WWII: The Army Ground Forces, the Organization of Ground Combat Troops.* Washington, DC: Historical Division, Department of the Army, 1947.

Harman, Nicholas. *Dunkirk: The Patriotic Myth.* New York: Simon and Schuster, 1980.

Hart, B. H. Liddell. *History of the Second World War.* New York: G. P Putnam's Sons, 1970.

———. *The Real War: 1914–1918.* Boston: Little Brown, 1964.

Heckmann, Wolf. *Rommel's War in Africa.* Translated by Stephen Seago. Garden City, NY: Doubleday, 1981.

Heiber, Helmut. *Hitler and His Generals: Military Conferences, 1942–1945.* New York: Enigma Books, 2003.

Heller, Charles E., and William Stofft, eds. *America's First Battles, 1776–1965.* Lawrence: University Press of Kansas, 1986.

Hoffmann, George. *Through Mobility We Conquer: The Mechanization of US Cavalry.* Lexington: University Press of Kentucky, 2006.

Hoffschmidt, E. J., and W. H. Tantum IV, eds. *Tank Data 2*. Proving Ground Series. Old Greenwich, CT: WE, 1969.

Icks, Robert Joseph. *Famous Tank Battles*. New York: Doubleday, 1972.

Jarymowycz, Roman Johann. *Tank Tactics: From Normandy to Lorraine*. Mechanicsburg, PA: Stackpole Books, 2009.

Jensen, Marvin. *Strike Swiftly!: The 70th Tank Battalion from North Africa to Normandy to Germany*. Novato, CA: Presidio Press, 1997.

Keegan, John. *The First World War*. New York: Alfred A. Knopf, 1999.

———. *History of Warfare*. New York: Vintage Books, 1993.

Kennett, Lee B. *G.I.: The American Soldier in World War II*. New York: Scribner, 1987.

Kershaw, Robert. *Tank Men: The Human Story of Tanks at War*. London: Hodder & Stoughton, 2009.

Macksey, Kenneth. *Tank Warfare*. New York: Stein and Day, 1971.

Moynihan, Michael. *People at War, 1914–1918*. Newton Abbot, Eng.: David & Charles, 1973.

Peterson, Harold L. *Round Shot and Rammers*. Harrisburg, PA: Stackpole Books, 1969.

Stokesbury, James L. *A Short History of World War II*. New York: Perennial, 2001.

Stoler, Mark A. "George C. Marshall and the Europe-First Strategy." *Journal of Military History* 79, no. 2 (April 2015).

To Hell and Back, DVD. Directed by Jesse Hibbs. 1955. Universal City, CA: Universal Studios Home Entertainment, 2004.

Van Creveld, Martin. *Supplying War: Logistics from Wallenstein to Patton*. New York: Cambridge University Press, 1987.

Weeks, John. *Men against Tanks: A History of Anti-Tank Warfare*. New York: Mason/Charter Publishers, 1975.

Wheldon, John. *Machine Age Armies*. London: Abelard-Schuman, 1968.

Williamson, Porter B. *General Patton's Principles for Life and Leadership*. Tuscon: Management and Systems Consultants, 1988.

Wilson, Dale E. *Treat 'Em Rough!: The Birth of American Armor, 1917–1920*. Novato, CA: Presidio, 1989.

Yeide, Harry. *Steel Victory: The Heroic Story of America's Independent Tank Battalions at War in Europe*. Novato, CA: Presidio, 2003.

———. *Weapons of the Tankers: American Armor in World War II*. St. Paul, MN: Zenith, 2006.

Yockelson, Mitchell. "The United States Armed Forces and the Mexican Punitive Expedition: Part 2." *Prologue Magazine* 29, no. 4 (Winter 1997). Available online, http://www.archives.gov/publications/prologue/1997/winter/mexican-punitive-expedition-2.html.

Zaloga, Steven J. *M4 (76mm) Sherman Medium Tank, 1943–1965*. Long Island City, NY: Osprey, 2003.

Zoepf, Wolf T. *Seven Days in January with the 6th SS-Mountain Division in Operation Norwind*. Bedford, PA: Aberjona, 2001.

Index